European Imperialism, 1830–1930

PROBLEMS IN EUROPEAN CIVILIZATION SERIES

European Imperialism, 1830–1930

CLIMAX AND CONTRADICTION

Edited and with an introduction by

Alice L. Conklin

University of Rochester

Ian Christopher Fletcher

Georgia State University

WADSWORTH
CENGAGE Learning·

Australia · Brazil · Japan · Korea · Mexico · Singapore · Spain · United Kingdom · United States

European Imperialism, 1830–1930: Climax and Contradiction
Edited and with an introduction by Alice L. Conklin, Ian Christopher Fletcher

Editor-in-Chief: Jean Woy

Assistant Editor: Leah Strauss

Associate Project Editor: Amy Johnson

Associate Production/ Design Coordinator: Jodi O'Rourke

Manufacturing Coordinator: Andrea Wagner

Marketing Manager: Sandra McGuire

Cover Image: Hulton Getty

Cover Design: Sarah Melhado

For product information and technology assistance, contact us at **Cengage Learning Customer & Sales Support, 1-800-354-9706**

For permission to use material from this text or product, submit all requests online **www.cengage.com/ permissions** Further permissions questions can be emailed to **permissionrequest@cengage.com**

Library of Congress Control Number: 98-72011

ISBN-13: 978-0-395-90385-8

ISBN-10: 0-395-90385-8

Wadsworth
20 Channel Center Street
Boston, MA 02210
USA

Cengage Learning is a leading provider of customized learning solutions with office locations around the globe, including Singapore, the United Kingdom, Australia, Mexico, Brazil, and Japan. Locate your local office at **www.cengage.com/global**

Cengage Learning products are represented in Canada by Nelson Education, Ltd.

To learn more about Wadsworth, visit **www.cengage.com/wadsworth**

Purchase any of our products at your local college store or at our preferred online store **www.cengagebrain.com**

Printed in the United States of America
3 4 5 6 7   18 17 16 15 14

Contents

V Anticolonial Resistance   181

Preface

The 1980s and 1990s have witnessed an explosion of new and innovative scholarship on the age of empire, dealing with the European metropole as well as the African, Asian, and American colonies. There are two major reasons for this revival of interest. First, the end of the Cold War has opened a space for reconsidering the course of modern history and, in particular, for reexamining the epic stories of empire and decolonization. Scholars increasingly recognize that the global world we now inhabit has a history, and much of that history concerns the complex interaction of Europe with many parts of the world since the fifteenth century. The second, and related, reason is the rise of multicultural and multiracial societies, not just in the United States, but also in former imperial powers like Britain, France, and Germany as well as in many of the former colonies. The sense of dislocation and the multiple identities that these societies are currently experiencing are now seen as effects of colonialism. Not surprisingly, scholars are addressing these issues in part by emphasizing the centrality of imperialism and its legacies of racism and nationalism to modern European history.

This book consists principally of thematically organized selections from the most recent historical work on French, British, and Dutch imperialism. We begin the volume with a section devoted to several of the classic interpretations and criticisms of empire so that students might better judge for themselves how recent scholarship has changed. The introduction provides a brief overview of a century of historical writing on the subject to orient the reader at the outset. Our chronology and bibliography highlight the critical moments in European expansion and the resistance that the colonizers met from the colonized. We also take note of key dates in the history of American, Russian, and Japanese empire building in this period to call attention to the global climate of expansionism in which modern European imperialism operated. Finally, although the selections of the book are organized into five sections, the "boundaries" between each section are meant to be porous. Readers are encouraged to find their own connections between the many different selections presented in this volume.

Many people helped make this book possible. We would like to thank all of our colleagues in the field who generously responded to our request for suggestions on what selections to include and who enthusiastically endorsed this project from its inception. Since the literature is enormous, we could not have proceeded in a timely fashion without their help. Several individuals contributed great amounts of their time and energy; in particular we thank Stanley Engerman, Jean Fletcher, Yael Fletcher, Barbara Brooks, Hugh Hudson, Matt Payne, Brenda Meehan, and Jeff Jackson. Valuable comments provided by the following reviewers helped to shape this volume: Antoinette Burton, Johns Hopkins University; Frederick Cooper, University of Michigan; Krystyna von Henneberg, University of California at Davis; and Margaret Strobel, University of Illinois. At Wadsworth, Cengage Learning we owe a special debt to Jean Woy, for her timely recognition of how important a topic imperialism has become in undergraduate curriculae, and to Leah Strauss and Amy Johnson for their expert editing. Still, when all is said and done, it is our own students at the University of Rochester and Georgia State University who have unwittingly done the most to inspire this volume and determine much of its content. We thus dedicate the book to them.

Alice L. Conklin
Ian Christopher Fletcher

Chronology of Events

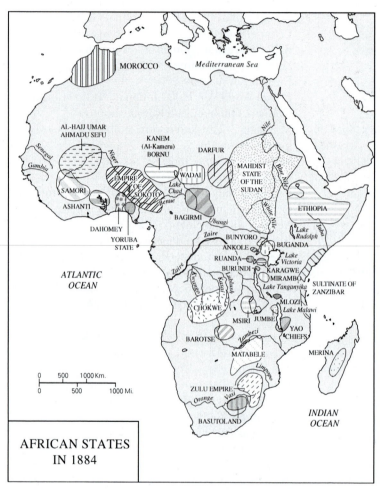

AFRICAN STATES IN 1884

Note: This map does not show existing British, French, Italian, Portugese, and Spanish colonies, or Boer republics.

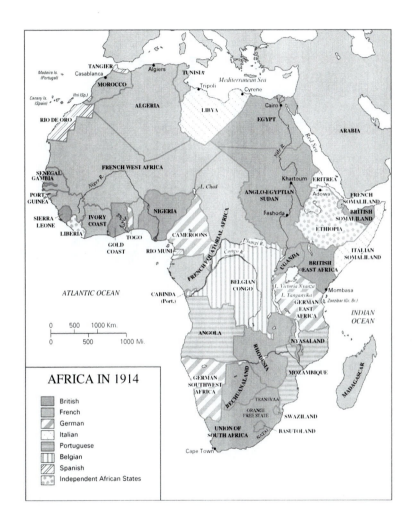

Madeira Is.
(Portugal)

TANGIER
Casablanca
MOROCCO

Canary Is.
(Spain)

Ifni (Sp.)

Algiers

TUNISIA

Mediterranean Sea

Tripoli

Cyrene

RIO DE ORO

ALGERIA

LIBYA

Cairo

EGYPT

Nile R.

Red Sea

ARABIA

SENEGAL
GAMBIA

FRENCH WEST AFRICA

Niger R.

L. Chad

Khartoum

ERITREA

Adowa

FRENCH
SOMALILAND

PORT.
GUINEA

ANGLO-EGYPTIAN
SUDAN

BRITISH
SOMALILAND

SIERRA
LEONE

IVORY
COAST

NIGERIA

Fashoda

ETHIOPIA

LIBERIA

GOLD
COAST

TOGO

RIO MUNI

CAMEROONS

FRENCH EQUATORIAL AFRICA

Ubangi R.

Congo R.

UGANDA

BRITISH
EAST AFRICA

ITALIAN
SOMALILAND

ATLANTIC OCEAN

CABINDA
(Port.)

BELGIAN
CONGO

L. Victoria Nyanza

L. Tanganyika

Mombasa

Zanzibar (Gr. Br.)

GERMAN
EAST
AFRICA

INDIAN
OCEAN

| 0 | 500 | 1000 Km. |

| 0 | 500 | 1000 Mi. |

ANGOLA

NYASALAND

RHODESIA

MOZAMBIQUE

MADAGASCAR

GERMAN
SOUTHWEST
AFRICA

BECHUANALAND

TRANSVAAL

ORANGE
FREE STATE

SWAZILAND

UNION OF
SOUTH AFRICA

BASUTOLAND

NATAL

Cape Town

AFRICA IN 1914

	British
	French
	German
	Italian
	Portuguese
	Belgian
	Spanish
	Independent African States

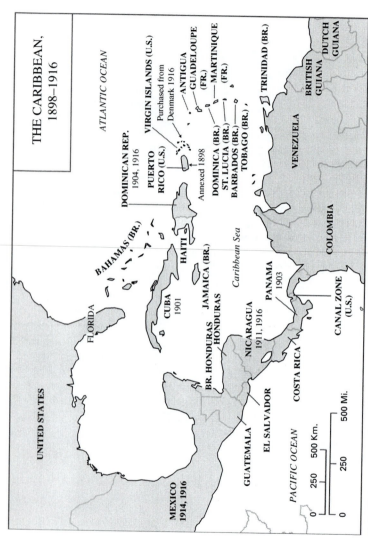

THE CARIBBEAN, 1898–1916

ATLANTIC OCEAN

UNITED STATES

FLORIDA

BAHAMAS (BR.)

CUBA
1901

HAITI

DOMINICAN REP.
1904, 1916

PUERTO
RICO (U.S.)
Annexed 1898

VIRGIN ISLANDS (U.S.)
Purchased from
Denmark 1916

ANTIGUA

GUADELOUPE
(FR.)

DOMINICA (BR.)
MARTINIQUE
(FR.)

ST. LUCIA (BR.)
BARBADOS (BR.)

TOBAGO (BR.)

TRINIDAD (BR.)

JAMAICA (BR.)

Caribbean Sea

BR. HONDURAS
HONDURAS

NICARAGUA
1911, 1916

PANAMA
1903

CANAL ZONE
(U.S.)

COSTA RICA

EL SALVADOR

GUATEMALA

MEXICO
1914, 1916

PACIFIC OCEAN

COLOMBIA

VENEZUELA

BRITISH
GUIANA

DUTCH
GUIANA

0   250   500 Km.

0   250   500 Mi.

Note: Dates on map refer to U.S. interventions

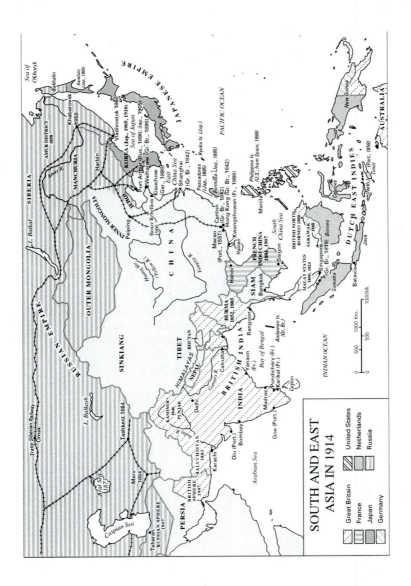

SOUTH AND EAST ASIA IN 1914

Great Britain
France
Japan
Germany
United States
Netherlands
Russia

Introduction

Imperialism is the process by which an expanding state dominates the territory, population, and resources of less powerful states or regions. Sometimes this process takes a colonial form including: the imposition of direct military and administrative control, the influx of settlers from the imperialist country, and the systematic subordination of indigenous peoples. Sometimes it takes less overt forms including: the establishment of "spheres of influence," commercial concessions, special financial and legal privileges, and other manifestations of dependency. Modern European imperialism transformed global political, economic, and cultural relationships and laid the foundations for the interdependent world we inhabit today. By the early twentieth century, Britain, France, Germany, Italy, Belgium, the Netherlands, Denmark, Spain, and Portugal together held sway over almost 84 percent of the earth's surface. The British alone ruled over one-fourth of the world's land and a third of its population. Rising American, Japanese, and Russian imperialism only accentuated this unprecedented combination of overland and overseas (*outremer* as the French put it) conquest.

Although these empires have disappeared, their legacies remain. Thanks to recent waves of immigration from former colonies, European societies have become multicultural and multiracial in ways that resemble Australia or the United States. Musical hybrids such as Afro-pop or *bhangra* are drawing diverse audiences, suggesting the creative potential of a world made smaller by cultural interactions and technology transfers that began in the age of empire. At the same time extreme-right political parties in Europe are gaining adherents by playing on fears of immigrants, reviving old racisms and inventing new ones. In the postcolonial world many new states have emerged from colonies whose borders were drawn by European imperialists either ignorant of, or indifferent to, precolonial political, cultural, and ethnic boundaries. These countries have had little choice but to accept not only the borders, but also the languages, administrative and legal systems, and economic infrastructures of their former colonial rulers. The results have been mixed. Some countries have suffered chronic ethnic strife, continued economic dependence on the West, and a pattern of authoritarian government whose origins lie at least in part in the colonial period. Others have become major financial and industrial powers in their own right or have embarked on remarkable experiments in political and social renovation.

The modern expansion of Europe into Africa, Asia, the Caribbean, and the Pacific did not, of course, begin in 1830. It was arguably the Iberian navigators of the fifteenth century, reaching the Americas in 1492 and India in 1498, who inaugurated this process. Nor did European imperialism reach its climax in 1930. This occurred slightly earlier, during the convulsive scrambles for Africa and Asia between 1880 and 1900. However, the hundred years between 1830 and 1930 have a particular unity in the general sweep of European global conquest that sets this century off from what came before and from what followed.

Beginning in the 1830s, the outlines of a new kind of European imperialism began to emerge. This imperialism was deeply influenced by the advent of two developments in particular in the West: industrialization and the rise of three related ideologies: liberalism, nationalism, and scientific racism. One hundred years later, the grand edifice of empire still appeared to be firmly in place. Indeed, the French Colonial Exposition of 1931 was dedicated to the proposition that Europe continued to hold uncontested sway over the "uncivilized" masses of Africa and Asia, and that it was currently developing the material resources of the rest of the world for the mutual benefit of colonizer and colonized. European hegemony was, however, much less secure than contemporaries realized. Anticolonial protest was already challenging colonial rule in many places, and the upheavals of world war, revolution, and depression had shaken the imperial self-confidence of many Europeans. Japanese, Italian, and German aggression in the 1930s further undermined the post-World War I international order that had sustained imperialism. Although decolonization would not officially begin until the 1947 transfer of power from Britain to India and Pakistan, the process of imperial dissolution had already been initiated by the contradictory tendencies of the period between the world wars.

How did the "typical" European statesman seeking to promote the interests of his nation view imperialism in 1830? What colonies already existed, and how and why did Europe's position in the world expand so dramatically over the course of the next one hundred years? How can we best characterize this century of imperial expansion? Colonies in 1830 were a well-established fixture of European politics. Three centuries of imperial rule in the Americas—valuable for their gold, silver, sugar, and other resources, whose extraction or cultivation led to the enslavement of millions of Africans and their descendants— had accustomed metropolitan Europeans to overseas sources of wealth. Yet the period from 1775 to 1825—the age of revolution—witnessed a major setback for European imperial fortunes. Most of British North America, the French island colony of St. Domingue (Haiti), and mainland Portuguese and Spanish America all successfully won independence at this time. While this left what was to become Canada as well as much of the Caribbean (the "West Indies") under British, Danish, Dutch, French, and Spanish rule, the shock administered by these colonial losses reinvigorated imperial expansion elsewhere, particularly in Asia.

South and Southeast Asia (the "East Indies") had long been a source of spices, silk, and other luxury goods for Europe. Here rule by trading companies responsible to metropolitan parliaments was the norm. By the mid-eighteenth century, the British East India Company had achieved a virtual monopoly of trade between India and Europe, and its agents ruled the vital province of Bengal. The Dutch East India Company—by far the major component of the Dutch empire—appeared to have achieved a similarly commanding position in Java. Yet when revolutionary turmoil threatened British and Dutch hegemony in this part of the world, local European authorities, backed by their home governments, successfully solidified and extended their holdings in the region, turning them into virtual colonies. Still smarting from its losses in the Caribbean, France made a disastrous attempt to colonize Egypt in 1798. Thirty years later it turned to the neighboring province of Algeria in quest of a "jewel" comparable to British India and an antidote for revolution at home.

In the 1830s, then, three "old" colonial powers—Britain, France, and the Netherlands—were strengthening their empires in what was then commonly called "the Orient" without relinquishing control of their remaining American colonies. As a glance at the Chronology indicates, for the next fifty years each of these nations continued to extend its overseas possessions piecemeal. In a period of relative peace, free trade, and rapid capitalist development, colonialism was fueled by the search for raw materials and new markets and concomitant resistance from native rulers to imperial "protection." All parts of the non-Western world beckoned, and all except the African interior suffered European territorial encroachment. Abruptly, however, the pace of conquest quickened in the 1880s. Several factors explain this shift. Economic depression, aggressive nationalism in the wake of the unifications of Italy and Germany, and increased rivalry and competition as two late industrializers—Germany and the United States—surged forward, helped to destabilize the European balance of power. The desire to distract newly enfranchised masses and intensifying strife among indigenous rulers in Africa and Asia further tempted Europeans into imperialist adventures, particularly where they already had "interests" to protect. The result was a final colonizing frenzy as panicky, yet supremely confident, European nations hurriedly passed protective tariffs at home (Britain and Belgium excepted) and rushed to carve out new dominions and "sheltered markets" for themselves overseas. By 1900, these same nations, in what is commonly called the "new imperialism," had partitioned all of Africa, most of Asia, and that part of the Pacific that had not been claimed by the United States. Between 1900 and 1930, the European powers struggled to make real the political mastery they had claimed during the two previous decades of whirlwind conquest and to force their newest colonies to "yield" the anticipated economic dividends.

Despite the uneven pace of European imperialism between 1830 and 1930, expansion over these years shared certain characteristics. First, beginning early in the nineteenth century new technologies and medical knowledge developed in the course of industrialization dramatically shifted the global balance of power in favor of Europeans. From 1830 to 1870, the invention of the steam engine and discovery of quinine prophylaxis gave Europeans easy access to the waterways of Asia and their first chance to survive in tropical Africa. The arms revolution of the end of the century made it possible for relatively small forces equipped with new weapons like the Gatling gun to decimate much larger armies. Thanks in part to technology, Europeans, Americans, Japanese, and Russians acquired empire at low financial and human cost to themselves. They also readily assumed that their newfound mastery of nature made them morally superior to the rest of the globe's inhabitants.

Second, the ages of enlightenment and revolution altered European identity, society, and culture in ways that critically shaped the colonial encounters of the nineteenth century. Greater contact with other cultures in the eighteenth century encouraged Europeans to take a closer—and often more admiring—look at themselves than had earlier been the case, thus laying the foundation for scientific racism in the century to follow. The rise of liberal and nationalist ideals also contributed to empire-building. Paradoxically, the abolition of colonial slavery in the British (1833) and French (1848) empires only heightened Europeans' sense of moral superiority over others. It is one of the central contradictions of European imperialism—as it reached its climax—that every colonizing power insisted both that conquest by their particular nation was a force for universal human progress, and that the peoples of the rest of the world were organized into immutable racial hierarchies that justified their subjugation.

Historians, needless to say, have not always approached the study of European imperialism in the same way. Modern historical writing on the subject began in the early twentieth century. As we shall see in Part I, much of this early writing was critical of the "new imperialism" of 1880–1900. Many intellectuals, in the Western metropole and in the colonies, were profoundly disturbed by the scale, brutality, and rapidity of the colonial scrambles they had just witnessed. Not surprisingly, they attempted to explain what had happened. These critics made connections between specific abuses of conquest, commerce, and administration, and wider patterns of military, economic, and racial domination. They spoke from many different political and moral perspectives, and therefore did not interpret the facts in the same way—or even agree on the facts in the first place. At home and overseas, there were those who imagined the world in terms of the permanence of empires, races, and nations, and those who did not. For some there were better and worse forms of imperialism; for others imperialism could not be reformed but instead had to be overthrown.

Out of these early critiques a few European texts—especially Hobson's *Imperialism*, Lenin's *Imperialism, the Highest Stage of Capitalism*, and Schumpeter's "The Sociology of Imperialisms" (the latter two borrowing heavily from Hobson)—quickly gained canonical status. Each of these works assessed the relative weight of economic forces, social classes, and politics and ideology in triggering overseas expansion; each reached a different conclusion. Their competing and influential explanations set the terms of debate for decades. Following their lead, many historians continued to argue about the determinacy of economics or politics, the agency of elites and masses, and the role of organized interests and fractions of capital in the rise of the new imperialism. With the advantage of hindsight, we can see that despite real differences of interpretation, there were three assumptions that no one in this school of historiography ever questioned: first, that imperialism was a distinctive phenomenon of the late nineteenth century preceded by a long anti-imperialist period; second, that it was primarily political and economic in origin, and that it was the origins of imperialism in particular that required explaining; and third, that its principal actors were capitalists, politicians, diplomats, soldiers, and ideologues. While these assumptions opened up certain rich fields of research, they also closed off other possible lines of inquiry regarding the chronological limits of, the character of, and the many additional participants in, modern imperialism.

In the interwar period, the historiography of imperialism saw little innovation or revision. The dissolution of the German and Ottoman empires did not in the short run loosen the grip of colonial rule, as the British and French empires actually expanded under the League of Nations mandatory system. In these years, most academic historians still approached imperialism as an annex to the history of protectionism, nationalism, war, and diplomacy within Europe. It was only with the onset of decolonization after the Second World War that the first of several dramatic revisionist turns significantly altered the course of scholarship.

The initial break with the canon will always be associated with the names of the British imperial historians Ronald Robinson and John Gallagher. In "The Imperialism of Free Trade" (1953), they took issue with the neat division of the nineteenth century into anti-imperialist and imperialist periods. They not only emphasized continuing territorial expansion in the middle decades of the century but also argued that Britain expanded its global reach through an informal trading empire as well as a formal colonial empire. In a subsequent study with Alice Denny, *Africa and the Victorians* (1961), they treated the partition of Africa as the outcome of instability and crisis in Africa rather than in Europe. They claimed that the statesmen who oversaw the scramble acted from political and strategic rather than narrowly economic motives. According to this interpretation, Britain seized new colonies in Africa to protect the routes to India and Australia; the "new imperialism" thus represented less a break with the past than the continuation of empire by other means. Robinson further challenged old assumptions when he suggested in "Non-European Foundations of European Imperialism" (1972) that imperialism could not be understood without a full appraisal of the motives and actions of collaborating Asian and African elites.

Far from producing a new synthesis, the contributions of Robinson and Gallagher shook up the whole field of imperial history. Historians of French and German imperialism as well as British imperialism eagerly took up this new research agenda. Their findings did not always substantiate Robinson and Gallagher's arguments. A. Kanya-Forstner showed that France's drive for control of West Africa did not coincide with the timetable proposed for the partition of the continent. Studying the German case, Hans-Ulrich Wehler reasserted the primacy of domestic politics by stressing Bismarck's manipulation of the masses through social imperialism. Recently, P.J. Cain and A.G. Hopkins have proposed a sweeping new interpretation of British imperialism, grounded on the longstanding "gentlemanly capitalism" of merchants, bankers, and aristocrats concentrated in the City of London. Unlike Robinson and Gallagher's "excentric" interpretation, with its emphasis on the breakdown of order overseas as a precipitant of conquest, Cain and Hopkins' thesis is firmly recentered on the metropole.

Nevertheless, Robinson and Gallagher helped begin an ongoing process of reorienting historiography from its original Eurocentric assumptions towards a radically decentered conception of imperialism. This process was accelerated in the 1960s and 1970s by nationalist historiographies in the former colonies that traced the rise of anticolonial movements, Marxist analyses of neocolonialism in the Third World, and, more broadly, a concern among social historians, anthropologists, and other scholars to recover the experiences of workers, peasants, women, and marginalized communities under colonialism. Although these actors were not completely absent from the older historiography, they had rarely been considered historical agents in their own right. Without discounting the continuing importance of research into imperial policy and strategy, the administrative and military apparatuses of the colonial state, and the firms and sectors involved in colonial trade and industry, this reorientation of scholarship opened the way for the historiography of imperialism to take fundamentally new directions in the 1980s and 1990s. It is these innovations in research and interpretation that Parts II, III, IV, and V of *European Imperialism* highlight.

Perhaps the most important of these new directions has been a growing interest in the discourses and ideologies animating both European domination and resistance and accommodation on the part of the colonized. Of course, historians have long been aware that ideas and values shaped the colonial encounter, but these intellectual and moral underpinnings have received relatively little systematic analysis until recently. We now recognize that imperialism had a much greater reciprocal impact upon the populations of both the European metropole and the overseas colonies than was once thought. Rather than being the sole concern of a narrow elite of businessmen and statesmen, the imperial project involved the entire nation-state. In the colonies, European rulers sought to insure hegemony by penetrating the most intimate domains of their colonial subjects. Consequently, traces of empire can be found in the cultural artifacts of daily life of colonizer and colonized alike. The current approach to imperial culture is thus quite different from that of earlier studies. Where scholars once focused on official doctrines alone, they now scrutinize a much broader array of texts, images, and practices for insights into how empire was imagined, represented, and experienced. These new sources from material and visual culture include household goods, architecture and design, advertising, fashion, literature, and the press, to name but a few that appear in *European Imperialism*.

This new interest in the cultural history of empire has been inspired at least in part by the innovative work of two interdisciplinary groups of scholars. The first is the school of postcolonial cultural studies inaugurated by the literary scholar Edward Said, the historians and anthropologists grouped around the journal *Subaltern Studies*, and other analysts of discourse. Postcolonial cultural critics have emphasized how important the production of "Orientalist" knowledge about the colonized was to the maintenance of colonial rule. According to Said, "Orientalism" amounted to a discourse, or ideological and institutional framework that guided the ways in which Europeans understood and acted towards "others." This discourse was replete with negative stereotypes that served to create the very "Orient" it purported only to describe. Much of this discourse, Said has argued, is still influential today. This group has also highlighted the importance of literary texts and popular culture for consolidating European rule, and many historians have responded to their insights. The second influential group that has given a major impetus to imperial history has been feminist scholars. They began by calling attention to the important role women played in both the maintenance of empire and the anticolonial and nationalist struggles against it. More recently, feminist scholars have studied the interplay between the construction of gender roles and the regulation of sexuality between colonizers and colonized. In showing how sexuality was racialized and race was sexualized, this group has demonstrated the ways in which cultural ideals of femininity and masculinity served to subordinate women and people of color.

In addition to this "cultural" turn over the last twenty years, there has been one other major departure from the older historiography of imperialism. This is an increasing acknowledgment of the close relationship between developments in modern science, medicine, and urban-planning in Europe, and imperialism. Reflecting late-twentieth-century skepticism about the objectivity or even progressive nature of modern science, a number of historians have shown that the colonies often served as either "laboratories" or outposts for repressive social and hygienic policies formulated by various European states. Colonial administrators concerned with managing deadly diseases in their capital cities experimented with new forms of social control for the local populations — including segregation on the basis of ethnicity and race. Some of these policies later surfaced in Europe, as bureaucrats sought to regulate the health habits of their own poor and working classes. Moreover, colonial authorities depended heavily upon engineers and botanists to build public works and improve crop yields that benefited colonizers but not always the colonized. In short, science in a variety of guises facilitated imperialism, while the advance of social engineering and research in the West depended on the existence of the colonial laboratory.

As this brief Introduction suggests, the study of modern imperialism now assumes a more dynamic, expansive, and complex model of interaction between metropole and colonies than was once the case. It is no longer sufficient to frame the question around the causes of the "new imperialism," or to limit its agents to male elites, whether in Europe or overseas. Nor can historians argue that the same economic, political, and cultural conditions pertained across time and space in an empire's many different colonies. Modern imperialism was extraordinarily diverse, and its overall impact upon metropole and colonies was truly dramatic. These selections seek to emphasize this diversity and impact, still visible today, so that students might better understand how the world we inhabit was made.

African workers in a South African gold mine in 1896. Colonial labor—enslaved, indentured, forced, or "free" under the color bar—made an enormous contribution to the expansion of the world economy under imperialism. (Hulton Getty/Liaison Agency)

PART

I The "New Imperialism"

European imperialisms had existed long before the great powers met in Berlin to partition Africa in 1884. Portugal, Spain, France, Britain, and the Netherlands had held overseas possessions for several centuries, and had been extensively involved in both the slave trade and the trade in commodities produced by slave labor. The Spanish withdrawal from the American mainlands in the early nineteenth century was balanced by British, Dutch, and French expansion in North Africa, Southern Africa, South Asia, and Southeast Asia. But the "scrambles" for Africa and Asia in the last decades of the nineteenth century marked a massive territorial increase of European empire, with enormous economic, social, cultural, and political consequences for people on both sides of the divide between metropole and colonies. This intensification of imperialism eventually became the subject of critical analysis, both at home and overseas. The nationalist Dadabhai Naoroji argued as early as the 1870s that the unequal exchanges of imperialism were maldeveloping India by systematically draining the country of its wealth. When wars, rebellions, and protest broke out in many parts of Africa and Asia around the turn of the century, the question of imperialism took center stage in European politics and public life. These conflicts provided disturbing evidence not only

11

of disorder in the colonial world but also of its dangerous repercussions in the metropole—from jingo mobs in London to revolutionary crowds in St. Petersburg.

J.A. Hobson's *Imperialism* (1902, 1905) was one of the first full-fledged critiques of the "new imperialism." A political economist, Hobson contended that imperialism only benefited certain classes of British society, chiefly investors and financiers, and their allies in the state. The capitalism of manufacturing industry and free trade was not imperialistic by necessity. Hobson was a "little Englander" who believed that empire and democracy were incompatible. He advocated social and economic reforms that would raise domestic consumption and alleviate poverty. Hobson's radicalism included an unmistakably anti-Semitic component. His humanitarian regard for Africans and Asians suffering under the yoke of colonialism did not, however, lead him to reject invidious distinctions between Europeans and the "lower races" or to question the essential nature of "Western civilization."

The critique of the "new imperialism" was not limited to Europe. In "The Color Line Belts the World" (1906), W.E.B. Du Bois connected the development of racial segregation in the United States to the global process of colonial domination. Like Hobson and other contemporaries, Du Bois assumed the prior existence of races and civilizations rather than seeing them, at least in part, as effects of imperialism. In *Hind Swaraj* (1910), Mohandas K. Gandhi also held "Western civilization" largely responsible for imperialism's destructive spread. He argued that India was a nation, and that its "true civilization" offered a tolerant and nonviolent basis for Indian *swaraj*, or self-government. Nevertheless, he pointed out the complicity of Indians in British rule. Gandhi recognized that colonialism was virtually impossible without collaboration.

Some socialists, particularly Marxist opponents of reformism and revisionism, rejected the suggestion that imperialism was simply the policy of statesmen or the preference of certain organized economic interests. They sought instead to explain it as the most modern manifestation of the capitalist system as a whole. In *The Accumulation of Capital* (1913), the Polish-German Marxist Rosa Luxemburg argued that the continued profitable expansion of capitalism required a widening penetration and transformation of the non-capitalist world, which was virtually synonymous with the colonial and semicolonial countries of Africa, Asia, Latin America, and the Middle East. In *Imperialism, the Highest Stage of Capitalism* (1916), the Russian Marxist Vladimir Illych Lenin asserted that imperialism represented the supersession of competitive, entrepreneurial capitalism by the monopolistic corporate capitalism of cartels, combines, and banks. While Luxemburg focused on the periphery of the capitalist world-system, and Lenin focused on its core, both emphasized the apocalyptic tendencies of imperialism. Needless to say, European militarism in the era of World War I seemed to justify this sense of crisis.

In an iconoclastic essay, "The Sociology of Imperialisms" (1919), the Austrian political economist Joseph A. Schumpeter linked contemporary militarism and imperialism in a different way. The persistence of aristocracy and the popularity of patriotism indicated to him that imperialism was an atavistic survival of premodern political and social forces. At least in Europe, the formative historical background of capitalism, especially the mercantilist nature of autocratic states, shaped the outlook of supposedly progressive capitalists and workers and made them supporters of empire. If Europe's long past continued to influence its present, so too did its manifold interactions with the rest of the world. In "The Struggle Lies in the Colonies" (1924), the Vietnamese revolutionary Ho Chi Minh urged the Communist International to recognize the centrality of colonialism for both revolution and reaction in the West. The weight of the colonies' peasants, laborers, and soldiers could be thrown in favor of the European workers' movement, or against it.

The original analyses of Hobson and others still influence our understanding of imperialism. Indeed, they gave rise to a continuing debate about the relative importance of economic and political factors in the development of imperialism. But each year brings new narrative histories, comparative analyses, and thematic treatments of the imperial experience. No longer confining themselves to the "new imperialism," between the 1870s and 1910s, historians have recently begun to emphasize the cross-cultural encounters and exchanges of empire. A careful reading of Hobson and his contemporaries should shed light on this dimension of imperialism as well.

J. A. Hobson

Imperialism

Quibbles about the modern meaning of the term Imperialism are best resolved by reference to concrete facts in the history of the last sixty years. During that period a number of European nations, Great Britain being first and foremost, annexed or otherwise asserted political sway over vast portions of Africa and Asia, and over numerous islands in the Pacific and elsewhere. . . .

Though, for convenience, the year 1870 has been taken as indicative of the beginning of the conscious policy of Imperialism, it will be evident that the movement did not attain its full impetus until the middle of the eighties. The vast increase of territory, and the method of wholesale partition which assigned to us great tracts of African land, may be dated from about 1884. Within fifteen years some three and three-quarter millions of square miles were added to the British Empire.

Nor did Great Britain stand alone in this enterprise. The leading characteristic of that modern Imperialism, the competition of rival Empires, was the product of this same period. . . .

. . . The new Imperialism nowhere extended the political and civil liberties of the mother country to any part of the vast territories which, after 1870, fell under the government of Western civilized Powers. Politically, the new Imperialism was an expansion of autocracy. . . .

Thus this recent imperial expansion stands entirely distinct from the colonization of sparsely peopled lands in temperate zones, where white colonists carry with them the modes of government, the industrial and other arts of the civilization of the mother country. The "occupation" of these new territories was comprised in the presence of a small minority of white men, officials, traders, and industrial organisers, exercising political and economic sway over great hordes of popu-

lation regarded as inferior and as incapable of exercising any considerable rights of self-government in politics or industry. . . .

Although the new Imperialism has been bad business for the nation, it has been good business for certain classes and certain trades
within the nation. The vast expenditure on armaments, the costly
wars, the grave risks and embarrassments of foreign policy, the checks
upon political and social reforms within Great Britain, though fraught
with great injury to the nation, have served well the present business
interests of certain industries and professions. . . .

By far the most important economic factor in Imperialism is the
influence relating to investments. The growing cosmopolitanism of
capital has been the greatest economic change of recent generations.
Every advanced industrial nation has been tending to place a larger
share of its capital outside the limits of its own political area, in foreign
countries, or in colonies, and to draw a growing income from this
source. . . .

It is not too much to say that the modern foreign policy of Great
Britain has been primarily a struggle for profitable markets of investment. To a larger extent every year Great Britain has been becoming a
nation living upon tribute from abroad, and the classes who enjoy this
tribute have had an ever-increasing incentive to employ the public
policy, the public purse, and the public force to extend the field of
their private investments, and to safeguard and improve their existing
investments. This is, perhaps, the most important fact in modern politics, and the obscurity in which it is wrapped has constituted the
gravest danger to our State. . . .

Aggressive Imperialism, which costs the taxpayer so dear, which is
of so little value to the manufacturer and trader, which is fraught with
such grave incalculable peril to the citizen, is a source of great gain to
the investor who cannot find at home the profitable use he seeks for
his capital, and insists that his Government should help him to profitable and secure investments abroad. . . .

If the special interest of the investor is liable to clash with the public interest and to induce a wrecking policy, still more dangerous is the
special interest of the financier, the general dealer in investments. In
large measure the rank and file of the investors are, both for business
and for politics, the cat's-paws of the great financial houses, who use
stocks and shares not so much as investments to yield them interest,

but as material for speculation in the money market. In handling large masses of stocks and shares, in floating companies, in manipulating fluctuations of values, the magnates of the Bourse find their gain. These great businesses—banking, broking, bill discounting, loan floating, company promoting—form the central ganglion of international capitalism. . . .

In view of the part which the non-economic factors of patriotism, adventure, military enterprise, political ambition, and philanthropy play in imperial expansion, it may appear that to impute to financiers so much power is to take a too narrowly economic view of history. And it is true that the motor-power of Imperialism is not chiefly financial: finance is rather the governor of the imperial engine, directing the energy and determining its work: it does not constitute the fuel of the engine, nor does it directly generate the power. Finance manipulates the patriotic forces which politicians, soldiers, philanthropists, and traders generate; the enthusiasm for expansion which issues from these sources, though strong and genuine, is irregular and blind; the financial interest has those qualities of concentration and clear-sighted calculation which are needed to set Imperialism to work. An ambitious statesman, a frontier soldier, an overzealous missionary, a pushing trader, may suggest or even initiate a step of imperial expansion, may assist in educating patriotic public opinion to the urgent need of some fresh advance, but the final determination rests with the financial power. The direct influence exercised by great financial houses in "high politics" is supported by the control which they exercise over the body of public opinion through the Press, which, in every "civilised" country, is becoming more and more their obedient instrument. . . .

The play of these forces does not openly appear. They are essentially parasites upon patriotism, and they adapt themselves to its protecting colours. In the mouth of their representatives are noble phrases, expressive of their desire to extend the area of civilisation, to establish good government, promote Christianity, extirpate slavery, and elevate the lower races. Some of the business men who hold such language may entertain a genuine, though usually a vague, desire to accomplish these ends, but they are primarily engaged in business, and they are not unaware of the utility of the more unselfish forces in furthering their ends. . . .

Every improvement of methods of production, every concentration of ownership and control, seems to accentuate the tendency. As one nation after another enters the machine economy and adopts advanced industrial methods, it becomes more difficult for its manufacturers, merchants, and financiers to dispose profitably of their economic resources, and they are tempted more and more to use their Governments in order to secure for their particular use some distant undeveloped country by annexation and protection.

The process, we may be told, is inevitable, and so it seems upon a superficial inspection. Everywhere appear excessive powers of production, excessive capital in search of investment. It is admitted by all business men that the growth of the powers of production in their country exceeds the growth in consumption, that more goods can be produced than can be sold at a profit, and that more capital exists than can find remunerative investment.

It is this economic condition of affairs that forms the taproot of Imperialism. If the consuming public in this country raised its standard of consumption to keep pace with every rise of productive powers, there could be no excess of goods or capital clamorous to use Imperialism in order to find markets: foreign trade would indeed exist, but there would be no difficulty in exchanging a small surplus of our manufacturers for the food and raw material we annually absorbed, and all the savings that we made could find employment, if we chose, in home industries. . . .

The fallacy of the supposed inevitability of imperial expansion as a necessary outlet for progressive industry is now manifest. It is not industrial progress that demands the opening up of new markets and areas of investment, but mal-distribution of consuming power which prevents the absorption of commodities and capital within the country. . . .

Everywhere the issue of quantitative *versus* qualitative growth comes up. This is the entire issue of empire. A people limited in number and energy and in the land they occupy have the choice of improving to the utmost the political and economic management of their own land, confining themselves to such accessions of territory as are justified by the most economical disposition of a growing population; or they may proceed, like the slovenly farmer, to spread their power and energy over the whole earth, tempted by the speculative value or the quick profits of some new market, or else by mere greed of territorial acquisition, and ignoring the political and economic wastes and risks involved by this imperial career. . . .

Imperialism—whether it consists in a further policy of expansion or in the rigorous maintenance of all those vast tropical lands which have been ear-marked as British spheres of influence—implies militarism now and ruinous wars in the future. . . .

Modern British colonialism has been no drain upon our material and moral resources, because it has made for the creation of free white democracies, a policy of informal federation, of decentralisation, involving no appreciable strain upon the governmental faculties of Great Britain. Such federation, whether it remains informal with the slight attachment of imperial sovereignty which now exists, or voluntarily takes some more formal shape, political or financial, may well be regarded as a source of strength, political and military.

Imperialism is the very antithesis of this free, wholesome colonial connection, making, as it ever does, for greater complications of foreign policy, greater centralisation of power, and a congestion of business which ever threatens to absorb and overtax the capacity of parliamentary government. . . .

The order and progress of Great Britain during the nineteenth century was secured by the cultivation and practise of the ordinary civic and industrial virtues, assisted by certain advantages of natural resources and historical contingencies. Are we prepared to substitute the military code of ethics or to distract the national mind and conduct by a perpetual conflict of two warring principles, the one making for the evolution of the good citizen, the other for the evolution of the good soldier? . . .

. . . The new Imperialism has been, we have seen, chiefly concerned with tropical and sub-tropical countries where large "lower races" are brought under white control. Why should Englishmen fight the defensive or offensive wars of this Empire, when cheaper, more numerous, and better-assimilated fighting material can be raised upon the spot, or transferred from one tropical dominion to another? As the labour of industrial development of tropical resources is put upon the "lower races" who reside there, under white superintendence, why should not militarism be organized upon the same basis, black or brown or yellow men, to whom military discipline will be "a wholesome education," fighting for the British Empire under British officers? . . .

This mode of militarism, while cheaper and easier in the first instance, implies less and less control from Great Britain. Though reducing the strain of militarism upon the population at home, it enhances the risks of wars, which become more frequent and more barbarous in proportion as they involve to a less degree the lives of Englishmen. The expansion of our Empire under the new Imperialism has been compassed by setting the "lower races" at one another's throats, fostering tribal animosities and utilising for our supposed benefit the savage propensities of the peoples to whom we have a mission to carry Christianity and civilization.

That we do not stand alone in this ignominious policy does not make it better, rather worse, offering terrible prophetic glimpses into a not distant future, when the horrors of our eighteenth century struggle with France in North America and India may be revived upon a gigantic scale, and Africa and Asia may furnish huge cock-pits for the struggles of black and yellow armies representing the imperialist rivalries of Christendom. The present tendencies of Imperialism plainly make in this direction, involving in their recoil a degradation of Western States and a possible *débâcle* of Western civilization. . . .

The antagonism with democracy drives to the very roots of Imperialism as a political principle. Not only is Imperialism used to frustrate those measures of economic reform now recognized as essential to the effectual working of all machinery of popular government, but it operates to paralyse the working of that machinery itself. Representative institutions are ill adapted for empire, either as regards men or methods. The government of a great heterogeneous medley of lower races by departmental officials in London and their nominated emissaries lies outside the scope of popular knowledge and popular control. The Foreign, Colonial, and Indian Secretaries in Parliament, the permanent officials of the departments, the governors and staff who represent the Imperial Government in our dependencies, are not, and cannot be, controlled directly or effectively by the will of the people. This subordination of the legislative to the executive, and the concentration of executive power in an autocracy, are necessary consequences of the predominance of foreign over domestic politics. . . . So long as

Imperialism is allowed to hold the field, the only real political conflict is between groups representing the divergent branches of Imperialism, the men upon the spot and the Home Government, the Asiatic interests of India and China and the forward policy in Africa, the advocates of a German alliance or a Franco-Russian alliance.

. . . As our free self-governing colonies have furnished hope, encouragement, and leading to the popular aspirations in Great Britain, not merely by practical successes in the arts of popular government, but by the wafting of a spirit of freedom and equality, so our despotically ruled dependencies have ever served to damage the character of our people by feeding the habits of snobbish subservence, the admiration of wealth and rank, the corrupt survivals of the inequalities of feudalism. This process began with the advent of the East Indian nabob and the West Indian planter into English society and politics, bringing back with his plunders of the slave trade and the gains of corrupt and extortionate officialism the acts of vulgar ostentation, domineering demeanour and corrupting largesse to dazzle and degrade the life of our people. . . .

. . . As the despotic portion of our Empire has grown in area, a larger and larger number of men, trained in the temper and methods of autocracy as soldiers and civil officials in our Crown colonies, protectorates, and Indian Empire, reinforced by numbers of merchants, planters, engineers, and overseers, whose lives have been those of a superior caste living an artificial life removed from all the healthy restraints of ordinary European society, have returned to this country, bringing back the characters, sentiments, and ideas imposed by this foreign environment. The South and South-West of England is richly sprinkled with these men, many of them wealthy, most of them endowed with leisure, men openly contemptuous of democracy, devoted to material luxury, social display, and the shallower arts of intellectual life. The wealthier among them discover political ambitions, introducing into our Houses of Parliament the coarsest and most selfish spirit of "Imperialism," using their imperial experience and connexions to push profitable companies and concessions for their private benefits, and posing as authorities so as to keep the yoke of Imperialism firmly fixed upon the shoulders of the "nigger.". . .

It is, indeed, a nemesis of Imperialism that the arts and crafts of tyranny, acquired and exercised in our unfree Empire, should be turned against our liberties at home.

W. E. B. Du Bois

The Color Line Belts the World

We have a way in America of wanting to be "rid" of Problems. It is not so much a desire to reach the best and largest solution as it is to clean the board and start a new game. For instance, most Americans are simply tired and impatient over our most sinister social problem, the Negro. They do not want to solve it, they do not want to understand it, they want simply to be done with it and hear the last of it. Of all possible attitudes this is the most dangerous, because it fails to realize the most significant fact of the opening century, viz.; The Negro Problem in America is but a local phase of a world problem. "The problem of the twentieth century is the problem of the Color Line." Many smile incredulously at such a proposition, but let us see.

The tendency of the great nations of the day is territorial, political, and economic expansion, but in every case this has brought them in contact with darker peoples, so that we have to-day England, France, Holland, Belgium, Italy, Portugal, and the United States in close contact with brown and black peoples, and Russia and Austria in contact with the yellow. The older idea was that the whites would eventually displace the native races and inherit their lands, but this idea has been rudely shaken in the increase of American Negroes, the experience of the English in Africa, India, and the West Indies, and the development of South America. The policy of expansion, then, simply means world problems of the Color Line. The color question enters into European imperial politics and floods our continents from Alaska to Patagonia.

This is not all. Since 732, when Charles Martel beat back the Saracens at Tours, the white races have had the hegemony of civilization—so far so that "white" and "civilized" have become synonymous

From *A W. E. B. Du Bois Reader* (Macmillan, 1971) by Andrew G. Paschal, pp. 263–264.

in everyday speech; and men have forgotten where civilization started. For the first time in a thousand years a great white nation has measured arms with a colored nation and has been found wanting. The Russo-Japanese War has marked an epoch. The magic of the word "white" is already broken, and the Color Line in civilization has been crossed in modern times as it was in the great past. The awakening of the yellow races is certain. That the awakening of the brown and black races will follow in time, no unprejudiced student of history can doubt. Shall the awakening of these sleepy millions be in accordance with, and aided by, the great ideals of white civilization, or in spite of them and against them? This is the problem of the Color Line. Force and Fear have hitherto marked the white attitude toward darker races; shall this continue or be replaced by Freedom and Friendship?

M. K. Gandhi

The Disease of Civilization

[In this dialogue, the "Editor" articulates Gandhi's views.]

READER: [W]ill you tell me something of what you have read and thought of this [modern] civilisation?

EDITOR: Let us first consider what state of things is described by the word "civilisation." Its true test lies in the fact that people living in it make bodily welfare the object of life. We will take some examples. The people of Europe today live in better built houses than they did a hundred years ago. This is considered an emblem of civilisation, and this is also a matter to promote bodily happiness. Formerly, they wore skins, and used as their weapons spears. Now, they wear long trousers, and, for embellishing their bodies, they wear a variety of clothing, and, instead of spears, they carry with them revolvers containing five or more chambers. If people of a certain country, who have hitherto not been in the habit of wearing much clothing, boots, etc., adopt European clothing, they are supposed to have become civilised out of savagery. Formerly, in Europe, people ploughed their lands mainly by manual labour. Now, one man can plough a vast tract by means of steam-engines, and can thus amass great wealth. This is called a sign of civilisation. Formerly, the fewest men wrote books that were most valuable. Now, anybody writes and prints anything he likes and poisons people's mind. Formerly, men travelled in wagons; now they fly through the air in trains at the rate of four hundred and more miles per day. This is considered the height of civilisation. It has been stated that, as men progress, they shall be able to travel in airships and reach any part of the world in a few hours. Men will not need the use of their hands and feet. They will press a button and they will have their clothing by their side. They will press another button and they will have their newspaper. A third, and a motorcar will be in waiting for them. They will have a variety of delicately dished-up food. Everything will be done by machinery. Formerly, when people wanted to fight with one another, they measured between them their bodily strength; now it is possible to take away thousands of lives by one man working behind a gun from a hill. This is civilisation. Formerly, men worked in the open air only so much as they liked. Now, thousands of workmen meet together and for the sake of maintenance work in factories or mines. Their condition is worse than that of beasts. They are obliged to work, at the risk of their lives, at most dangerous occupations, for the sake of millionaires. Formerly, men were made slaves under physical compulsion, now they are enslaved by temptation of money and of the luxuries that money can buy. There are now diseases of which people never dreamt before, and an army of doctors is engaged in finding out their cures, and so hospitals have increased. This is a test of civilisation. Formerly, special messengers were required and much expense was incurred in order to send letters; today, anyone can abuse his fellow by means of a letter for one penny. True, at the same cost, one can send one's thanks also. Formerly, people had two or three meals consisting of homemade bread and vegetables; now, they require something to eat every two hours, so that they have hardly leisure for anything else. What more need I say? All this you can ascertain from several authoritative books. These are all true tests of civilisation. And, if anyone speaks to the contrary, know that he is ignorant. This civilisation takes note neither of morality nor of religion. Its votaries calmly state that their business is not to teach religion. Some even consider it to be a superstitious growth. Others put on the cloak of religion, and prate about morality. But, after twenty years' experience, I have come to the conclusion that immorality is often taught in the name of morality. Even a child can understand that in all I have described above there can be no inducement to morality. Civilisation seeks to increase bodily comforts, and it fails miserably even in doing so.

This civilisation is irreligion, and it has taken such a hold on the people in Europe that those who are in it appear to be half mad. They lack real physical strength or courage. They keep up their energy by intoxication. They can hardly be happy in solitude. Women, who should be the queens of households, wander in the streets, or they slave away in factories. For the sake of a pittance, half a million women in England alone are labouring under trying circumstances in factories or similar institutions. This awful fact is one of the causes of the daily growing suffragette movement. . . .

READER: . . . If civilisation is a disease, and if it has attacked the English nation, why has she been able to take India, and why is she able to retain it?

EDITOR: . . . The English have not taken India; we have given it to them. They are not in India because of their strength, but because we keep them. Let us now see whether these propositions can be sustained. They came to our country originally for purposes of trade. Recall the [East India] Company. . . . Who made it [powerful]? . . . They had not the slightest intention at the time of establishing a kingdom. Who assisted the Company's officers? Who was tempted at the sight of their silver? Who bought their goods? History testifies that we did all this. In order to become rich all at once, we welcomed the Company's officers with open arms. . . .

EDITOR: . . . When our princes fought among themselves, they sought the assistance of [East India] Company. . . . That corporation was versed alike in commerce and war. It was unhampered by questions of morality. Its object was to increase its commerce and to make money. It accepted our assistance, and increased the number of its warehouses. To protect the latter it employed an army which was utilised by us also. Is it not then useless to blame the English for what we did at that time? The Hindus and the Mohammedans were at daggers drawn. This, too, gave the Company its opportunity, and thus we created the circumstances that gave the Company its control over India. Hence it is truer to say that we gave India to the English than that India was lost.

READER: Will you now tell me how they are able to retain India?

EDITOR: The causes that gave them India enable them to retain it. Some Englishmen state that they took, and they hold, India by the sword. Both these statements are wrong. The sword is entirely useless for holding India. We alone keep them. Napoleon is said to have described the English as a nation of shopkeepers. It is a fitting description. They hold whatever dominions they have for the sake of their commerce. Their army and their navy are intended to protect it. When the Transvaal offered no such attractions, the late Mr. Gladstone discovered that it was not right for the English to hold it. When it became a paying proposition, resistance led to war. Mr. Chamberlain soon discovered that England enjoyed a suzerainty over the Transvaal. It is related that someone asked the late President Kruger whether there was gold in the moon? He replied that it was highly unlikely, because, if there were, the English would have annexed it. Many problems can be solved by remembering that money is their God. Then it follows that we keep the English in India for our base self-interest. We like their commerce, they please us by their subtle methods, and get what they want from us. To blame them for this is to perpetuate their power. We further strengthen their hold by quarrelling amongst ourselves. If you accept the above statements, it is proved that the English entered India for the purposes of trade. They remain in it for the same purpose, and we help them to do so. Their arms and ammunition are perfectly useless. In this connection, I remind you that it is the British flag which is waving in Japan, and not the Japanese. The English have a treaty with Japan for the sake of their commerce, and you will see that, if they can manage it, their commerce will greatly expand in that country. They wish to convert the whole world into a vast market for their goods. That they cannot do so is true, but the blame will not be theirs. They will leave no stone unturned to reach the goal. . . .

EDITOR: It must be manifest to you that, but for the railways, the English could not have such a hold on India as they have. The railways, too, have spread the bubonic plague. Without them, masses could not move from place to place. They are the carriers of plague germs. Formerly we had natural segregation. Railways have also increased the frequency of famines, because, owing to facility of means of locomotion, people sell out their grain, and it is sent to the dearest markets. People become careless, and so the pressure of famine increases. They accentuate the evil nature of man. Bad men fulfil their evil designs with greater rapidity. The holy places of India have become unholy. Formerly, people went to these places with very great difficulty. Generally, therefore, only the real devotees visited such places. Nowadays, rogues visit them in order to practise their roguery. . . .

[T]he greatest injury they [lawyers] have done to the country is that they have tightened the English grip. Do you think that it would be possible for the English to carry on their government without law courts? It is wrong to consider that courts are established for the bene-fit of the people. Those who want to perpetuate their power do so through the courts. If people were to settle their own quarrels, a third party would not be able to exercise any authority over them. Truly, men were less unmanly when they settled their disputes either by fighting or by asking their relatives to decide upon them. They be-came more unmanly and cowardly when they resorted to the courts of law. It was certainly a sign of savagery when they settled their dis-putes by fighting. Is it any the less so if I ask a third party to decide be-tween you and me? Surely, the decision of a third party is not always right. The parties alone know who is right. We, in our simplicity and ignorance, imagine that a stranger, by taking our money, gives us justice.

The chief thing, however, to be remembered is that, without lawyers, courts could not have been established or conducted, and without the latter the English could not rule. Supposing that there were only English judges, English pleaders and English police, they could only rule over the English. The English could not do without Indian judges and Indian pleaders. How the pleaders were made in the first instance and how they were favoured you should understand well. Then you will have the same abhorrence for the profession that I have. If pleaders were to abandon their profession and consider it just as degrading as prostitution, English rule would break up in a day. They have been instrumental in having the charge laid against us that we love quarrels and courts, as fish love water. What I have said with reference to the pleaders necessarily applies to the judges; they are first cousins, and the one gives strength to the other. . . .

Doctors have almost unhinged us. Sometimes I think that quacks are better than highly qualified doctors. Let us consider: the business of a doctor is to take care of the body, or, properly speaking, not even that. Their business is really to rid the body of diseases that may afflict it. How do these diseases arise? Surely by our negligence or indulgence. I over-eat, I have indigestion, I go to a doctor, he gives me medicine, I am cured, I over-eat again, and I take his pills again. Had I not taken the pills in the first instance, I would have suffered the punishment deserved by me, and I would not have over-eaten again. The doctor intervened and helped me to indulge myself. My body thereby certainly felt more at ease, but my mind became weakened. A continuance of a course of a medicine must, therefore, result in loss of control over the mind.

I have indulged in vice, I contract a disease, a doctor cures me, the odds are that I shall repeat the vice. Had the doctor not intervened, nature would have done its work, and I would have acquired mastery over myself, would have been freed from vice, and would have become happy.

Hospitals are institutions for propagating sin. Men take less care of their bodies, and immorality increases. European doctors are the worst of all. For the sake of a mistaken care of the human body, they kill annually thousands of animals. They practise vivisection. No religion sanctions this. All say that it is not necessary to take so many lives for the sake of our bodies. . .

It is worth considering why we take up the profession of medicine. It is certainly not taken up for the purpose of serving humanity. We become doctors so that we may obtain honours and riches. I have endeavoured to show that there is no real service of humanity in the profession, and that it is injurious to mankind. Doctors make a show of their knowledge, and charge exorbitant fees. Their preparations, which are intrinsically worth a few pennies, cost shillings. The populace in its credulity and in the hope of ridding itself of some disease, allows itself to be cheated. Are not quacks then, whom we know, better than the doctors who put on an air of humaneness?

READER: When you speak of driving out Western civilisation, I suppose you will say that we want no machinery.

EDITOR: . . . It is machinery that has impoverished India. It is difficult to measure the harm that Manchester has done to us. It is due to Manchester that Indian handicraft has all but disappeared.

But I make a mistake. How can Manchester be blamed? We wore Manchester cloth, and that is why Manchester wove it. I was delighted when I read about the bravery of Bengal. There are no cloth mills in that Presidency. They were, therefore, able to restore the original handweaving occupation. It is true, Bengal encourages the mill industry of Bombay. If Bengal had proclaimed a boycott of *all* machine-made goods, it would have been much better.

Machinery has begun to desolate Europe. Ruination is now knocking at the English gates. Machinery is the chief symbol of modern civilisation; it represents a great sin.

The workers in the mills of Bombay have become slaves. The condition of the women working in the mills is shocking. When there were no mills, these women were not starving. If the machinery craze grows in our country, it will become an unhappy land. It may be considered a heresy, but I am bound to say that it were better for us to send money to Manchester and to use flimsy Manchester cloth, than to multiply mills in India. By using Manchester cloth, we would only waste our money, but, by reproducing Manchester in India, we shall keep our money at the price of our blood, because our very moral being will be sapped, and I call in support of my statement the very mill-hands as witnesses. And those who have amassed wealth out of factories are not likely to be better than other rich men. It would be folly to assume that an Indian Rockefeller would be better than the American Rockefeller. Impoverished India can become free, but it will be hard for an India made rich through immorality to regain its freedom. I fear we will have to admit that moneyed men support British rule; their interest is bound up with its stability. Money renders a man helpless. The other thing as harmful is sexual vice. Both are poison. A snake-bite is a lesser poison than these two, because the former merely destroys the body, but the latter destroy body, mind and soul. We need not, therefore, be pleased with the prospect of the growth of the mill industry. . . .

READER: You have so far spoken about machine-made cloth, but there are innumerable machine-made things. We have either to import them or to introduce machinery into our country.

EDITOR: Indeed, our goods even are made in Germany. What need, then, to speak of matches, pins, and glassware? My answer can be only one. What did India do before these articles were introduced?

Precisely the same should be done today. As long as we cannot make pins without machinery, so long will we do without them. The tinsel splendour of glassware we will have nothing to do with, and we will make wicks, as of old, with home-grown cotton, and use hand-made earthen saucers for lamps. So doing, we shall save our eyes and money, and will support Swadeshi, and so shall we attain Home Rule.

It is not to be conceived that all men will do all these things at one time, or that some men will give up all machine-made things at once. But, if the thought is sound, we will always find out what we can give up, and will gradually cease to use this.

Rosa Luxemburg

Capitalism Depends on the Non-Capitalist World

. . . After many centuries of development, the capitalist mode of production still constitutes only a fragment of total world production. Even in the small Continent of Europe, where it now chiefly prevails, it has not yet succeeded in dominating entire branches of production, such as peasant agriculture and the independent handicrafts; the same holds true, further, for large parts of North America and for a number of regions in the other continents. In general, capitalist production has hitherto been confined mainly to the countries in the temperate zone, whilst it made comparatively little progress in the East, for instance, and the South. Thus, if it were dependent exclusively on elements of production obtainable within such narrow limits, its present level and indeed its development in general would have been impossible. From the very beginning, the forms and laws of capitalist production aim to comprise the entire globe as a store of productive forces.

Excerpted from *The Accumulation of Capital* by Rosa Luxemburg. Translated by Agnes Schwarzchild. Copyright © 1963 by Routledge & Keegan Paul, Ltd. Used by permission of Routledge, Ltd.

Capital, impelled to appropriate productive forces for purposes of exploitation, ransacks the whole world, it procures its means of production from all corners of the earth, seizing them, if necessary by force, from all levels of civilisation and from all forms of society. The problem of the material elements of capitalist accumulation, far from being solved by the material form of the surplus value that has been produced, takes on quite a different aspect. It becomes necessary for capital progressively to dispose ever more fully of the whole globe, to acquire an unlimited choice of means of production, with regard to both quality and quantity, so as to find productive employment for the surplus value it has realised. . . .

Since capitalist production can develop fully only with complete access to all territories and climes, it can no more confine itself to the natural resources and productive forces of the temperate zone than it can manage with white labour alone. Capital needs other races to exploit territories where the white man cannot work. It must be able to mobilise world labour power without restriction in order to utilise all productive forces of the globe—up to the limits imposed by a system of producing surplus value. This labour power, however, is in most cases rigidly bound by the traditional pre-capitalist organisation of production. It must first be "set free" in order to be enrolled in the active army of capital. The emancipation of labour power from primitive social conditions and its absorption by the capitalist wage system is one of the indispensable historical bases of capitalism. For the first genuinely capitalist branch of production, the English cotton industry, not only the cotton of the Southern states of the American Union was essential, but also the millions of African Negroes who were shipped to America to provide the labour power for the plantations, and who later, as a free proletariat, were incorporated in the class of wage labourers in a capitalist system. Obtaining the necessary labour power from non-capitalist societies, the so-called "labour-problem", is ever more important for capital in the colonies. All possible methods of "gentle compulsion" are applied to solving this problem, to transfer labour from former social systems to the command of capital. . . .

. . . [W]hen the history of capitalism in Europe began, and right into the nineteenth century, dispossessing the peasants in England and on the Continent was the most striking weapon in the large-scale transformation of means of production and labour power into capital. Yet capital in power performs the same task even to-day, and on an

even more important scale—by modern colonial policy. It is an illusion to hope that capitalism will ever be content with the means of
production which it can acquire by way of commodity exchange. In
this respect already, capital is faced with difficulties because vast tracts
of the globe's surface are in the possession of social organisations that
have no desire for commodity exchange or cannot, because of the
entire social structure and the forms of ownership, offer for sale the productive forces in which capital is primarily interested. The most important of these productive forces is of course the land, its hidden
mineral treasure, and its meadows, woods and water, and further the
flocks of the primitive shepherd tribes. If capital were here to rely on
the process of slow internal disintegration, it might take centuries. To
wait patiently until the most important means of production could be
alienated by trading in consequence of this process were tantamount
to renouncing the productive forces of those territories altogether.
Hence derives the vital necessity for capitalism in its relations with
colonial countries to appropriate the most important means of
production. Since the primitive associations of the natives are the
strongest protection for their social organisations and for their material
bases of existence, capital must begin by planning for the systematic
destruction and annihilation of all the non-capitalist social units
which obstruct its development. With that we have passed beyond the
stage of primitive accumulation; this process is still going on. Each
new colonial expansion is accompanied, as a matter of course, by a relentless battle of capital against the social and economic ties of the natives, who are also forcibly robbed of their means of production and
labour power. Any hope to restrict the accumulation of capital exclusively to "peaceful competition," i.e. to regular commodity exchange
such as takes place between capitalist producer-countries, rests on the
pious belief that capital can accumulate without mediation of the
productive forces and without the demand of more primitive organisations, and that it can rely upon the slow internal process of a dis-
integrating natural economy. Accumulation, with its spasmodic
expansion, can no more wait for, and be content with, a natural internal disintegration of non-capitalist formations and their transition to
commodity economy, than it can wait for, and be content with, the
natural increase of the working population. Force is the only solution
open to capital; the accumulation of capital, seen as an historical process, employs force as a permanent weapon, not only at its genesis, but

further on down to the present day. From the point of view of the primitive societies involved, it is a matter of life or death; for them there can be no other attitude than opposition and fight to the finish — complete exhaustion and extinction. Hence permanent occupation of the colonies by the military, native risings, and punitive expeditions are the order of the day for any colonial regime. The method of violence, then, is the immediate consequence of the clash between capitalism and the organisations of a natural economy which would restrict accumulation. Their means of production and their labour power no less than their demand for surplus products is necessary to capitalism. Yet the latter is fully determined to undermine their independence as social units, in order to gain possession of their means of production and labour power and to convert them into commodity buyers. This method is the most profitable and gets the quickest results, and so it is also the most expedient for capital. . . .

The second condition of importance for acquiring means of production and realising the surplus value is that commodity exchange and commodity economy should be introduced in societies based on natural economy as soon as their independence has been abrogated, or rather in the course of this disruptive process. Capital requires to buy the products of, and sell its commodities to, all non-capitalist strata and societies. Here at last we seem to find the beginnings of that "peace" and "equality," the *do ut des*, mutual interest, "peaceful competition" and the "influences of civilisation." For capital can indeed deprive alien social associations of their means of production by force, it can compel the workers to submit to capitalist exploitation, but it cannot force them to buy its commodities or to realise its surplus value. In districts where natural economy formerly prevailed, the introduction of means of transport — railways, navigation, canals — is vital for the spreading of commodity economy, a further hopeful sign. The triumphant march of commodity economy thus begins in most cases with magnificent constructions of modern transport, such as railway lines which cross primeval forests and tunnel through the mountains, telegraph wires which bridge the deserts, and ocean liners which call at the most outlying ports. But it is a mere illusion that these are peaceful changes. Under the standard of commerce, the relations between the East India Company and the spice-producing countries were quite as piratical, extortionate, and blatantly fraudulent as present-day relations between American capitalists and the Red

Indians of Canada whose furs they buy, or between German merchants and the Negroes of Africa. Modern China presents a classical example of the "gentle," "peace-loving" practices of commodity exchange with backward countries. Throughout the nineteenth century, beginning with the early forties, her history has been punctuated by wars with the object of opening her up to trade by brute force. Missionaries provoked persecutions of Christians, Europeans instigated risings, and in periodical massacres a completely helpless and peaceful agrarian population was forced to match arms with the most modern capitalist military technique of all the Great Powers of Europe. Heavy war contributions necessitated a public debt, China taking up European loans, resulting in European control over her finances and occupation of her fortifications; the opening of free ports was enforced, railway concessions to European capitalists extorted. By all these measures commodity exchange was fostered in China, from the early thirties of the last century until the beginning of the Chinese revolution. . . .

The general result of the struggle between capitalism and simple commodity production is this: after substituting commodity economy for natural economy, capital takes the place of simple commodity economy. Non-capitalist organisations provide a fertile soil for capitalism; more strictly: capital feeds on the ruins of such organisations, and although this non-capitalist *milieu* is indispensable for accumulation, the latter proceeds at the cost of this medium nevertheless, by eating it up. Historically, the accumulation of capital is a kind of metabolism between capitalist economy and those pre-capitalist methods of production without which it cannot go on and which, in this light, it corrodes and assimilates. Thus capital cannot accumulate without the aid of non-capitalist organisations, nor, on the other hand, can it tolerate their continued existence side by side with itself. Only the continuous and progressive disintegration of non-capitalist organisations makes accumulation of capital possible. . . .

The imperialist phase of capitalist accumulation which implies universal competition comprises the industrialisation and capitalist emancipation of the *hinterland* where capital formerly realised its surplus value. Characteristic of this phase are: lending abroad, railroad constructions, revolutions, and wars. The last decade, from 1900 to 1910, shows in particular the world-wide movement of capital, especially in Asia and neighbouring Europe: in Russia, Turkey, Persia,

India, Japan, China, and also in North Africa. Just as the substitution of commodity economy for a natural economy and that of capitalist production for a simple commodity production was achieved by wars, social crises, and the destruction of entire social systems, so at present the achievement of capitalist autonomy in the *hinterland* and backward colonies is attained amidst wars and revolutions. Revolution is an essential for the process of capitalist emancipation. The backward communities must shed their obsolete political organisations, relics of natural and simple commodity economy, and create a modern state machinery adapted to the purposes of capitalist production. The revolutions in Turkey, Russia, and China fall under this heading. . . .

In the Imperialist Era, the foreign loan played an outstanding part as a means for young capitalist states to acquire independence. The contradictions inherent in the modern system of foreign loans are the concrete expression of those which characterise the imperialist phase. Though foreign loans are indispensable for the emancipation of the rising capitalist states, they are yet the surest ties by which the old capitalist states maintain their influence, exercise financial control and exert pressure on the customs, foreign and commercial policy of the young capitalist states. Pre-eminently channels for the investment in new spheres of capital accumulated in the old countries, such loans widen the scope for the accumulation of capital; but at the same time they restrict it by creating new competition for the investing countries. . . .

. . . The case of Egypt, just as that of China and, more recently, Morocco, shows militarism as the executor of the accumulation of capital, lurking behind international loans, railroad building, irrigation systems, and similar works of civilisation. The Oriental states cannot develop from natural to commodity economy and further to capitalist economy fast enough and are swallowed up by international capital, since they cannot perform these transformations without selling their souls to capital. Their feverish metamorphoses are tantamount to their absorption by international capital. . . .

Imperialism is the political expression of the accumulation of capital in its competitive struggle for what remains still open of the non-capitalist environment. Still the largest part of the world in terms of geography, this remaining field for the expansion of capital is yet insignificant as against the high level of development already attained by the productive forces of capital; witness the immense masses of capital accumulated in the old countries which seek an outlet for their surplus product and strive to capitalise their surplus value, and the rapid change-over to capitalism of the pre-capitalist civilisations. On the international stage, then, capital must take appropriate measures. With the high development of the capitalist countries and their increasingly severe competition in acquiring non-capitalist areas, imperialism grows in lawlessness and violence, both in aggression against the non-capitalist world and in ever more serious conflicts among the competing capitalist countries. But the more violently, ruthlessly and thoroughly imperialism brings about the decline of non-capitalist civilisations, the more rapidly it cuts the very ground from under the feet of capitalist accumulation. Though imperialism is the historical method for prolonging the career of capitalism, it is also a sure means of bringing it to a swift conclusion. . . .

When the Free Trade era opened, Eastern Asia was only just being made accessible by the Chinese wars, and European capital had but begun to make headway in Egypt. In the eighties the policy of expansion became ever stronger, together with a policy of protective tariffs. . . . The inherent contradictions of an international policy of protective tariffs, exactly like the dual character of the international loan system, are just a reflection of the historical antagonism which has developed between the dual interests of accumulation: expansion, the realisation and capitalisation of surplus value on the one hand, and, on the other, an outlook which conceives of everything purely in terms of commodity exchange. . . .

Thus capitalist accumulation as a whole, as an actual historical process, has two different aspects. One concerns the commodity market and the place where surplus value is produced—the factory, the mine, the agricultural estate. Regarded in this light, accumulation is a purely economic process, with its most important phase a transaction between the capitalist and wage labourer. . . .

The other aspect of the accumulation of capital concerns the relations between capitalism and the non-capitalist modes of production which start making their appearance on the international stage. Its predominant methods are colonial policy, an international loan system—a policy of spheres of interest—and war. Force, fraud, oppression, looting are openly displayed without any attempt at concealment, and it requires an effort to discover within this tangle of political violence and contests of power the stern laws of the economic process. . . .

In reality, political power is nothing but a vehicle for the economic process. The conditions for the reproduction of capital provide the organic link between these two aspects of the accumulation of capital. The historical career of capitalism can only be appreciated by taking them together. "Sweating blood and filth with every pore from head to toe" characterises not only the birth of capital but also its progress in the world at every step, and thus capitalism prepares its own downfall under ever more violent contortions and convulsions.

V. I. Lenin

Imperialism, the Highest Stage of Capitalism

Typical of the old capitalism, when free competition held undivided sway, was the export of *goods*. Typical of the latest stage of capitalism, when monopolies rule, is the export of *capital*. . . .

It goes without saying that if capitalism could develop agriculture, which today is everywhere lagging terribly behind industry, if it could raise the living standards of the masses, who in spite of the amazing technical progress are everywhere still half-starved and poverty-stricken, there could be no question of a surplus of capital. This "argument" is very often advanced by the petty-bourgeois critics of capitalism. But if capitalism did these things it would not be capitalism; for both uneven development and a semi-starvation level of existence of the masses are fundamental and inevitable conditions and constitute premises of this mode of production. As long as capitalism remains what it is, surplus capital will be utilised not for the purpose

Vladimir I. Lenin, excerpted from *Selected Works* (Moscow: Progress Publishers, 1975). Reprinted by permission of Progress Publishing Group Corporation.

of raising the standard of living of the masses in a given country, for this would mean a decline in profits for the capitalists, but for the purpose of increasing profits by exporting capital abroad to the backward countries. In these backward countries profits are usually high, for capital is scarce, the price of land is relatively low, wages are low, raw materials are cheap. The export of capital is made possible by a number of backward countries having already been drawn into world capitalist intercourse; main railways have either been or are being built in those countries, elementary conditions for industrial development have been created, etc. The need to export capital arises from the fact that in a few countries capitalism has become "overripe" and (owing to the backward state of agriculture and the poverty of the masses) capital cannot find a field for "profitable" investment. . . .

The export of capital influences and greatly accelerates the development of capitalism in those countries to which it is exported. While, therefore, the export of capital may tend to a certain extent to arrest development in the capital-exporting countries, it can only do so by expanding and deepening the further development of capitalism throughout the world. . . .

. . . [T]he characteristic feature of the period under review is the final partitioning of the globe—final, not in the sense that *repartition* is impossible; on the contrary, repartitions are possible and inevitable—but in the sense that the colonial policy of the capitalist countries has *completed* the seizure of the unoccupied territories on our planet. For the first time the world is completely divided up, so that in the future *only* redivision is possible, i.e., territories can only pass from one "owner" to another, instead of passing as ownerless territory to an "owner."

Hence, we are living in a peculiar epoch of world colonial policy, which is most closely connected with the "latest stage in the development of capitalism," with finance capital. . . .

Finance capital is interested not only in the already discovered sources of raw materials but also in potential sources, because present-day technical development is extremely rapid, and land which is useless today may be improved tomorrow if new methods are devised (to this end a big bank can equip a special expedition of engineers, agricultural experts, etc.), and if large amounts of capital are invested. This also applies to prospecting for minerals, to new methods of processing up and utilising raw materials, etc. Hence, the inevitable striving of finance capital to enlarge its spheres of influence and even its actual territory. In the same way that the trusts capitalise their property at two or three times its value, taking into account its "potential" (and not actual) profits and the further results of monopoly, so finance capital in general strives to seize the largest possible amount of land of all kinds in all places, and by every means, taking into account potential sources of raw materials and fearing to be left behind in the fierce struggle for the last remnants of independent territory, or for the repartition of those territories that have been already divided. . . .

We must now try to sum up, to draw together the threads of what has been said . . . on the subject of imperialism. Imperialism emerged as the development and direct continuation of the fundamental characteristics of capitalism in general. But capitalism only became capitalist imperialism at a definite and very high stage of its development, when certain of its fundamental characteristics began to change into their opposites, when the features of the epoch of transition from capitalism to a higher social and economic system had taken shape and revealed themselves in all spheres. Economically, the main thing in this process is the displacement of capitalist free competition by capitalist monopoly. Free competition is the basic feature of capitalism, and of commodity production generally; monopoly is the exact opposite of free competition, but we have seen the latter being transformed into monopoly before our eyes, creating large-scale industry and forcing out small industry, replacing large-scale by still larger-scale industry, and carrying concentration of production and capital to the point where out of it has grown and is growing monopoly: cartels, syndicates and trusts, and merging with them, the capital of a dozen or so banks, which manipulate thousands of millions. At the same time the monopolies, which have grown out of free competition, do not eliminate the latter, but exist above it and alongside it, and thereby give rise to a number of very acute, intense antagonisms, frictions and conflicts. Monopoly is the transition from capitalism to a higher system.

If it were necessary to give the briefest possible definition of imperialism we should have to say that imperialism is the monopoly stage of capitalism. Such a definition would include what is most important, for, on the one hand, finance capital is the bank capital of a few very big monopolist banks merged with the capital of the monopolist associations of industrialists; and, on the other hand, the division of the world is the transition from a colonial policy which has extended without hindrance to territories unseized by any capitalist power, to a colonial policy of monopolist possession of the territory of the world, which has been completely divided up.

But very brief definitions, although convenient, for they sum up the main points, are nevertheless inadequate, since we have to deduce from them some especially important features of the phenomenon that has to be defined. And so, without forgetting the conditional and relative value of all definitions in general, which can never embrace all the concatenations of a phenomenon in its full development, we must give a definition of imperialism that will include the following five of its basic features:

(1) the concentration of production and capital has developed to such a high stage that it has created monopolies which play a decisive role in economic life; (2) the merging of bank capital with industrial capital, and the creation, on the basis of this "finance capital," of a financial oligarchy; (3) the export of capital as distinguished from the export of commodities acquires exceptional importance; (4) the formation of international monopolist capitalist associations which share the world among themselves; and (5) the territorial division of the whole world among the biggest capitalist powers is completed. Imperialism is capitalism at that stage of development at which the dominance of monopolies and finance capital is established; in which the export of capital has acquired pronounced importance; in which the division of the world among the international trusts has begun; in which the division of all territories of the globe among the biggest capitalist powers has been completed. . . .

As we have seen, the deepest economic foundation of imperialism is monopoly. This is capitalist monopoly, i.e., monopoly which has grown out of capitalism and which exists in the general environment of capitalism, commodity production, and competition, in permanent and insoluble contradiction to this general environment. Nevertheless, like all monopoly, it inevitably engenders a tendency of stagnation and decay. Since monopoly prices are established, even temporarily, the motive cause of technical and, consequently, of all other progress disappears to a certain extent and, further, the *economic* possibility arises of deliberately retarding technical progress. For instance, in America, a certain Owens invented a machine which revolutionised the manufacture of bottles. The German bottle-manufacturing cartel purchased Owens's patent, but pigeon-holed it, refrained from utilising it. Certainly, monopoly under capitalism can never completely, and for a very long period of time, eliminate competition in the world market (and this, by the by, is one of the reasons why the theory of ultra-imperialism is so absurd). Certainly, the possibility of reducing the cost of production and increasing profits by introducing technical improvements operates in the direction of change. But the *tendency* to stagnation and decay, which is characteristic of monopoly, continues to operate, and in some branches of industry, in some countries, for certain periods of time, it gains the upper hand.

The monopoly ownership of very extensive, rich or well-situated colonies operates in the same direction.

Further, imperialism is an immense accumulation of money capital in a few countries, amounting, as we have seen, to 100,000–150,000 million francs in securities. Hence the extraordinary growth of a class, or rather, of a stratum of rentiers, i.e., people who live by "clipping coupons," who take no part in any enterprise whatever, whose profession is idleness. The export of capital, one of the most essential economic bases of imperialism, still more completely isolates the rentiers from production and sets the seal of parasitism on the whole country that lives by exploiting the labour of several overseas countries and colonies. . . .

The enormous dimensions of finance capital concentrated in a few hands and creating an extraordinarily dense and widespread network of relationships and connections which subordinates not only the small and medium, but also the very small capitalists and small masters, on the one hand, and the increasingly intense struggle waged against other national state groups of financiers for the division of the world and domination over other countries, on the other hand, cause the propertied classes to go over entirely to the side of imperialism. "General" enthusiasm over the prospects of imperialism, furious defence of it, and painting it in the brightest colours—such are the signs of the times. Imperialist ideology also penetrates the working class. No Chinese Wall separates it from the other classes. The leaders of the present-day, so-called, "Social-Democratic" Party of Germany are justly called "social-imperialists," that is, socialists in words and imperialists in deeds; but as early as 1902, Hobson noted the existence in Britain of "Fabian imperialists" who belonged to the opportunist Fabian Society. . . .

We have seen that in its economic essence imperialism is monopoly capitalism. This in itself determines its place in history, for monopoly that grows out of the soil of free competition, and precisely out of free competition, is the transition from the capitalist system to a higher socio-economic order. We must take special note of the four principal types of monopoly, or principal manifestations of monopoly capitalism, which are characteristic of the epoch we are examining.

Firstly, monopoly arose out of the concentration of production at a very high stage. This refers to the monopolist capitalist associations, cartels, syndicates, and trusts. We have seen the important part these play in present-day economic life. At the beginning of the twentieth century, monopolies had acquired complete supremacy in the advanced countries, and although the first steps towards the formation of the cartels were taken by countries enjoying the protection of high tariffs (Germany, America), Great Britain, with her system of free trade, revealed the same basic phenomenon, only a little later, namely, the birth of monopoly out of the concentration of production.

Secondly, monopolies have stimulated the seizure of the most important sources of raw materials, especially for the basic and most highly cartelised industries in capitalist society: the coal and iron industries. The monopoly of the most important sources of raw materials has enormously increased the power of big capital, and has sharpened the antagonism between cartelised and non-cartelised industry.

Thirdly, monopoly has sprung from the banks. The banks have developed from modest middleman enterprises into the monopolists of finance capital. Some three to five of the biggest banks in each of the foremost capitalist countries have achieved the "personal link-up" between industrial and bank capital, and have concentrated in their hands the control of thousands upon thousands of millions which form the greater part of the capital and income of entire countries. A financial oligarchy, which throws a close network of dependence relationships over all the economic and political institutions of present-day bourgeois society without exception—such is the most striking manifestation of this monopoly.

Fourthly, monopoly has grown out of colonial policy. To the numerous "old" motives of colonial policy, finance capital has added the struggle for the sources of raw materials, for the export of capital, for spheres of influence, i.e., for spheres for profitable deals, concessions, monopoly profits, and so on, economic territory in general. When the colonies of the European powers, for instance, comprised only one-tenth of the territory of Africa (as was the case in 1876), colonial policy was able to develop by methods other than those of monopoly—by the "free grabbing" of territories, so to speak. But when nine-tenths of Africa had been seized (by 1900), when the whole world had been divided up, there was inevitably ushered in the era of monopoly possession of colonies and, consequently, of particularly intense struggle for the division and the redivision of the world.

The extent to which monopolist capital has intensified all the contradictions of capitalism is generally known. It is sufficient to mention the high cost of living and the tyranny of the cartels. This intensification of contradictions constitutes the most powerful driving force of the transitional period of history, which began from the time of the final victory of world finance capital.

Monopolies, oligarchy, the striving for domination and not for freedom, the exploitation of an increasing number of small or weak nations by a handful of the richest or most powerful nations—all these have given birth to those distinctive characteristics of imperialism which compel us to define it as parasitic or decaying capitalism. More and more prominently there emerges, as one of the tendencies of imperialism, the creation of the "rentier state," the usurer state, in which the bourgeoisie to an ever-increasing degree lives on the proceeds of capital exports and by "clipping coupons." It would be a mistake to believe that this tendency to decay precludes the rapid growth of capitalism. It does not. In the epoch of imperialism, certain branches of industry, certain strata of the bourgeoisie, and certain countries betray, to a greater or lesser degree, now one and now another of these tendencies. On the whole, capitalism is growing far more rapidly than before; but this growth is not only becoming more and more uneven in general, its unevenness also manifests itself, in particular, in the decay of the countries which are richest in capital (Britain).

. . . In its turn, this finance capital which has grown with such extraordinary rapidity is not unwilling, precisely because it has grown so quickly, to pass on to a more "tranquil" possession of colonies which have to be seized—and not only by peaceful methods—from richer nations. In the United States, economic development in the last decades has been even more rapid than in Germany, *and for this very reason,* the parasitic features of modern American capitalism have stood out with particular prominence. On the other hand, a comparison of, say, the republican American bourgeoisie with the monarchist Japanese or German bourgeoisie shows that the most pronounced political distinction diminishes to an extreme degree in the epoch of imperialism — not because it is unimportant in general, but because in all these cases we are talking about a bourgeoisie which has definite features of parasitism.

The receipt of high monopoly profits by the capitalists in one of the numerous branches of industry, in one of the numerous countries, etc. makes it economically possible for them to bribe certain sections of the workers, and for a time a fairly considerable minority of them, and win them to the side of the bourgeoisie of a given industry or given nation against all the others. The intensification of antagonisms between imperialist nations for the division of the world increases this urge. And so there is created that bond between imperialism and opportunism, which revealed itself first and most clearly in Great Britain, owing to the fact that certain features of imperialist development were observable there much earlier than in other countries. . . . As a matter of fact the extraordinary rapidity and the particularly revolting character of the development of opportunism is by no means a guarantee that its victory will be durable: the rapid growth of a painful abscess on a healthy body can only cause it to burst more quickly and thus relieve the body of it. The most dangerous of all in this respect are those who do not wish to understand that the fight against imperialism is a sham and humbug unless it is inseparably bound up with the fight against opportunism. . . .

Joseph A. Schumpeter

The Sociology of Imperialisms

No one calls it imperialism when a state, no matter how brutally and vigorously, pursues concrete interests of its own; and when it can be

From Joseph A. Schumpeter, *Imperialism and Social Classes* (New York: Augustus M. Kelley, Inc., 1951) © Copyright 1951 Augustus M. Kelley. Excerpted by permission.

expected to abandon its aggressive attitude as soon as it has attained what it was after. The word "imperialism" has been abused as a slogan to the point where it threatens to lose all meaning, but up to this point our definition is quite in keeping with common usage, even in the press. For whenever the word imperialism is used, there is always the implication—whether sincere or not—of an aggressiveness, the true reasons for which do not lie in the aims which are temporarily being pursued; of an aggressiveness that is only kindled anew by each success; of an aggressiveness for its own sake, as reflected in such terms as "hegemony," "world dominion," and so forth. And history, in truth, shows us nations and classes—most nations furnish an example at some time or other—that seek expansion for the sake of expanding, war for the sake of fighting, victory for the sake of winning, dominion for the sake of ruling. This determination cannot be explained by any of the pretexts that bring it into action, by any of the aims for which it seems to be struggling at the time. It confronts us, independent of all concrete purpose or occasion, as an enduring disposition, seizing upon one opportunity as eagerly as the next. It shines through all the arguments put forward on behalf of present aims. It values conquest not so much on account of the immediate advantages—advantages that more often than not are more than dubious, or that are heedlessly cast away with the same frequency—as because it *is* conquest, success, action. Here the theory of concrete interest in our sense fails. What needs to be explained is how the will to victory itself came into being.

Expansion for its own sake always requires, among other things, concrete objects if it is to reach the action stage and maintain itself, but this does not constitute its meaning. Such expansion is in a sense its own "object," and the truth is that it has no adequate object beyond itself. Let us therefore, in the absence of a better term, call it "objectless." It follows for that very reason that, just as such expansion cannot be explained by concrete interest, so too it is never satisfied by the fulfillment of a concrete interest, as would be the case if fulfillment were the motive, and the struggle for it merely a necessary evil—a counterargument, in fact. Hence the tendency of such expansion to transcend all bounds and tangible limits, to the point of utter exhaustion. This, then, is our definition: imperialism is the objectless disposition on the part of a state to unlimited forcible expansion.

Now it may be possible, in the final analysis, to give an "economic explanation" for this phenomenon, to end up with economic factors. Two different points present themselves in this connection: First, an attempt can be made, following the basic idea of the economic interpretation of history, to derive imperialist tendencies from the economic-structural influences that shape life in general and from the relations of production. I should like to emphasize that I do not doubt in the least that this powerful instrument of analysis will stand up here in the same sense that it has with other, similar phenomena—if only it is kept in mind that customary modes of political thought and feeling in a given age can never be mere "reflexes" of, or counterparts to, the production situation of that age. . . .

Imperialism thus is atavistic in character. It falls into that large group of surviving features from earlier ages that play such an important part in every concrete social situation. In other words, it is an element that stems from the living conditions, not of the present, but of the past—or, put in terms of the economic interpretation of history, from past rather than present relations of production. It is an atavism in the social structure, in individual, psychological habits of emotional reaction. Since the vital needs that created it have passed away for good, it too must gradually disappear, even though every warlike involvement, no matter how non-imperialist in character, tends to revive it. It tends to disappear as a structural element because the structure that brought it to the fore goes into a decline, giving way, in the course of social development, to other structures that have no room for it and eliminate the power factors that supported it. It tends to disappear as an element of habitual emotional reaction, because of the progressive rationalization of life and mind, a process in which old functional needs are absorbed by new tasks, in which heretofore military energies are functionally modified. If our theory is correct, cases of imperialism should decline in intensity the later they occur in the history of a people and of a culture. . . .

1.   Throughout the world of capitalism, and specifically among the elements formed by capitalism in modern social life, there has arisen a fundamental opposition to war, expansion, cabinet diplomacy, armaments, and socially-entrenched professional armies. . . .

2.   Wherever capitalism penetrated, peace parties of such strength arose that virtually every war meant a political struggle on the

domestic scene. . . . In the distant past, imperialism had needed no disguise whatever, and in the absolute autocracies only a very transparent one; but today imperialism is carefully hidden from public view — even though there may still be an unofficial appeal to warlike instincts. No people and no ruling class today can openly afford to regard war as a normal state of affairs or a normal element in the life of nations. . . .

3. The type of industrial worker created by capitalism is always vigorously anti-imperialist. In the individual case, skillful agitation may persuade the working masses to approve or remain neutral — a concrete goal or interest in self-defense always playing the main part — but no initiative for a forcible policy of expansion ever emanates from this quarter. On this point official socialism unquestionably formulates not merely the interests but also the conscious will of the workers. Even less than peasant imperialism is there any such thing as socialist or other working-class imperialism.

4. Despite manifest resistance on the part of powerful elements, the capitalist age has seen the development of methods for preventing war, for the peaceful settlement of disputes among states. The very fact of resistance means that the trend can be explained only from the mentality of capitalism as a mode of life. It definitely limits the opportunities imperialism needs if it is to be a powerful force. . . .

5. Among all capitalist economies, that of the United States is least burdened with precapitalist elements, survivals, reminiscences, and power factors. Certainly we cannot expect to find imperialist tendencies altogether lacking even in the United States, for the immigrants came from Europe with their convictions fully formed, and the environment certainly favored the revival of instincts of pugnacity. But we can conjecture that among all countries the United States is likely to exhibit the weakest imperialist trend. . . . Leading industrial and financial circles in the United States had and still have an evident interest in incorporating Mexico into the Union. There was more than enough opportunity for such annexation — but Mexico remained unconquered. Racial catch phrases and working-class interests pointed to Japan as a possible danger. Hence possession of the Philippines was not a matter of indifference — yet surrender of this possession is being discussed. Canada was an almost defenseless prize — but Canada re-

mained independent. Even in the United States, of course, politicians need slogans—especially slogans calculated to divert attention from domestic issues. Theodore Roosevelt and certain magnates of the press actually resorted to imperialism—and the result, in that world of high capitalism, was utter defeat, a defeat that would have been even more abject, if other slogans, notably those appealing to anti-trust sentiment, had not met with better success. . . .

It may be stated as being beyond controversy that where free trade prevails *no* class has an interest in forcible expansion as such. For in such a case the citizens and goods of every nation can move in foreign countries as freely as though those countries were politically their own— free trade implying far more than mere freedom from tariffs. In a genuine state of free trade, foreign raw materials and foodstuffs are as accessible to each nation as though they were within its own territory. Where the cultural backwardness of a region makes normal economic intercourse dependent on colonization, it does not matter, assuming free trade, which of the "civilized" nations undertakes the task of colonization. Dominion of the seas, in such a case, means little more than a maritime traffic police. Similarly, it is a matter of indifference to a nation whether a railway concession in a foreign country is acquired by one of its own citizens or not—just so long as the railway *is* built and put into efficient operation. . . .

A protectionist policy, however, does facilitate the formation of cartels and trusts. . . . What happens when the entrepreneurs successfully pursue such a policy is something that did not occur in the cases discussed so far—a conflict of interests between nations that becomes so sharp that it cannot be overcome by the existing basic community of interests. . . .

In such a struggle among "dumped" products and capitals, it is no longer a matter of indifference who builds a given railroad, who owns a mine or a colony. Now that the law of costs is no longer operative, it becomes necessary to fight over such properties with desperate effort and with every available means, including those that are not economic in character, such as diplomacy. The concrete objects in question often become entirely subsidiary considerations; the anticipated profit may be trifling, because of the competitive struggle—a struggle that has very little to do with normal competition. What matters is to gain a foothold of some kind and then to exploit this foothold as a base for the conquest of new markets. . . .

. . . In this context, the conquest of colonies takes on an altogether different significance. Nonmonopolist countries, especially those adhering to free trade, reap little profit from such a policy. But it is a different matter with countries that function in a monopolist role *vis-à-vis* their colonies. There being no competition, they can use cheap native labor without its ceasing to be cheap; they can market their products, even in the colonies, at monopoly prices; they can, finally, invest capital that would only depress the profit rate at home and that could be placed in other civilized countries only at very low interest rates. . . .

Thus we have here, within a social group that carries great political weight, a strong, undeniable, economic interest in such things as protective tariffs, cartels, monopoly prices, forced exports (dumping), an aggressive economic policy, an aggressive foreign policy generally, and war, including wars of expansion with a typically imperialist character. . . .

Yet the final word in any presentation of this aspect of modern economic life must be one of warning against overestimating it. The conflicts that have been described, born of an export-dependent monopoly capitalism, may serve to submerge the real community of interests among nations; the monopolist press may drive it underground; but underneath the surface it never completely disappears. Deep down, the normal sense of business and trade usually prevails. . . .

. . . Export monopolism does *not* grow from the inherent laws of capitalist development. The character of capitalism leads to large-scale production, but with few exceptions large-scale production does *not* lead to the kind of unlimited concentration that would leave but one or only a few firms in each industry. On the contrary, any plant runs up against limits to its growth in a given location; and the growth of combinations which would make sense under a system of free trade encounters limits of organizational efficiency. Beyond these limits there is no tendency toward combination inherent in the competitive system. In particular, the rise of trusts and cartels—a phenomenon quite different from the trend to large-scale production with which it is often confused—can never be explained by the automatism of the competitive system. This follows from the very fact that trusts and cartels can attain their primary purpose — to pursue a monopoly policy — only behind protective tariffs, without which they would lose their essential significance. But protective tariffs do not automatically grow from the competitive system. They are the fruit of political action — *a type of action that by no means reflects the objective interests of all those concerned* but that, on the contrary, becomes impossible as soon as the majority of those whose consent is necessary realize their true interests. To some extent it is obvious, and for the rest it will be presently shown, that the interests of the minority, quite appropriately expressed in support of a protective tariff, do not stem from capitalism as such. It follows that *it is a basic fallacy to describe imperialism as a necessary phase of capitalism, or even to speak of the development of capitalism into imperialism.* . . .

Since we cannot derive even export monopolism from any tendencies of the competitive system toward big enterprise, we must find some other explanation. . . .

Trade and industry of the early capitalist period thus remained strongly pervaded with precapitalist methods, bore the stamp of autocracy, and served its interests, either willingly or by force. . . . Existing economic interests, "artificially" shaped by the autocratic state, remained dependent on the "protection" of the state. . . . This explains why the features and trends of autocracy — including imperialism — proved so resistant, why they exerted such a powerful influence on capitalist development, why the old export monopolism could live on and merge into the new.

These are facts of fundamental significance to an understanding of the soul of modern Europe. Had the ruling class of the Middle Ages — the war-oriented nobility — changed its profession and function and become the ruling class of the capitalist world; or had developing capitalism swept it away, put it out of business, instead of merely clashing head-on with it in the agrarian sphere — then much would have been different in the life of modern peoples. But as things actually were, neither eventuality occurred; or, more correctly, both are taking place, only at a very slow pace. . . . The social pyramid of the present age has been formed, not by the substance and laws of capitalism alone, but by two different social substances, and by the laws of two different epochs. Whoever seeks to understand Europe must not forget this and concentrate all attention on the indubitably basic truth that one of these substances tends to be absorbed by the other and thus the sharpest of all class conflicts tends to be eliminated. Whoever seeks to understand Europe must not overlook that even today its life, its ideology, its politics are greatly under the influence of the feudal "substance," that while the bourgeoisie can assert its interests everywhere, it "rules" only in exceptional circumstances, and then only briefly. . . . The "feudal" elements, on the other hand, have both feet on the ground, even psychologically speaking. Their ideology is as stable as their mode of life. They believe certain things to be really true, others to be really false. This quality of possessing a definite character and cast of mind as a class, this simplicity and solidity of social and spiritual position extends their power far beyond their actual bases, gives them the ability to assimilate new elements, to make others serve their purposes—in a word, gives them *prestige*, something to which the bourgeois, as is well known, always looks up, something with which he tends to ally himself, despite all actual conflicts. . . .

Here we find that we have penetrated to the historical as well as the sociological sources of modern imperialism. It does not *coincide* with nationalism and militarism, though it *fuses* with them by supporting them as it is supported by them. It too is—not only historically, but also sociologically—a heritage of the autocratic state, of its structural elements, organizational forms, interest alignments, and human attitudes, the outcome of precapitalist forces which the autocratic state has reorganized, in part by the methods of early capitalism. It would never have been evolved by the "inner logic" of capitalism itself. This is true even of mere export monopolism. It too has its sources in absolutist policy and the action habits of an essentially precapitalist environment. That it was able to develop to its present dimensions is owing to the momentum of a situation once created, which continued to engender ever new "artificial" economic structures, that is, those which maintain themselves by political power alone. In most of the countries addicted to export monopolism it is also owing to the fact that the old autocratic state and the old attitude of the bourgeoisie toward it were so vigorously maintained. But export monopolism, to go a step further, is not yet imperialism. And even if it had been able to arise without protective tariffs, it would never have developed into imperialism in the hands of an unwarlike bourgeoisie. If this did happen, it was only because the heritage included the war machine, together with its socio-psychological aura and aggressive bent, and because a class oriented toward war maintained itself in a ruling position. This class clung to its domestic interest in war, and the pro-military interests among the bourgeoisie were able to ally themselves with it. This alliance kept alive war instincts and ideas of overlordship, male supremacy, and triumphant glory—ideas that would have otherwise long since died. It led to social conditions that, while they ultimately stem from the conditions of production, cannot be explained from capitalist production methods alone. And it often impresses its mark on present-day politics, threatening Europe with the constant danger of war.

Ho Chi Minh

The Struggle Lies in the Colonies

I am here in order to continuously remind the International of the existence of the colonies and to point out that the revolution faces a colonial danger as well as a great future in the colonies. It seems to me that the comrades do not entirely comprehend the fact that the fate of the world proletariat and especially that of the proletariat in the colonies is closely tied to the fate of the oppressed peoples of the colonies. Since this is the case I will take every opportunity that presents itself or, if necessary, create opportunities to point out to you the importance of the colonial question. For this purpose it would be sufficient if I repeated the talk given yesterday by Comrade Roy, changing

From *International Communism in the Era of Lenin* by Helmut Gruber. Copyright © 1972 by Helmut Gruber. Used by permission of Doubleday, a division of Bantam Doubleday Dell Publishing Group, Inc.

only names where appropriate, e.g., substituting for the word "England" the words "France," "Belgium," "America," "Japan," "Italy," etc. But since I come from a French colony, I will, for brevity's sake, speak only of French imperialism and about the French party in the French colonies, just as Comrade Roy spoke of English imperialism, our English party, and English colonies. You must excuse my frankness, but I cannot help but observe that the speeches by comrades from the mother countries give me the impression that they wish to kill a snake by stepping on its tail. You all know that today the poison and life energy of the capitalist snake is concentrated more in the colonies than in the mother countries. The colonies supply the raw materials for industry. The colonies supply soldiers for the armies. In the future, the colonies will be bastions of the counter-revolution. Yet in your discussions of the revolution you neglect to talk about the colonies. If one wants to break an egg or a stone, one will be careful to find an instrument whose strength corresponds to the object one wishes to break. Why is it that you are not equally careful when you want to destroy capitalism? Why is it that where the revolution is concerned you do not wish to make your strength, your propaganda, equal to the enemy whom you wish to fight and defeat? Why do you neglect the colonies, while capitalism uses them to support itself, defend itself, and fight you?

I want to add a few words in answer to the speech by Comrade Treint. Comrade Treint spoke of an approaching revolutionary wave in France and about the growth of a fascist movement there. I fully share Comrade Treint's optimism concerning his first point. As far as his second argument is concerned, I hold the opposite opinion. I believe that the reactionary party in Italy, in Germany, and in other countries needs fascism to defend itself, but the reaction in France does not need that. It has stronger, better organized, and more disciplined defenders than the black shirts. It has black and yellow soldiers. You may know that currently the French Army consists of 458,000 young Frenchmen and 206,550 natives from the colonies. But what you may not know is that if you take into account the length of service and training period and the ease with which natives can be sent to the front, every native soldier is worth two French soldiers. Thus if nominally the strength of the combat-ready army is only 664,550 men, the real numbers are closer to a million soldiers, or, to give exact figures,

939,950 men. Although numerically French exceed native soldiers by 251,450, native soldiers serve 431,000 months longer than French-men. All of you, English comrades as well as French comrades and the comrades from all the other parties, when you discuss the possibility of revolution and the means for its realization, have left out of all your plans for the next struggle this momentously important strategic element. For this reason I use all my powers to call out a warning to you!

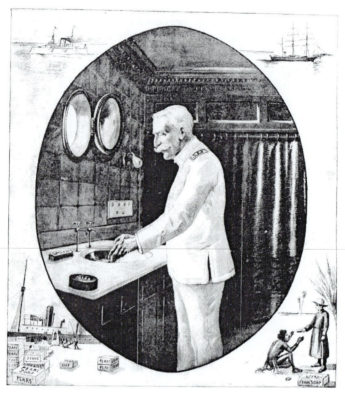

The first step towards lightening

The White Man's Burden

is through teaching the virtues of cleanliness.

Pears' Soap

is a potent factor in brightening the dark corners of the earth as civilization advances, while amongst the cultured of all nations it holds the highest place—it is the ideal toilet soap.

Advertisements such as this one from *McClure's Magazine* in 1899 show how the cult of Victorian domesticity and commodity capitalism were often intertwined in the civilizing mission overseas. (By permission of the British Library. PP6383 ae)

PART

II The Imperial Mission

The most common moral justification for nineteenth-century European expansion was that colonization would uplift the barbaric native peoples living outside the West. This section addresses the idea and the reality of this civilizing mission. Dismissed until relatively recently as mere rhetoric cloaking the "real" economic and political motives of imperialism, the civilizing language of European colonizers is now being analyzed more closely. Cultural assumptions, and occasional doubts, about the superior achievements of the white colonizers, and the ability of Africans and Asians to catch up under European tutelage, affected every policy choice in the colonies—from building schools, roads and hospitals, to justifying forced labor, selling new commodities, and enforcing strict segregation of the European and native populations.

We begin with one of the clearest, yet most ambivalent, celebrations of this civilizing mission in late-nineteenth-century Britain: Rudyard Kipling's "The White Man's Burden," a poem inspired by the American conquest of the Philippines. By turns determined, anxious, resentful, and self-sacrificing, the verses combine a racialized and gendered arrogance with a deeper uncertainty about the whole imperial project.

The remaining selections are drawn from new research on the ideology of the civilizing mission. Historical debate currently centers on this ideology's principal themes and its most important effects. Discussions of European civilizing rhetoric generally highlight two principal themes. The first emphasizes the degree to which Europeans responsible for governing or converting Africans and Asians hoped to transform these colonial subjects in their own image. According to Alice Conklin, even as French colonial officials in West Africa denied their subjects basic liberties, they also paradoxically promoted egalitarian social relations and liberal notions of "free labor." These officials thus replicated overseas, albeit in a diluted form, values and institutions that were deeply embedded in republican France.

In his examination of nineteenth-century European civilization ideology, Michael Adas pays special attention to the scientific and technological superiority of the West, and the imperial attitudes this superiority engendered. Europe's extraordinary communications and transportation revolution in the nineteenth century led the British in India and the French in Africa to view the construction of telegraphs, railroads, and ports as the most critical steps in the advancement of civilization overseas. An obsessive belief in the transformative power of technology has haunted Western development policies ever since.

Adrian Hastings considers the missionary discourse on civilization. Missionaries, a significant presence in all European colonies, readily accepted that the forward march of Christianity was also that of civilization. But did their concept of the term coincide with that of the secular authorities? Hastings shows that this group of colonial actors also initially defined civilization in terms that drew directly on their own life experiences in the West. European schooling, scientific farming techniques, and expanding needs and wants, along with Christian prayer, were the one true path to God, which Africans could and should now be made to adopt.

A belief that European values and lifestyles were universally desirable and imitable thus constituted one major aspect of colonial ideology and policy. A second theme, however, was in direct tension with this Western universalism. This was the belief that colonized peoples in their present state were fundamentally different from and inferior to Europeans. Current historical research has also revealed the myriad subtle and not-so-subtle differences that the colonizers "identified" between themselves and their subjects as part of their mission to uplift them.

In this context, the European medical and hygiene policies studied by David Arnold and Timothy Burke are particularly revealing. All Europeans accepted that it was part of their mission to improve health conditions in their colonies for themselves and the colonized. This belief, however, was usually predicated upon the assumption that Africans and Asians were dirty and diseased. These stereotypes, in turn, justified forced separation of the races in the name of better hygiene, and blatant disregard for indigenous standards regarding the proper care of the body. In his study of the response to the 1896 plague epidemic in India, David Arnold shows how coercive public-health measures led the colonial state to invade and police Indians' most private spaces in ways that did not always help diminish mortality rates. Timothy Burke illustrates how the British in colonial Rhodesia, oscillating between contradictory but equally racist notions of African bodies as dirty or pure, came to equate the civilizing process with cleanliness and the consumption of soap.

Despite differences of nationality or vocation, all European colonizers shared a common discourse of civilization. They targeted both the minds and the bodies of the colonized, who were expected to learn to think and act in new ways. European perceptions of the colonized were always contradictory, seeing the latter simultaneously like themselves and inescapably "other." Students of overseas expansion must consider how these conflicting assumptions worked together to sustain imperialism over the course of the nineteenth and twentieth centuries. Two final themes of this section that subsequent selections will bring out are that European ideas of civilization and barbarism changed over time in the face of colonial resistance and as social, economic, and political conditions in Europe evolved; and that Europeans were never fully in control of the consequences of their "civilizing" actions.

Rudyard Kipling

The White Man's Burden

1899
THE UNITED STATES AND THE
PHILIPPINE ISLANDS

Take up the White Man's burden—
    Send forth the best ye breed—
Go bind your sons to exile
    To serve your captives' need;
To wait in heavy harness
    On fluttered folk and wild—
Your new-caught, sullen peoples,
    Half devil and half child.

Take up the White Man's burden—
    In patience to abide,
To veil the threat of terror
    And check the show of pride;
By open speech and simple,
    An hundred times made plain.
To seek another's profit,
    And work another's gain.

Take up the White Man's burden—
    The savage wars of peace—
Fill full the mouth of Famine
    And bid the sickness cease;
And when your goal is nearest
    The end for others sought,
Watch Sloth and heathen Folly
    Bring all your hope to nought.

From *Rudyard Kipling's Verse* (Doubleday and Company) by Rudyard Kipling, pp. 321–323.

Take up the White Man's burden—
No tawdry rule of kings.
But toil of serf and sweeper—
The tale of common things.
The ports ye shall not enter,
The roads ye shall not tread,
Go make them with your living,
And mark them with your dead!

Take up the White Man's burden—
And reap his old reward:
The blame of those ye better,
The hate of those ye guard—
The cry of hosts ye humour
(Ah, slowly!) toward the light:—
"Why brought ye us from bondage,
"Our loved Egyptian night?"

Take up the White Man's burden—
Ye dare not stoop to less—
Nor call too loud on Freedom
To cloak your weariness;
By all ye cry or whisper,
By all ye leave or do,
The silent, sullen peoples
Shall weigh your Gods and you.

Take up the White Man's burden—
Have done with childish days—
The lightly proffered laurel,
The easy, ungrudged praise.
Comes now, to search your manhood
Through all the thankless years,
Cold-edged with dear-bought wisdom,
The judgment of your peers!

Alice L. Conklin

The French Republican Civilizing Mission

Civilization is a particularly French concept; the French invented the term in the eighteenth century and have celebrated the achievements of their own ever since. At no point in modern history, however, did the French make more claims for their civilization than during the "new" imperialism of the Third Republic. Of course all European powers at the end of the nineteenth century claimed to be carrying out the work of civilization in their overseas territories; but only in republican France was this claim elevated to the realm of official imperial doctrine. From about 1870, when France began to enlarge its holdings in Africa and Indochina, French publicists, and subsequently politicians, declared that their government alone among the Western states had a special mission to civilize the indigenous peoples now coming under its control—what the French called their *mission civilisatrice*.

This idea of a secular *mission civilisatrice* did not originate under the Third Republic; it nevertheless acquired a particularly strong resonance after the return of democratic institutions in France, as the new regime struggled to reconcile its aggressive imperialism with its republican ideals. The notion of a civilizing mission rested upon certain fundamental assumptions about the superiority of French culture and the perfectibility of humankind. It implied that France's colonial subjects were too primitive to rule themselves, but were capable of being uplifted. It intimated that the French were particularly suited, by temperament and by virtue of both their revolutionary past and their current industrial strength, to carry out this task. Last but not least, it assumed that the Third Republic had a duty and a right to remake "primitive" cultures along lines inspired by the cultural, political, and economic development of France.

Excerpted from *A Mission to Civilize: The Republican Idea of Empire in France and West Africa, 1895–1930*, by Alice L. Conklin, with the permission of the publishers, Stanford University Press. © 1997 by the Board of Trustees of the Leland Stanford Junior University.

The ideology of the civilizing mission could not but strike a responsive chord in a nation now publicly committed to institutionalizing the universal principles of 1789. At the end of the nineteenth century, few French citizens doubted that the French were materially and morally superior to—and that they lived in greater freedom than—the rest of the earth's inhabitants. Many may have scoffed at the idea that the Republic's empire was actually bestowing these blessings upon those ostensibly still oppressed. But no one questioned the premise of French superiority upon which the empire rested, or even that the civilizing mission could in fact be accomplished. Such convictions were part of what it meant to be French and republican in this period, and had a profound impact upon the way in which the French ran their colonies. Administrators—vastly outnumbered, and equipped with little more than their prejudices—relied upon the familiar categories of "civilization" and its inevitable opposite, "barbarism," to justify and maintain their hegemony overseas. These categories served to structure how officials thought about themselves as rulers and the people whom they ruled, with complex and often contradictory consequences for French colonial policy—and French republican identity—in the twentieth century.

This book demonstrates just how powerful an idea the *mission civilisatrice* was under the Third Republic by examining how a particular group of colonial officials in a specific context—the governors general of French West Africa from 1895 to 1930—understood this mission. Scholars have too often dismissed the *mission civilisatrice* as window dressing. Or they have been content to label the French as racist, without bothering to explain the insidious and persistent appeal of colonial ideology, or to consider its relationship to policy making. I begin from a different set of premises. I argue that republican France invested the notion of a civilizing mission with a fairly specific set of meanings that set limits on what the government could and could not do in the colonies. By officially acting within these limits, the French managed to obscure the fundamental contradiction between democracy and the forcible acquisition of an empire. A second theme . . . is that the content of the republican *mission civilisatrice* between 1895 and 1930 was not in any sense static; rather, it evolved as the colonial situation and conditions in the metropole changed. Although always a mirror of larger trends within *l'hexagone* (as mainland France has come to be called since the retreat from Algeria in 1962), the republican idea of empire was also at times decisively shaped by circumstances in the empire itself. Last but not least, I hope to demonstrate that as a vision of what the colonies could become and a reflection of how France saw itself, civilization ideology, its evolution, and its influence provide essential insights into the history of modern French republicanism. Through the prism of the *mission civilisatrice*, the shifting ideals, conceits, and fears of the Third Republic between 1895 and 1930 are both sharply revealed and better explained.

As a study of how the civilizing mission was interpreted in a specific colony, this book offers a new approach to empire studies and to the history of modern France. Both traditional imperial historiography and the newer field of African studies have underestimated the cultural and ideological dimension of modern French colonialism. Most discussions of French imperialism have tended to dwell either on the economic motivations for acquiring colonies or the nationalist, political, and military reasons leading to overseas expansion. And although there are numerous references to France's *mission civilisatrice* in case studies of colonial West African history, African historians have not systematically investigated its content. Modern African historiography has been more concerned with recovering the African experience of colonial rule than with analyzing French rationalizations of empire, or considering how colonial policy related to that of metropolitan France. This concern with African agency has made dramatically clear the limits of French hegemony in West Africa and given new visibility to the colonized; yet it has also had the paradoxical effect of making French rule appear more monolithic and unchanging than was actually the case.

Older studies of French imperial ideology have limited themselves to investigating the theories propounded by publicists or the ideas developed exclusively in France about Africa. More recently, newspapers, travel accounts, contemporary literature, geographical societies, colonial exhibitions, schoolbooks, and postcards and photographs have been mined for information about France's self-image as an imperial state and the rise (and fall) of public interest in the empire. And with the development of postcolonial studies, cultural critics (in fields outside history, for the most part) are reexamining the discourse of French imperialism in an effort to better understand how representations of the "other" helped define a French "national" identity. These older, more traditional histories as well as current research trends have carefully described the development and dissemination in France and the colonies of racial and cultural stereotypes regarding Africans and the evolution of competing imperialist doctrines in metropolitan circles. These studies, however, have not for the most part considered what relevance such ideas had for government officials whose task was to administer the "different" peoples within the French Empire. Nor have they adequately assessed the impact that changing political, social, and economic conditions in both the metropole and the colonies had upon the civilizing mission of the French. Here postcolonial theory, despite its innovative exploration of the way knowledge and identities have been constructed through colonialism, is particularly open to criticism. Its concept of "coloniality," ironically, risks depriving Africans of any agency and French actions of any specificity, because it presents all colonizing cultures as essentially the same. . . .

One way to address these neglected issues in the modern French experience of empire is to explore, in a particular imperial setting, what it was that a group of high-ranking republican administrators believed about themselves in relation to the "others" they encountered overseas, and how and why these beliefs evolved over time. This book proposes to do just that, through an analysis of thirty-five years of official rhetoric and decision making in French West Africa. Directly responsible to the colonial minister in Paris, yet strategically located in what the French deemed their most barbaric territory of all—sub-Saharan Africa—the office of the governor general in Dakar provides an ideal window onto the Third Republic's *mission civilisatrice* and its consequences. By scrutinizing the directives and policy initiatives of this office, but also—at crucial junctures—tacking either to relevant developments in France or to African social realities on the ground, I seek to decenter the history of modern France and open new perspectives on the symbiotic relationship between empire and metropole.

What, then, were France's official civilizing ideas in West Africa between 1895 and 1930? French imperial ideology consistently identified civilization with one principle more than any other: mastery. Mastery not of other peoples—although ironically this would become one of civilization's prerogatives in the age of democracy; rather, mastery of nature, including the human body, and mastery of what can be called "social behavior." To put it another way, to be civilized was to be free from specific forms of tyranny: the tyranny of the elements over man, of disease over health, of instinct over reason, of ignorance over knowledge and of despotism over liberty. Mastery in all these realms was integral to France's self-definition under the Third Republic. It was because the French believed that they had triumphed over geography, climate, and disease to create new internal and external markets, and because they before all other nations had overcome oppression and superstition to form a democratic and rational government, that republican France deemed itself so civilized. By the same token, it was because the inhabitants of the non-European world were perceived to have failed on these same fronts—because they appeared to lack the crucial ability to master—that they were just as obviously barbarians, in need of civilizing.

A conflation of civilization with mastery was thus a defining and permanent characteristic of French rhetoric; yet the meaning of the *mission civilisatrice* also evolved as the colonial situation itself changed during the period under study. Before 1914, two tenets dominated French civilization doctrine. . . . First, confronted with the economic poverty of the indigenous populations, the French believed that civilization required that they improve their subjects' standard of living through the rational development, or what the French called the *mise en valeur*, of the colonies' natural and human resources. This objective, they thought, could best be achieved by building railroads—because railroads would link the interior to the coast and promote the exchange of peoples, currencies, commodities, and ideas—and by improving hygiene to eliminate the parasites deadly to Europeans and Africans. Second, the French insisted that civilization required that the different West African peoples had to evolve within their own cultures, to the extent that these cultures did not conflict with the republican principles of French civilization. When a conflict arose, the offending African mores were to be suppressed and replaced by French ones. After a prolonged struggle with African leaders in the Western Sudan, four African institutions were singled out for eradication: indigenous languages, slavery, barbaric customary law, and "feudal" chieftaincies. The republican virtues of a common language, freedom, social equality, and liberal justice were to take their place.

In the aftermath of World War I, this definition of France's civilizing mission began to change in subtle ways. Although the French did not renounce their belief that Africans had to evolve along their own lines, the administration no longer dwelt on the theme of eradicating institutions antithetical to French civilization. Instead, it spoke increasingly of the need to "associate" traditional West African chiefs and the first generation of French-educated Africans in policy making. "Association" meant that the members of the African elite were now supposed to be consulted in all decisions regarding them. In the postwar years French imperial authorities also rejected the formerly held opinion that railroads alone would trigger the desired increase in the African standard of living. The key to tapping the economic potential of the West African territories, these authorities now believed, was the *mise en valeur* of Africa's human resources. In theory, human *mise en valeur* meant a more intensive focus upon improving the African producer's health and farming methods compared to conditions and practices in the prewar era. In reality, the term reflected a renewed conviction that Africans would never progress unless the French made them progress, and that forcibly inculcating a hitherto absent work ethic constituted a crucial part of the Third Republic's civilizing mission in West Africa. These changes in French civilizing tenets were not arbitrary, but causally linked in part to several local factors, such as gradually improving knowledge of African cultures, and a series of colonial revolts against France's earlier imperial policies. One result of this change was that, after World War I, French civilizing tenets better served French interests than had the ones they replaced.

The changes in French ideology, however, naturally reflected — and helped reinforce — trends within *l'hexagone* as much as they did developments within colonial West Africa. Along with documenting the unstable nature of French ideology, I explore what the shifting parameters of the civilizing mission in West Africa can tell us about the evolution of the Third Republic during the crucial transition from the Belle Epoque to the 1920s. The most important metropolitan trend to shape the *mission civilisatrice* in West Africa between 1895 and 1930 was the persistence of a certain liberal republican vision among France's governing elite before World War I and its decline after the war. French republicanism was always multifaceted. Nevertheless, a core set of values animated republicans of all camps up through the war: an emancipatory and universalistic impulse that resisted tyranny; an ideal of self-help and mutualism that included a sanctioning of state assistance to the indigent when necessary; anticlericalism, and its attendant faith in reason, science, and progress; an ardent patriotism founded on the creation of a loyal, disciplined, and enlightened citizenry; and a strong respect for the individual, private property, and morality. All these ideas were embedded in the very terms *mission* and *civilisatrice* and influenced French policy making in West Africa. It was, for example, republican principles as much as the experience of the conquest itself that led the Government General in West Africa to condemn slavery and "feudalism" among African tribes. The Government General also adopted France's latest technological improvements, partly out of the traditional republican belief that science held one key to regenerating humanity. After World War I, these same values weakened as the Third Republic attempted to come to terms with the losses and traumas of the war and the growth of nationalist protest throughout the empire. Colonial discourse echoed this shift: established republican verities now surfaced in a more attenuated form in Dakar, replaced by a more conservative vision of progress—as the new respect for the African aristocracy and the greater emphasis on human *mise en valeur* attest. . . .

There can, of course, be little doubt that colonization under the Third Republic was in large part an act of state-sanctioned violence. On the crudest level, the French forcibly "pacified" those West African groups who resisted colonization. On a more subtle level, French rule rested upon a set of coercive practices that violated their own democratic values. Africans were designated as subjects, not citizens. They had duties, but few rights. In neither case, however, did French republicans identify any contradiction between their democratic institutions and the acquisition and administration of their empire. This was because they viewed Africans as barbarians, and were continually undertaking—or claiming to undertake, as the case may be—civilizing measures on behalf of their subjects that appeared to make democracy and colonialism compatible. However misguided, self-deluding, or underfunded—indeed, because they were all these things—these claims merit our attention. As an enduring tension of French republicanism, the civilizing ideal in whose name the nation of the "rights of man" deprived so many people of their freedom deserves to be better understood. . . .

Michael Adas

The Machine as Civilizer

In the 1740s while the ship on which he was traveling was at anchor off the mouth of the Gambia River, William Smith went ashore to instruct one of the ship's mates in the use of surveying instruments. On a stretch of beach near a small town, Smith had begun to demonstrate how one could measure distances with his theodolite and hodometer when he noticed a sizable band of armed Africans gathering nearby. Troubled by their hostile gestures, Smith questioned the ship's slave, who had come along to help him operate the instruments, as to why they were so vexed by activities that Smith regarded as entirely peaceful and nonthreatening. The slave explained that the "foolish natives" were alarmed by Smith's strange devices, which they believed he would use to bewitch them. The Africans had driven off their cattle, sent the women and children from the town to hide in a nearby forest, and marched out to confront the dangerous strangers who had appeared so suddenly in their midst. Concluding that attempts to reason with "ignorant savages" would be futile, and observing that the Africans were afraid to approach the surveying party, Smith continued with his instruction—though he cautioned the mate to keep his blunderbuss ready. As the slave measured the distance along the beach with the hodometer, the frightened warriors tried to stop him by running in his path—but they were careful not to touch the wheel. The slave amused himself by trying to run into them. Smith and his companions found the Africans' fear of the wheel and their scrambling to avoid it a source of merriment which they wished the "other gentlemen" on board had been present to enjoy. But when Smith stopped to rest in the shade and sent the mate and slave off to make punch, the townsmen grew more and more threatening. Alone and surrounded by the angry and well-armed warriors, Smith began to fear that he might be attacked. Just as it occurred to him that he could be "cruelly torn asunder," the mate returned, and together they chased away the band of warriors by making threatening gestures and discharging the weapons that the terrified Africans had left behind on the beach. The mate pleaded to be allowed to pursue them, but Smith insisted on returning to the safety of the ship.

Though in itself a relatively insignificant encounter, this incident reveals much about European attitudes toward and interaction with non-Western peoples in the centuries since the fifteenth-century voyages of exploration. It was the Europeans who went out to the peoples of Africa, Asia, and the Americas, and never the reverse—though at times Africans and Amerindians were carried back to Europe to be exhibited and studied. For the Africans the ship from which Smith and his small party disembarked was a marvel of design and workmanship. It represented an area of technology in which the Europeans had few rivals by the fifteenth century and in which they reigned supreme by the seventeenth. Sailing ships with superior maneuverability and armament permitted the Europeans to explore, trade, and conquer all around the world. Smith's instruments and his reason for taking them ashore convey both a sense of the curiosity that provided a major motivation for the Europeans' overseas expansion and their compulsion to measure and catalogue the worlds they were "discovering." With little thought for the reaction of the people who lived there, Smith set out to measure a tiny portion of the vast continent he was exploring. Much more than his physical appearance and dress, it was Smith's unknown instruments and what the Africans perceived as strange behavior in employing these devices that became the focus of their concern. He delighted in dazzling and terrifying the townspeople with his strange machines and continued his activities despite their obvious hostility to his intrusion. When threatened, he relied on the Africans' fear of his technology to drive them off. As he informs the reader, the guns that the warriors dropped and he and the ship's mate fired into the air were of European manufacture. . . .

As Smith relates this encounter, it is superior technology—the surveying instruments and firearms—that set the European traveler and his companions off from the Africans and give them the upper hand in the confrontation that ensues. Taken in isolation, the incident overstates the importance of technology in an age when religion was still the chief source of western Europeans' sense of superiority. But it indicates how influential achievements in material culture had become, especially those relating to technology and science, in shaping

European perceptions of non-Western peoples even before the Industrial Revolution. From the very first decades of overseas expansion in the fifteenth century, European explorers and missionaries displayed a great interest in the ships, tools, weapons, and engineering techniques of the societies they encountered. They often compared these with their own and increasingly regarded technological and scientific accomplishments as significant measures of the overall level of development attained by non-Western cultures. By the mid-eighteenth century, scientific and technological gauges were playing a major and at times dominant role in European thinking about such civilizations as those of India and China and had begun to shape European policies on issues as critical as the fate of the African slave trade. In the industrial era, scientific and technological measures of human worth and potential dominated European thinking on issues ranging from racism to colonial education. They also provided key components of the civilizing-mission ideology that both justified Europe's global hegemony and vitally influenced the ways in which European power was exercised.

In view of their importance, it is remarkable that scientific and technological accomplishments as measures of European superiority and as gauges of the abilities of non-Western peoples have been so little studied. Most authors who have dealt with European attitudes toward African and Asian peoples in the industrial era acknowledge that Europe's transformation and the power differential that it created had much to do with the hardening of European assumptions of racial supremacy in the late nineteenth century. But few writers have examined these complex connections in any detail, and in all cases consideration of them has been subordinated to discussion of racist issues. The rare works that deal in any depth with the pervasive effects of the scientific and industrial revolutions on European perceptions of non-Western peoples are focused on Africa, the geographical area that elicited the most extreme responses. Because these studies cover a wide range of topics beyond the impact of European advances in science and technology, even for Africa we have only a partial view of one of the most critical dimensions of European interaction with non-Western peoples in the modern era. For China, India, the Islamic empires, and the Amerindian civilizations of the New World, we have little more than chance comments on the superiority of European weapons, tools, and mathematical techniques. The accounts that deal with these observations often give little sense of the material conditions and the cultural and ideological milieus that shaped them or their place in the broader, ongoing process of European exchange with non-Western peoples which has spanned the last half-millennium.

This book examines the ways in which European's perceptions of the material superiority of their own cultures, particularly as manifested in scientific thought and technological innovation, shaped their attitudes toward and interactions with peoples they encountered overseas. It is not a work in the history of science or technology as those fields are usually defined. The processes of invention and of scientific investigation which have traditionally occupied scholars in these fields and the patterns of institutional and disciplinary development which have more recently come into favor are crucial to the themes I explore. But for my purposes, these discoveries and developments are important only insofar as they influenced the ways in which Europeans viewed non-Western peoples and cultures and as these perceptions affected European policies toward the African and Asian societies they came to dominate in the industrial era. Though varying forms of interaction—including trade, proselytization, and colonial conquest—often resulted in the diffusion of European tools and scientific learning to overseas areas, my main concerns are the attitudes and ideologies that either promoted or impeded these transfers rather than the actual processes of diffusion. Because the spread of European science and technology has been central to the global transformations that Western expansion set in motion, the assumptions and policies that determined which and how many discoveries, machines, and techniques would be shared with which non-Western peoples have been critical determinants of the contemporary world order. . . .

The Machine as Civilizer

More than any other technological innovation, the railway embodied the great material advances associated with the first Industrial Revolution and dramatized the gap which that process had created between the Europeans and all non-Western peoples. Powered by the steam engines that were the core invention of the industrial transformation, locomotives boldly exhibited the latest advances in metallurgy and machine-tooling. Running on tracks that reshaped the landscape across vast swaths of Europe and later the Americas, Africa, and Asia; crossing great bridges that were themselves marvels of engineering skill; serviced in railway yards whose sheds and mounds of coal became familiar features of urban centers around the world, railways were at once "the most characteristic and most efficient form of the new technics." "The railroad as a system," as Leo Marx has observed, "incorporated most of the essential features of the emerging industrial order: the substitution of metal for wood construction; mechanized motive power; vastly enlarged geographical scale; speed, rationality, impersonality, and an unprecedented emphasis on precise timing.". . .

When railways were introduced in North America in the 1830s and India in the 1850s, many European observers fixed upon them as the key symbol of the superiority, material as well as moral, that Western societies had attained over all others. The great engines and thousands of miles of tracks provided pervasive and dramatic evidence of European power and material mastery. Railways (and the steamboat in heavily forested, riverine areas such as that which provides the setting for Conrad's *Heart of Darkness*) made it possible for Europeans to open vast stretches of "hinterland" and "undeveloped wilderness" to colonization, settlement, and economic exploitation. Most of these areas had been little affected by European activities during the early centuries of expansion which, except in the New World, had been concentrated in coastal and island regions. Trains and steamboats led to more direct and effective European rule in such areas as India, Egypt, and Vietnam and furthered colonial expansion throughout much of Africa, southeast Asia, and Australia. Officials and their families could be stationed in interior districts and troops moved about quickly to places where the "natives" showed signs of unrest. Perhaps the most impressive use of the railway for troop movement was the construction in the late 1880s of four hundred miles of track across the Nubian desert from Wadi Halfa to the Blue Nile to transport and supply the expeditionary force led by Lord Kitchener against the Mahdist state in the Sudan.

European officials and travelers delighted in the awe and, at times, outright terror that the dirty, noisy, and obviously powerful locomotives instilled in the peoples they sought to rule, convert, and recruit as laborers. At midcentury Harriet Martineau recorded an early encounter: "Under the Western Ghauts [mountains in southwest India] the villagers come out at the sound of the steam whistle, and the babies gasp and cry when the train rushes by; and nobody denies that the railway is a wonderful thing." More than half a century later Elspeth Huxley observed that even the slow and antiquated Uganda mail train was an object of awe for the Kikuyu of Kenya: "In fact our train made something of a triumphal progress, with long pauses to allow people to admire at close quarters a creature so strong and inexplicable, that brought to remote places a flavour of adventure, a whiff of the mystery of unknown lands."

In addition to the complexity, scale, and power that rendered locomotives such superb physical and symbolic manifestations of the European colonial presence, the railway also served as a reminder of more subtle sources of European dominance and the attributes that nineteenth-century thinkers believed set Western peoples off from all others. In the speed and regularity of their comings and goings, trains (and steamships) proclaimed the Europeans' mastery of time and space and demonstrated their capacity for precision and discipline. As the nineteenth century progressed, improvements in steam engines and railway carriages, and ultimately the shift to diesel or electric power, gave impressive evidence of the insatiable appetite for experiment, innovation, and technological change that had become defining characteristics of industrial European and North American societies.

As early as the 1830s, European colonial administrators and missionaries came to view railroads, steamships, and Western machines in general as key agents in their campaigns to revive "decadent" civilizations in Asia and uplift the "savage" peoples of Africa. Lord William Bentinck, the reform-minded Governor-General of India in this period, viewed the steamboat as a "great engine of moral improvement" in a land that at the time of his arrival he considered "cursed from one end to the other by the vice, the ignorance, the oppression, the despotism, the barbarous and cruel customs that have been the growth of ages under every description of Asiatic misrule." Bentinck judged that British plantations, factories, and mines, where Western technology was concentrated, would serve as the best "schools of instruction" through which the British might elevate the level of civilization in India. A decade later an editorial in *The Times* of London boasted that a combination of good government and the introduction of Western technology, particularly through railway construction, made it inevitable that the British would become "the greatest benefactors the Hindoo race had known." The "science and steadiness of the north," *The Times* predicted, would galvanize the "capabilities of the East" and result in the full development of India's resources and a great improvement in the condition of its peoples. . . .

In addition to undermining Indian adherence to what most of the British in India regarded as grotesque rituals and degrading superstitions, railways were considered a powerful way to introduce the Indian multitudes to the values and attitudes that the British believed were responsible for England's prosperity and global power. W. A. Rogers, an officer in the Indian Civil Service, noted some of the lessons in the late 1870s:

> *Railways are opening the eyes of the people who are within reach of them in a variety of ways. They teach them that time is worth money, and induce them to economise that which they had been in the habit of slighting and wasting; they teach them that speed attained is time, and therefore money, saved or made. They show them that others can produce better crops or finer works of art than themselves, and set them thinking why they should not have sugarcane or brocade equal to those of their neighbours. They introduce them to men of other ideas, and prove to them that much is to be learnt beyond the narrow limits of the little town or village which has hitherto been the world to them. Above all, they induce in them habits of self-dependence, causing them to act for themselves promptly and not lean on others. . . .*

The most resounding late Victorian affirmation of the role of technology in Britain's civilizing mission in India was Benjamin Kidd's in his discussion of the importance of altruism among the qualities that he believed were conducive to "social evolution." Dismissing the suggestion that Great Britain had developed India solely for its own advantage, Kidd listed the many benefits that the Indians had enjoyed as a result of British efforts to "share" their superior technology:

> *There has been for long in progress in India a steady development of the resources of the country which cannot be paralleled in any other tropical region of the world. Public works on the most extensive scale and of the most permanent character have been undertaken and completed; roads and bridges have been built; mining and agriculture have been developed; irrigation works, which have added considerably to the*

fertility and resources of large tracts of the country, have been con-
structed; even sanitary reform is beginning to make considerable prog-
ress. European enterprise too, attracted by security and integrity in the
government, has been active. Railways have been gradually extended
over the Peninsula. . . . The cotton industry of India has already en-
tered on friendly rivalry with that of Lancashire. Other industries,
suited to the conditions of the country, are in like manner rising into
prominence, without any kind of artificial protection or encourage-
ment.

G. O. Trevelyan, a civil servant who was famed for his satirical
sketches of British life in India, summed up a good deal more laconi-
cally the widespread sentiment that the railway was a key agent of Europe's civilizing mission: he simply observed that in India all signs of
civilization disappeared beyond one hundred yards on either side of
the railway track.

Adrian Hastings

Christianity, Civilization, and Commerce

. . . The nineteenth-century missionary fixation with civilization—and
it sometimes seems little less—requires proper explanation. And that
requires some return to eighteenth-century roots. A few quotations
may help.

In proportion to the Civilization, so will be the consumption of British
Manufactures. (Olaudah Equiano, 13 March 1788, in a letter to the
Committee of the Privy Council Examining the Question of the Slave
Trade) . . .

The authority of the British Crown is at this moment the most powerful
instrument under Providence of maintaining peace and order in many

Reprinted from *The Church in Africa, 1450–1950* by Adrian Hastings (1994). © Adrian
Hastings 1994. Reprinted by permission of Oxford University Press.

extensive regions of the earth, and thereby assists in diffusing amongst millions of the human race the blessings of Christianity and civilization. (Earl Grey, 1853)

There had been considerable advance in civilization since I left. Many cottages have sprung up to replace the windowless and chimneyless round conical-roofed huts. Trees have been planted, wagons purchased; the valley is nearly all reclaimed and cultivated. The effects of missionary influence are undeniable and striking. (John Moffat on Kuruman, 21 March 1859)

We sympathize with your desire to introduce the law and order of civilized life, but we doubt whether the very extensive and rapidly developed changes in Lagos will produce anything but a forced compliance as far as British power extends and beyond it a fixed hatred and hostility to Christianity, Civilization and the white man. (Memorial from British subjects and foreign residents in Abeokuta [including CMS missionaries], October 30, 1863 to Lieutenant-General Glover)

In the middle decades of the century almost everyone linked together Christianity and Civilization, adding—when occasion served—Commerce or Cultivation. It was by no means a specifically missionary characteristic. These Cs need some sorting out, if they are not to mislead. They represented the public values of the mid-Victorian age together with Science, for "Civilization and Science" could be as easily linked as "Civilization and Commerce." In fact, in these four terms Christianity was really the odd man out, despite the rhetoric.

The bond between Christianity and civilizing goes back to the conversion of Europe's northern tribes in the Dark Ages, and it was very clearly present in the Portuguese conception of their overseas mission in the sixteenth century. Yet for Protestants what was decisive was the new eighteenth-century preoccupation with "civilization"—a word which only then made its appearance in English. It was indicative of what the Enlightenment was all about. In 1728 Daniel Defoe in his *Plan of the English Commerce* declared that "The Savage Part" (of West Africa) "would be much civiliz'd . . . and the People learn to live to be cloth'd, and to be furnish'd with many things from Europe, which they now want; and by consequence would with their Manners change the very Nature of their commerce and fall in upon the consumption of the European Manufacturers.' Adam Ferguson, in his influential *Essay on the History of Civil Society* (1767), concerned with the advance of the human species "from rudeness to civilization," saw civilization as a complex thing, at once political, intellectual, and commercial. Commerce, it was generally agreed, had a great deal to do with the spread of civilization, but Enlightenment thinkers were unlikely to suggest that Christianity had much to do with it.

The new missionary movement for its part had exceedingly little concern with civilization. Its working-class, Free Church originators were interested in evangelism, in the spread of faith and piety but not in the fruits of the Enlightenment or of British commerce. The gospel was something quite different. In 1815 the Methodist Missionary Committee could still write emphatically to a missionary, "As men of God and Ambassadors for Christ you must have nothing to do with trade in any way whatever." Here were two very different worlds. It is important for us not to confuse them in their starting-points, though in due course they did for a time confuse themselves and, in consequence, their interpreters. It was the Clapham group, high-minded, upper-middle-class Anglican Evangelicals with strong commercial connections who, consciously or unconsciously, did what many thoughtful Christians try to do in every age: adapt the current secular ideology to the service of Christian morality. They argued that legitimate commerce would be far more profitable for everyone (both Africans and Liverpool merchants) than one in slavery, that it would redound far better to the advance of civilization—which, on current thinking, commerce was supposed to do—and would (here they put their own oar in) spread Christianity too. . . .

. . . Missionaries, working class or not, were people of their age, imbibing almost unconsciously the assumptions of its ideology. The rationale for Britain's greatness and, more generally, the world supremacy of western Europe was that of commerce and civilization. Commerce, it is true, could not mean much to the ordinary missionary, being for the most part too far removed from the opportunities of his station, but civilization was different. Missionaries were much concerned with vegetable gardens and fruit trees, clean houses and water, ploughs and forges, reading and writing, hats and shoes: the simple things which they had known at home but which were in no way new in Britain and hardly in the forefront of the minds of the civilization theorists. After all, many of them had been gardeners, hatters, or cobblers. Where the theorists thought of high international commerce, large companies, the development of factories in Manchester or

Leeds, the missionaries translated civilization into the simpler terms of the more homely things they themselves had some knowledge of. They no less readily adopted the jargon of civilization for what they were doing. In practice they turned "Christianity and commerce" into "gospel and plough." In this sense it was almost inevitable that they should be concerned with "civilization.". . . James Read . . . was unpreoccupied with clothes but very preoccupied with ploughs (he may, indeed, even have originated the "gospel and plough" formula) and with this or any other way of increasing the earning power of the Khoikhoi, with whom he had thrown in his lot.

By the 1830s "Civilization and Christianity" had become the catch-phrase used by everyone from Ministers of the Crown, quite uninterested in pushing missions but concerned to present acceptably Britain's world-wide colonial enterprise, to the humblest missionary explaining the tiny developments of his own corner. John Philip, the theorist in the field, expressed a middle-of-the-road missionary viewpoint with his customary precision in a statement of 1833:

> *The civilization of the people among whom we labour in Africa is not our highest object; but that object never can be secured and rendered permanent among them without their civilization. Civilization is to the Christian religion what the body is to the soul . . . The blessings of civilization are a few of the blessings which the Christian religion scatters in her progress to immortality; but they are to be cherished for their own sake as well as for ours . . .*

Of course, for many a non-missionary, colonial administrator or settler, it was very much the other way round: what mattered was "civilization" (meaning, very often, commercial employability). The missionary was to be welcomed only so long as he did not push religion too much but made certain requirements of "civilization" his first concern. . . .

For whatever reason and in whatever form nearly everyone seemed for a time agreed that the concern to civilize was incumbent upon a missionary, and not only Britons. French colonial officials were complaining that French Catholic missionaries, unlike the Protestants, did too little to civilize. Poor Père Lossedat, a Holy Ghost Father in Gabon, wrote home in 1852 that "Some Europeans (they say French Officers) have broken the rosaries of our catechumens. They object to our approach of teaching people to pray and to chant canticles. It is not thus, says M. Bouët, Commander of the

Adour, that one civilizes people." In fact in his massive *Mémoire* of 1846 for Propaganda Fide on African missions Libermann had already firmly asserted the absolute need for civilization, and not just some low-level technical skills but the inculcation of science, "les théories des choses." Turn to another sphere. In 1855 Alexander Crummell, a black clergyman from New York with a Cambridge degree, delivered an address on "The Duty of a Rising Christian State to Contribute to the World's Well-Being and Civilization" before the Common Council and citizens of Monrovia on the day of National Independence. This duty, he declared, would be chiefly fulfilled through "the elevating and civilizing influence of commerce." The citizens of Monrovia were assured that "The Carthaginians and the Roman merchants were noted for their sterling honesty and their love of justice. People who are uncommercial are given to dissimulation, fraud, and trickery. . . .

After 1841 the commerce model was once more set aside until Livingstone revived it in the late 1850s, on returning from his great transcontinental journey. For the next quarter-century his message of "the double influence of the spirit of commerce and Christianity" as being what was needed "to stay the bitter fountain of African misery" became again a widely accepted orthodoxy, especially in Scottish circles. . . .

If missionaries of the late nineteenth century were, in the main, pretty cool about any link between their work and commerce, it was drink more than anything else which made them so. In August, 1876 the steamer *Ethiopia* left Liverpool bound for the Nigerian coast, carrying one missionary, Mary Slessor, and a cargo of spirits. Six years later the *Ethiopia* was wrecked on rocks just off Loango and it is said that the rum seized as it was breaking up caused the deaths of 200 people. The first Baptist missionaries to the Congo arrived in 1879 on a boat loaded with gin. Earlier missionaries had arrived on slave-ships. Now "legitimate" commerce had been substituted. In place of slaves, gin. It is hardly surprising that the late Victorian Evangelical shied away from Livingstone's enthusiasm for the commercial model.

In missionary jargon the word "industrial" came much to be preferred to the word "commerce." "Industrial" was a step up from the plough. It signified a more systematic stress on technical skills in a way that was only possible in larger centres like Livingstonia and Lovedale, though the name would come to be adopted by many smaller enterprises as well. The central missionary "institute" became increasingly the ideal of the civilizing school—less ambitious and prone to corruption than the commercial company but rather more sophisticated than the "gospel and plough" formula. The Industrial Mission is the late nineteenth- and early twentieth-century favourite for people with this approach, aware of the dangers to which the commerce ideal almost inevitably led—drink, bankruptcy, or a takeover by European settlers. For white settlement is what Christianity and Commerce seemed inevitably to lead to if it was to succeed in terms of profit in the immediate term. And white settlement was, indeed, what Livingstone had had in mind. Maybe missionary recognition that this sort of culmination to the commercial pursuit would not be to the long-term advantage of Africans helped induce them to pull back from implementation of Livingstone's ideal. Yet in fact, on the west coast at least, the plough and the commercial marketing of its products by a new African farming class did actually succeed. We can see it particularly in the development of cocoa in Nigeria and then the Gold Coast at the turn of the century. In South Africa too and, later, in central Africa small-scale black commercial farming would have succeeded had it not been for white competitors determined that it should not do so. Settler farming needed black labour and did not want the rivalry of a profit-making black peasantry. Only where there were no settlers, as in the west or Uganda, did the commerce model finally work to black advantage: and to Christian advantage too, because in such cases the black community making profitable use of the plough was also the core of a local Church. So there proved to be, after all, a measure of sense in the commerce model. What was wrong with it was the narrow time-scale its backers in Britain inevitably looked for.

Nevertheless, there were always missionaries and, still more, missionary planners who had their doubts about this whole line of thought. "Civilization" meant something different to everyone who used it. It secularized the mission and idealized Europe. A highly intelligent, rather sceptical, Italian Franciscan missionary, in declaring his preference in 1850 for Ethiopia over Italy, could refer mockingly to "civilizzatissima Europa." The guide-lines of Propaganda Fide, ever since the seventeenth century, had been opposed to all unnecessary Europeanization, and what was the whole civilization school concerned with other than that? It is striking that Lavigerie, with all his devotion to the example of Livingstone, appears almost never to speak of civilization. On the contrary, he insisted, in his great *Instruction* to the missionaries of equatorial Africa of 1879:

> *From the material aspect we must leave Africans as they are, that is to say truly Africans. We must shut our eyes and hearts to a false pity . . . and resign ourselves to see the young negroes close to us maintain the customs of their land, their wattle huts instead of houses, their bare earth in place of beds, sorghum and manioc instead of bread, grass waist bands in place of shirt and trousers.*

If Protestant missionaries seem to have been rather easily carried away by the "civilization" model, it may be because they had so little of a real missionary doctrine to fall back upon, over and above a great enthusiasm for world evangelism. But so soon as they began to develop a doctrine, they started to recognize the danger. It is noticeable that Henry Venn had very little interest in civilizing, and indeed increasingly recognized how opposed it could be to the early realization of his ideal, the self—governing Church. The establishment of a native Church required the adoption of African ways, not the imposition of European ones. It is odd that it was Livingstone with all his African intuition who confused the whole movement by plunging back from a concern with native agency into one which ceaselessly harped on the vocabulary of civilization and pursued the goals of Western commerce and settlement. But at the very same time that he was reinvigorating the civilization school, Venn, Lavigerie, and others like Hudson Taylor, founder of the China Inland Mission, were guiding the central core of the missionary movement emphatically away from preoccupation with civilization towards the acceptance of cultural diversity and non-European ways as crucial to a missionary's central purpose. . . .

At the end of the day, Henri Junod, a remarkable Swiss missionary scholar, added up the pros and cons of "civilization" in the conclusion of his *Life of a South African Tribe*, published in 1912. He listed the blessings of civilization, among them the disappearance of deadly famines, improved clothing (which he thought only a "mixed blessing"), better seeds and agricultural implements, a broadening of ideas. But the "curses of civilization" he judged far to exceed the blessings, at least in South Africa, and first among them he listed "loss of political interest and responsibility." For Adam Ferguson, in the eighteenth century, it was the political which, more than anything else, defined civilization. . . . Perhaps the "anti-civilizers" had the deeper sense of civilization, even in terms of the Enlightenment, while the civilizers were continually in danger of disrupting civilization by concentrating upon the technical to the dissolution of the socio-political. . . .

The ideology of the nineteenth-century missionary movement began with a simple evangelical individualism grounded upon the Bible first and last. As we have seen, it quickly joined to this a second more worldly thread which may loosely be characterized as "civilization," an undefined additional component, formally rejected by rather few, but, equally, central to the thought of rather few. It seemed at least a happy way of persuading the secular scoffer that missionaries were a good thing earning their keep in terms of the public good. It also served to justify a great deal of highly "secular" activity on the mission station which, in strictly evangelical terms, might be hard to defend. A secular component to mission seemed a natural enough adjunct to anyone other than the narrowest evangelist; for a minority it became a quite central concern. It could take an anti-slavery form with some, a struggle for political rights with others, a general interest in benevolent improvement with a third group, an alliance with Western commerce for the opening-up of the world with a fourth . . . these were extremely different approaches to the business of spreading civilization, but they concur in showing that part of the missionary task was a secular and worldly one.

David Arnold

Medicine and the Colonization of the Body in India

The Indian plague epidemic which began in 1896 and claimed by 1930 more than 12 million lives was so massive in scale and so fraught with political, social, and demographic consequences that it could sustain many different approaches and interpretations. This essay is

From *Selected Subaltern Studies*, eds. Ranajit Guha and Gayatri C. Spivak (Oxford University Press, 1988). Reprinted by permission of Oxford University Press, New Delhi.

not an attempt at a comprehensive account of India's plague years. It examines only the epidemic's first, most turbulent phase, not its long, more quiescent coda. It seeks to understand the plague less as an epidemiological phenomenon than as a commentary upon the developing relationship between indigenous élites, subaltern classes and the colonial state. In these terms the plague was often of less importance than the state intervention that accompanied or preceded it. Tilak's *Mahratta* claimed with some justification in June, 1897 that no measure undertaken by the British in India had "interfered so largely and in such a systematic way with the domestic social and religious habits of the people" as the current plague administration. That the colonial government and colonial medicine attempted such forceful and far-reaching controls was indicative of the interventionist ambitions and capacity of India's mature colonial state. This was not the remote and shadowy presence British power in India is sometimes made out to be. It could (and during the early plague years commonly did) intervene directly in the lives of the people and elicit a potent response. And yet the very strength of the political and cultural backlash against the plague administration is a reminder of the practical limitations to that power and of the extent to which regulatory systems tend to be less absolute, less one-dimensional, than the writings of Foucault or Goffman would lead us to believe. Only through an awareness of the dialectical nature of such encounters is it possible to avoid assumptions of mass "passivity" and "fatalism."

The plague dramatized the importance of the body—the body, that is to say, of the colonized—as a site of conflict between colonial power and indigenous politics. During the early phase of the epidemic the body had a specific medical, administrative and social significance: much of the interventionist thrust of the state was directed towards its apprehension and control, just as much of the resistance to plague measures revolved around bodily evasion or concealment. The body, however, was also profoundly symbolic of a wider and more enduring field of contention between indigenous and colonial perceptions, practices, and concerns. The exercise of British power touched in many ways upon the issue of the Indian body. Moreover, as the early plague years demonstrated, the problematic was not only one of a colonial divide. It also deeply involved the growing assertion of a middle-class hegemony over the mass of the population and the equiv-

ocal responses—part resistance, part emulation—which such hegemonic aspirations evoked among the subaltern classes.

India's colonial state could never aspire to an absolute and exclusive control over the body of each and every one of its subjects. But
there existed a latent claim that became operative in certain administrative, judicial, and medical contexts. The early-nineteenth-century
attempts to abolish *sati* and female infanticide were preliminary
demonstrations of this arrogation of corporal power. Colonial penology is rich in other illustrations. Until well into the second half of the
nineteenth century exemplary punishments were meted out against
the living bodies and corpses of prominent rebels. Whipping persisted
as a colonial mode of punishment and deterrence as late as the Quit
India movement of 1942. Transportation, viewed with increasing dis-
favour in early-nineteenth-century Europe, was seized upon in India
as a "weapon of tremendous power," especially against Hindus with
their fear of crossing the "black water." Normally, however, the prison
regime respected caste differences and sensibilities, seeking, for example, to devise forms of employment that would not be unduly offensive
or demeaning to higher-caste convicts. And while exemplary punishments were in times of crisis and rebellion deemed necessary and
legitimate, the British sought to demonstrate a superiority over precolonial "barbarity" by condemning torture, mutilation, and indefi-
nite imprisonment without trial. The introduction of *habeas corpus*
was one expression of this colonial concern. T.B. Macaulay conveyed
the duality of British attitudes in 1835 when he called for a penal system in India that would be free from "any circumstances shocking to
humanity" and yet still "a terror to wrong-doers."

For most of the nineteenth century colonial medicine was loath to
venture where colonial penology had led. Although from early in the
century attempts were made to supplant the indigenous (and reput-
edly dangerous) practice of smallpox inoculation with Jenner's cow-
pox vaccination, it was not until the 1870s and 1880s that this policy
received legislative sanction. Even then compulsory vaccination was
confined to major towns and cantonments. Still more restricted and
controversial was the Contagious Diseases Act of 1868, introduced to
check the spread of venereal disease between Indian prostitutes and
European soldiers. It was repealed in 1886. As this latter example suggests, the primary responsibility of Western medicine in India until

late in the century was still to minister to the health of the colonizers, not the colonized, except in so far as Indian soldiers, servants, plantation labourers, and prostitutes constituted an apparent danger to European well-being. Financial as well as political constraints discouraged the colonial state from a greater degree of medical intervention.

There was, however, a substantial shift in state attitudes in the late nineteenth century. European health in India, it was increasingly argued, could only be assured through wider medical and sanitary measures. Epidemics, like the famines with which they frequently allied, were an unwelcome tax upon the profitability of empire. Sanitary reform and the curbing of epidemic smallpox and cholera in Britain created pressure for similar campaigns in India, while the advances made by Pasteur, Koch, and others in the new science of bacteriology created a confidence among British medical men in India that epidemic diseases could be "conquered" through the application of Western scientific knowledge and reason. It was at this juncture that the plague arrived in India. The first deaths occurred at Bombay in August, 1896, and within three or four years the disease had spread to every province of the Indian empire. Before 1900 mainly an urban phenomenon, the epidemic was moving steadily, seemingly remorselessly, into the countryside. The urban focus of the disease in the early years was reflected in the greater intensity of plague operations in the towns and cities. This in turn partly explains the urban character of much of the early resistance to plague measures, though it had also been remarked in earlier decades that vaccination too often encountered greater opposition in the towns than in the rural areas.

After a brief period of medical uncertainty and administrative hesitancy, the provincial government in Bombay, backed by the Government of India, introduced measures which, in the words of W.C. Rand, Pune's Plague Commissioner, were "perhaps the most drastic that had ever been taken in British India to stamp out an epidemic." On October 6, 1896, the Bombay government sanctioned a programme for the disinfection and destruction of infected property under the Bombay Municipal Act of 1888. Four months later the Epidemic Diseases Act gave the government the power to detain and segregate plague suspects, to destroy property, inspect, disinfect, evacuate, and even demolish dwellings suspected of harbouring the plague, to prohibit fairs and pilgrimages, to examine road and rail travellers—in short, to do almost anything medical and official opinion believed to be necessary for the suppression of the disease. In Bombay, Pune, Karachi, and Calcutta responsibility for health and sanitation was taken away from municipal councils and entrusted to small committees of European doctors and civil servants. In practice, even if not in theory, Indian opinion was brushed aside. Caste and religion were afforded scant recognition except as obstacles to the implementation of the necessary sanitary programme. The proclamation issued by Bombay's Municipal Commissioner on October 6, 1896 announced that all plague cases would be hospitalized, by force if necessary. It was not explained that relatives would be permitted to visit the sick nor that caste was to be respected in the hospital arrangements. A directive from the city's Surgeon-General in December, 1896 stated that while caste "prejudices" would be observed as far as possible, they could not be allowed to stand in the way of essential sanitary and medical measures. Never before had the medical profession in British India commanded such public power and exercised it with such administrative arrogance.

Behind the urgent and far-reaching nature of these measures lay several considerations. Plague, although present in some parts of India during the nineteenth century, was seen in 1896 as an invading disease which had to be checked before it could establish itself. Appearing first in Bombay (probably as a result of importation from Hong Kong), the plague challenged the prosperity of one of British India's premier ports and administrative centres. Apart from the threat to Bombay's own commerce and industry, the economic pressure for prompt action was increased by the possibility of an European embargo on Indian trade unless the epidemic was quickly brought under control. But no less powerful was the medical pressure from experts in Britain and India who argued that the disease could be stopped from spreading if only the appropriate measures were promptly and thoroughly implemented.

At this stage, too, the etiology of the plague was not fully understood. The role of rats in its transmission was still generally thought secondary to that of man: the part played by rats' fleas was not finally established until 1908. The human body—and the clothes, bedding and habitations associated with it—was thought to be the disease's principal vector. The perceived centrality of the human body was further emphasized by the difficulty at first experienced in identifying the disease. A physical examination was made to try to find the characteristic buboes or swellings; in dubious cases post mortems were used to search for internal evidence. The body was thus both the presumed vector of the disease and the bearer of its diagnostical signs. It followed that anti-plague measures concentrated upon the interception, examination, and confinement of the body. This entailed a form of direct medical intervention that swept aside the rival or preferential claims of relatives and friends, *vaids* and *hakims* (Hindu and Muslim medical practitioners respectively), religious and caste leaders. The body, as in the West, was treated as a secular object, not as sacred territory, as an individual entity, not as an element integral to a wider community. The body, moreover, was exposed not just to the "gaze" of Western medicine but also to its physical touch, an intrusion of the greatest concern to a society in which touch connoted possession or pollution.

Timothy Burke

Colonialism, Cleanliness, and Civilization in Colonial Rhodesia

On the Monday following the 1990 repeal of the Separate Amenities Act in South Africa, *The Weekly Mail* sent two reporters to the town of Ermelo. The reporters, Philip Molefe and Phillip Van Niekerk, discovered that access to previously forbidden facilities was still difficult. The most intense confrontation concerned access to the town's swimming pool. After trying to prevent Molefe's entrance, Ermelo's white swimmers were enraged when he entered the pool: "While Molefe splashed around . . . he [the white lifeguard] screamed angrily, 'Swim.

From Timothy Burke, *Lifebuoy Men, Lux Women: Commodification, Consumption, and Cleanliness in Modern Zimbabwe*, pp. 17, 18, 19, 19–23, 84, 85, 86, 86–87, 151, 151–152, 152–153. Copyright © 1996 by Duke University Press. Excerpted by permission of the publisher.

See page 229 for selection notes.

De Klerk said you can swim. . . . I'll give you some soap to wash with.'" Later, at another stop, one man muttered "*Die plek gaan nou vuil word* [This place is going to be dirty now]."[1]

These sorts of visceral feelings about the bodies of Africans, visions of them as dirty or diseased, have been among the most intensely expressed aspects of racist sentiment in southern Africa over the course of the twentieth century. . . .

In mid-nineteenth-century south-central Africa, Robert Moffat, the prominent missionary representative to the Ndebele court, occasionally commented on his hosts' hygiene or bodily practices, but he did not seem to imagine his own practices to be particularly superior. Indeed, he was shocked and irritated on one occasion when asked for soap by a Khoisan man during his travels: "A likely thing, to carry soap . . . to sell to a _____! What wonderful ideas shoot out of the depraved heart!"[2] His contemporary, Thomas Morgan Thomas, described the Ndebele people as "generally clean" and "not wanting in good taste in respect to beauty, cleanliness, and dress."[3] A trader, Herbert David Crook, echoed Thomas's complimentary description of Ndebele physical customs, though he found Shona-speaking peoples the opposite, "utterly regardless of personal cleanliness."[4] Another contemporary, Henry Stabb, was repelled by the lack of cleanliness in an Afrikaner household in Zeerust, but found Lobengula, his court, and the Ndebele generally attractive and well-groomed. . . .[5]

Racism and African Bodies after 1890

The somewhat fitful interest in the bodies of Africans expressed by pre-colonial European travelers to south-central Africa contrasted noticeably with accounts written after the 1890 invasion of Matabeleland and Mashonaland. White settlers vehemently and repeatedly characterized Africans as filthy, depraved, and ugly. Most whites, regardless of their institutional or professional affiliations, agreed with the first Anglican bishop of Mashonaland, G. W. H. Knight-Bruce, that Africans were a "repulsive degradation of humanity."[6] The Native Commissioner of Gutu District in 1909 argued, "before European influence . . . natives lived more or less like wild animals and in a general state of filth."[7] His contemporary in Hartley District agreed: "They have no idea of cleanliness. . . . They rarely bathe themselves and only during the warm weather and never wash their clothes or

blankets . . . their kraals are swarming with vermin of every description."[8] By contrast, European hygienic practices were defined as the
essence of "civilization," coinciding with the cementing of intensive
personal and social cleanliness as normative in English social life.
Cleanliness was described typically by one official in the 1920s as a
"primary art of civilised life."[9] For most whites living or traveling in
Zimbabwe after 1890, the African world was a world of universal dirt
and filth, while their own social world was its opposite, cleansed and
pure.

Such sentiments stand out as a distinctive aspect of colonial
racism not merely because of their omnipresence and vehemence, but
because of their physicality, the manner in which they influenced
whites to react with revulsion or avoidance in the presence of Africans.
For example, many early Native Commissioners represented their
African charges as generically "syphilitic," though their concept of
"syphilis" was clearly vague and quasi-metaphorical. Many of them
believed this "syphilis" could be spread to whites through shaking
hands, physical proximity, or handling hut taxes—leading some officials to routinely disinfect tax money after collecting it.[10] The intensity
of similar hygienic fears is suggested by Nathan Shamuyarira's recol-
lection that at Waddilove mission, "the wife of one missionary was
known to have sprayed a chair on which an African teacher had been
sitting, and broken a cup from which another had drunk tea."[11] As the
example of the *Weekly Mail* reporters' trip to Ermelo suggests, the
physicality of racism has retained its grip over time, even as other expressions of official and unofficial racism have been called into question, in both South Africa and Zimbabwe. C. Frantz and Cyril
Rogers's study of Rhodesian racial thought, done in the 1960s, cited
many whites continuing to offer hygienic explanations for segregation,
such as: "This is not really a color bar, it is a hygiene bar, as most
Africans do not have the facilities for proper cleanliness" and "The answer therefore to the question of sharing lots of things would be no.
Simply because of the ordinary African's ideas of hygiene."[12] A similar
argument appeared in *The Citizen* in 1956: "the native African is not
clean enough, physically, to make social intercourse with him pleas-
ant or even hygienically safe."[13]

The intimate materiality of these readings of race through images
of hygiene and appearance were reflected in a number of particular
obsessions of whites in colonial society. Odor, for example, was a regu-

lar feature of white representations of their interactions with Africans, not only in Zimbabwe but throughout southern Africa. One South African ethnographer commented, "no description of the outward appearance of the Kafirs would be complete if we failed to refer to the omnipresent odour which streams from these people."[14] A Rhodesian farmer wrote, "For it's oh! ye odorous Rhodesian natives . . . Mr. Rhodes spoke of you as 'Africa's greatest asset,' but so far as house-boys were concerned, you were Africa's greatest and smelliest ass."[15] Another lamented, "the unforgettable scent of a bush store—a mingled aroma of coarse native tobacco, 'Manchester goods,' and unwashed nigger."[16] David Caute quoted one Rhodesian professor teaching French at the university in the 1970s: "I cannot tolerate ze smell of zem! Zumtimes I geeve zum black students a leeft in my car and I tell you I can hardly bear ze smell of zem!"[17]

Domestic service formed another critical nexus for the intimate interpenetration of race, bodies, and hygiene. As Jacklyn Cock has so ably demonstrated, the interlocking of domestic space, privacy, racial identity, labor, and power that pertains in domestic service in southern Africa has been immensely potent.[18] Among Rhodesian texts, the books of Jeannie Boggie on farm life and domestic servants provide the clearest testament to the white perception of these relationships. Boggie endlessly catalogued the supposed errors of her servants, which with critical hindsight look more like deliberate sabotage—allowing meat to rot or putting dung into milk. She also described her own deep-rooted antipathy toward the bodily habits of her servants. In one case she wrote: "I rang the bell three times for Mike. . . . I noticed his hands were dirty, and pictured them foul with—maybe tobacco, or snuff, or maybe nose pickings or beer, or nasty microbes from handling dirty cards at card playing. So I said quite calmly: 'Mike. Go wash hands first.' He continued to place the parts together where the cream goes through. 'Ouch! Go wash hands. Go WASHEE hands.' No result. I said it a fourth time, accompanied by a smack on his back with a home-made brush made from the stalks of some weed, and used for swilling the dairy floor with water."[19] In another case, Boggie described servants as "breathing out beer . . . breathing out perspiration . . . breathing out roast meat . . . take sixteen strips of unwashed tripe hanging from the roof . . . put the total breathings into a 'scent bottle' to get breakfast ready and make toast. . . . Imagination seems to picture that native-handled toast as too absolutely smelly."[20] Similarly, in Frantz and Rogers's study, numerous apprehensions about the hygiene of domestic workers cropped up.[21]

As with all aspects of racist thought and behavior, such physical revulsion was at least partly performative, part of the public theater of segregation. The pervasiveness of sexual relationships between white men and black women simultaneous with racist visions of "dirty Africans" underlined the flexible and relative nature of such attitudes.[22] Moreover, some colonial texts also drew upon tropes of "noble savagery" to describe African bodies. "Probably the first thing," wrote one visitor, "which strikes a new-comer in Rhodesia is the unexpected beauty of the black race—the beauty, that is, of their bodies."[23] In such descriptions, African bodies emerge as aesthetically pleasing examples of "primitive physiques." Some practices that particularly revolted Europeans at one moment, like smearing oil mixtures on the skin, were then inverted and seen as "splendid."[24] Felix Bryk, in his ethnographic study of African bodies and sexuality, wrote:

> *The Negro is not satisfied with the beauty that nature has bestowed upon his skin. . . . He adds to his chocolate brown, black skin new erotic values by painting it, oiling it, and branding it. Painting with various earths and vegetable color is only used for temporary purposes. . . . Sometimes they rub themselves, from head to foot, wearing all their clothes and ornaments, with an animal fat mixed with red earth, so that they shine like red copper in the sun. This is a pleasant sight to behold, which does not discount the natural beauty of their unpainted bodies. Others satisfy themselves with just oiling their bodies. This blends the various copper hues of the skin into full force like a freshly varnished oil painting by Rembrandt.*[25]

Though seemingly at odds with beliefs that Africans were inherently dirty and diseased, such visions were often placed without any evident sense of contradiction right alongside expressions of disgust. African bodies, in these depictions, were beautiful as long as they remained pure and untouched by "civilization" or change. Africans "kept in their place" were more beautiful than those who accepted civilization. In this light, clothing in particular was seen as something that spoiled the image of the "primitive": "there are many Mashonas on the road, for the most part undisfigured by European dress. A leopard skin is the ideal costume for these bronze figures, with their fine free carriage and movement."[26] The spectacle provided by wild nature in Africa was increasingly prominent in travelers' tales by the late 1800s; Africans clothed or washed like Europeans violated hegemonic presumptions held by such travelers about the unity between "savage" peoples and the "natural world." As one hunter commented in his diary, it was "an outrage to the beautiful wild bush veldt, a native clad in his shabby unbecoming European clothes, and a hat that he lifted. Ugh."[27]

Both tropes, the dirty, unredeemed African body and the noble, pure, "savage" body, were pervasive parts of colonial sentiment and of white subjectivity. As such, they had a powerful and fairly obvious influence on both colonial institutions and colonial culture. . . .

Merchant Capital, "New Needs," and Colonial Society

The issue of the "needs" of Africans and the alteration of those needs was an important part of metropolitan British thought about colonialism. "We must be prepared to take the requisite measures to open new markets for ourselves among the half-civilized or uncivilized nations of the globe," declared Lord Salisbury in 1895. Lord Salisbury's sentiment was echoed around the turn of the century by many key figures in British imperialism: Cecil Rhodes, Joseph Chamberlain, and others. Chamberlain and his supporters particularly invoked the image of "new markets" abroad to woo support for their imperial ambitions among the British working class. Access to new markets, they assured the voting public, would secure the future of British capitalism and thus British jobs. There would always be a place to buy raw materials and a place to sell the products made by the factories.

The imperial imagining of overseas markets rested on the domestic transformation of market culture and modes of consumption in England during the eighteenth and nineteenth centuries. This was a world in which "the commodity literally came alive."[28] Recent historical works have clarified the importance of commodification in the cultural world of the industrializing West, especially in nineteenth-century England.[29] The expansion of "need" was seen by various Enlightenment philosophers, economists, and polemicists as one of the key components of the social engine that would drive the world to "progress" and "satisfaction." As the desire for more and better goods was increasingly understood in the metropolis as a key attribute of a "civilized" society, the societies of Africa, Asia, and Latin America were increasingly understood as societies that lacked desire and thus lacked aspiration and ambition. With Africa, furthermore, desire was understood by nineteenth-century Westerners to be inert, absent, never present. . . .

However, it was also taken as generally axiomatic . . . that the imitation of European material culture, the adoption of new consuming habits by Africans . . . would perform the work of "civilizing" Africans. For those who sought less provocative methods of obtaining workers and promoting the broader mission of "civilizing," "the desire of the natives" was potentially an attractive approach. Such a solution rested on the presumption that autonomous desires implanted in the heart of every African would "voluntarily" lead him or her to comply with settler rule. . . . If Africans "wanted" European things, and "wanted" to work to obtain them, this would preserve the façade of high-mindedness on which British colonialism relied so heavily. For example, the mayor of Salisbury responded to Earl Grey's speech by saying,

> the first thing that should be done . . . was to get them [Africans] out of their rugged hills and put them into . . . well-defined areas where they could be kept under control. They would then be brought into more frequent touch with the white man, and consequently they would try to adapt themselves to a certain extent to civilisation. If they wanted to follow more or less civilised methods of living they would want these items of European manufacture and would want to work in order to be able to purchase them. . . .[30]

In the same vein, government official Hugh Marshall Hole wrote, "the only means by which he [the native] could be weaned from this idyllic existence was the creation of a desire for European manufactured goods purchaseable with money."[31]

The Rhodesian state turned both to . . . merchants and to other colonial institutions to try to encourage the development of "new needs" among Africans. For example, a 1934 editorial in the *Native Mirror* typically concluded that the "objective of native education" was "to raise the whole standard of living of the African people. . . . Africans should aim at better homes, better furniture, better utensils, better dress, better wagon carts and ploughs, better stock and better gardens."[32] Traders naturally were key participants in these early colonial characterizations of the role of consumption in "civilizing" Africans, but were divided on how to interpret their own role. Some merchants boasted of their worth as a "civilizing influence," seeing their stores as a form of missionary work that brought Africans into the bosom of the West by altering their material culture. One such trader crowed about the change in African tastes: "The trader changes it for him really . . . we started selling the Natives knives and forks, cups and saucers, china plates, bedsteads. . . . We did it for them."[33] Other traders shared these beliefs: "Ploughs, bicycles, donkey carts, sewing machines, mealgrinders, etc. have all been introduced to the Native by outside Native Traders, with admitted benefit to him. The Traders have helped to get him away from un-hygienic skins and the introduction of clothes has done away with the "muchi"—beads, bangles, and other useless ornaments had their day but have been educated out of the native largely by trader influence."[34] Another trader claimed, "When I realised it was impossible to do trade in the Reserve and make a living, I decided to create what you might call necessities for the natives."[35] Representatives of the Mashonaland Kafir Truck Association piously declared, "The trader brought life into the reserve at a high cost to his health."[36] The Salisbury Chamber of Commerce echoed this sentiment: "But for such people the native would still be wearing skins.". . .[37]

Ad Campaigns for Soap

Lifebuoy is a brand-name version of a type of cheap soap often sold to African consumers all over the continent from the early part of this century: carbolic or "red" soaps. With the disinfectant carbolic added to them, these soaps all have a distinctive, unforgettable odor. Given the established weight of the settler vision of "dirty" Africans, it is unsurprising that soaps with extra disinfectant, soaps that give users a distinctive odor connoting cleanliness, were thought by white manufacturers to be particularly appropriate for use by Africans. . . .

The first soap brands advertised in African media, in the mid-1940s, were actually RMM's Atlas Soaps (which included a carbolic variety). RMM used rhetoric drawn straight from colonial doctrines of cleanliness, telling readers: "Nature's greatest gift is perhaps water—and one of civilization's greatest gifts—SOAP. The day of the witch-doctor's craft and all its evils are over. Today educated Africans know that disease is spread by germs—and that germs live in dirt. Be educated—be healthy—keep your body, clothes, and house clean by regular washing with soap and water. If you are wise you will make sure it is ATLAS Soap—the Best. There is an ATLAS Soap for each and every use. Ask for it by name—ATLAS SOAPS."[38] "Each and every use" was the space that Lever Brothers smoothly stepped into with its various well-defined brand images after its acquisition of RMM's facilities in 1947. Men were Lifebuoy's appointed target among urban African consumers, in advertisements running from about 1950 onward. One of the two predominant campaign slogans for the next two decades was "Successful Men Use Lifebuoy," which went through a number of subtle permutations as time went on; the other major campaign played variously on Lifebuoy's ability to "give health.". . .

. . . [M]arketers actively sought to give public expression to the anxieties and complaints that characterized African daily life in the cities. Obtaining work, staying employed, fending off crippling sickness, and achieving upward mobility were all major portions of these anxieties, especially during the years when strongly segregationist municipal administrators in Salisbury and Bulawayo took a hard line against stabilizing labor. At the same time, these advertisements also played very strongly, especially in the 1940s and 1950s, to white preconceptions about lazy and indolent African laborers. For example, a mid-1940s' ad for Parton's Purifying Pills features a comic strip in which a worker is castigated by his white boss for being too slow. His friend tells him, "The Boss never grumbles at *me*. If you're feeling lazy, you're probably constipated. Take Parton's Purifying Pills. I did." The worker later tells his wife, having followed this advice, "I'm glad I'm looking better . . . I'm certainly feeling better. And the boss is pleased, too."[39] A similar ad for B. B. Tablets featured an African man sighing, "I feel too weak to work. . . . I wonder if B. B. Tablets will help me?" A doctor fortunately steps in to give the protagonist the medicine, and the worker triumphantly declares, "It's good to feel well and strong again!"[40] These messages were connected with other products as well. The Tea Marketing Board's advertisements in the 1940s frequently harped on the same themes. In one ad, a son tells his father that he is always exhausted and will lose his job soon. His father wisely suggests, "Do as I do, my son. Drink a cup of refreshing tea when you feel tired." The son's white employer notes the subsequent improvement and tells him, "I am going to give you a better job."[41]

The "Successful Man" campaign for Lifebuoy fit neatly into this strain of promotions. Its first incarnation, in the 1950s, featured the aforementioned slogan accompanied by drawings of an African man dressed smartly in a suit and tie, sometimes holding a pen, beaming from ear to ear. At the end of the decade, these pictures were replaced by an alternating series of photographs featuring African men in various "typical" work clothes. One of the photographs still featured a well-dressed clerk, but others showed a miner, a brick-layer, and a teacher. The slogan remained the same, simultaneously recalling established associations between African masculinity and dirt, between labor and pollution, between professional success within the colonial system and rigorous hygienic purification. This later version of the campaign also featured one image of the "successful man *and* his family" using Lifebuoy, broadening the stakes involved. The other Lifebuoy campaign used in the 1960s and 1970s in African media played in a different way on the same ideas, with the message "Keep Healthy . . . Keep Clean . . . Use Lifebuoy, the *Health* Soap." Again, the ads almost always featured men, this time often already lathered up and in the shower, clutching a bar of Lifebuoy. In the first campaign, the soap was offered as the guarantor of the potential for success under the social rules of the white-controlled workplace; this campaign stressed Lifebuoy's power to guarantee the ability of men to work by securing continuous good health.

A mixed-race Dutch East Indies colonial family in 1922. The young Indonesian woman on the far right is probably the family's nursemaid. (Koninklijk Instituut Voor de Tropen, Amsterdam, The Netherlands)

Europe in the Empire

Current research on the civilizing mission is part of a reviving interest in the lives of European men and women overseas and the relationship between culture and empire. This section considers those aspects of European culture that the colonizer reproduced in the colonies, as well as the changes this culture underwent when enrolled in the service of colonialism. Society in Europe in this period was divided along sexual, racial, and class lines. The empire was no different. Colonial culture, even more so than metropolitan culture, was profoundly gendered, subordinating women to men and assigning different imperial roles to each sex. While gender divisions strengthened male white rule, class tensions among whites, and sexual unions between whites and natives, often threatened to destabilize it. All colonizers nevertheless felt racially superior to the colonized, and daily life overseas was carefully organized to preserve the distance between the races.

Through her study of one imperial man, the English administrator Edward Eyre, Catherine Hall reveals the central role played by Victorian ideals of masculinity and gentlemanliness in colonial strategies of rule. Good governance was thought to require manly attributes at all times: courage, strength, and sexual restraint. Administrators conceived of themselves as "fathers" to "childlike natives." Hall demonstrates first, how critically these ideals influenced the policies of Governor Eyre throughout his career. Second, she shows how Eyre's notions of the proper manly way to treat colonial subjects shifted depending on whether the imperialist was dealing with Australian Aboriginals or emancipated slaves and their descendants in the British West Indies.

As Frances Gouda's study of white women in the Dutch East Indies reveals, most European women overseas were dependent spouses of settlers or colonial administrators until World War II. Despite their dependency, they were also critical players in maintaining European hegemony. White women were expected to create European-style homes for their husbands, to prevent the latter from becoming "decivilized" in the tropics, and to keep a proper distance from their "black" servants. Imperial man, in turn, believed that he had to protect the white woman from supposedly sexually predatory "natives." Both roles positioned women first and foremost as guardians of the imperial nation's health and purity of race.

Gwendolyn Wright also considers the relationship between European rulers and their colonial subjects. She views it from the perspective of colonial urbanism and architecture in French Morocco. In their quest to maintain cultural and racial boundaries between themselves and native peoples, the French realized that their new imperial cities (where most whites lived) had to be planned very carefully. European districts were always to be physically separated from native towns; they had to look modern, while native ones were to be kept more traditional—thus underscoring the power, rationality, and scientific prowess of the West vs. the exoticism and backwardness of the colonized cultures. The French built several cities embodying these principles. This made colonial Morocco a laboratory for European urban modernism and racial segregation in the early twentieth century.

Europeans sought to maintain boundaries between themselves and their subjects because these boundaries often blurred in practice. Ann Stoler lays bare the many race and class tensions that characterized European colonial society, particularly in the settler communities of Southeast Asia. Although interracial sex became officially frowned upon, male white concubinage with a "native" woman was common in all colonies. The "mixed-blood" children that resulted were a great source of anxiety to officials, since their cultural and racial status was ambiguous. Administrators also worried about the poor whites in their midst; racially they appeared to be European, but their lifestyle was closer to that of the "native." Colonial society, in short, was much less homogeneous and secure in its identity than governmental ideology at the time, and historians since, have suggested.

Europeans worried about who belonged to their community and who did not, but what identity did mixed-bloods, in fact, claim for themselves? Owen White turns to this question with respect to the métis in French West Africa. Although it took time for the métis to articulate a sense of who they were, by the early 1930s they were organizing themselves into voluntary associations, and by the 1940s they had come to proudly adopt the label "Eurafrican." Thus was born a new historical personality—an amalgamation of African and French cultural traditions that denied one had to be either African or French. Whether this claim to a mixed cultural identity subverted colonial norms or represented an accommodation to the colonial system is an open question.

"Europe in the Empire" was thus fraught with contradictions. European men and women overseas were in daily contact with the colonized who were servants, employees, or (for men especially) sexual partners. Such contact only heightened the need for a set of cultural practices and living spaces that would preserve at all moments the proper hierarchy among the races. Within the white community itself, women were clearly the inferior sex of the superior race; they had power over the natives, but were themselves subject to male authority. White males were all-powerful in theory, but as a tiny minority ruling vast foreign populations, they were never as secure as they appeared on the surface. And the issue of identity—where Europe began and where it ended—was omnipresent for colonizer and colonized alike.

Catherine Hall

An Imperial Man in Australasia and the West Indies

The Morant Bay Rebellion

In October, 1865 a riot occurred outside the court house in the small town of Morant Bay on the south-eastern coast of Jamaica. Months of tensions between blacks and whites over land, labour, and law erupted after an unpopular verdict from magistrates which led to a demonstration and attempted arrests. . . . The local official had already asked the British Governor, Edward John Eyre, for troops and they were on their way by sea. . . . In the subsequent violence eighteen officials and members of the militia were killed, thirty-one wounded. The next day Eyre received a message, "the blacks have risen." The 13,000 whites on the island had constantly feared a rising from the 350,000 blacks. More troops were immediately sent in and martial law declared. In the month that followed horrific reprisals took place. Despite the absence of organized resistance, troops under British command executed 439 people, flogged more than 600 men and women and burnt over 1,000 homes. A mixed-race member of the Jamaican House of Assembly, George William Gordon, was hanged.

The initial response from the British government was cautiously to endorse Eyre's actions. Jamaica, conquered almost by chance by the troops of Oliver Cromwell in 1655, had become the jewel in the British crown during the halcyon days of Caribbean slave-sugar in the eighteenth century. By the 1780s, however, the anti-slavery movement was challenging the permanence of the plantation economy built on slave labour and the island increasingly became a source of difficulty and dispute for the Colonial Office. The abolition of the slave trade in

Excerpted from "Imperial Man: Edward Eyre in Australasia and the West Indies, 1833–66" by Catherine Hall, in *The Expansion of England: Race, Ethnicity and Cultural History*, Bill Schwarz, ed. Copyright © 1996 by Routledge & Keegan Paul, Ltd. Used by permission of Routledge, Ltd. and the author.

1807, and of slavery and apprenticeship in 1833 and 1838, put Jamaica, as the largest of the British Caribbean islands, at the heart of the great experiment of the abolitionists—the attempt to construct a successful free-labour economy with black labour. By mid-century this experiment looked, from the British line of vision, as less than successful and Jamaica increasingly appeared in Britain as a source of trouble and strife, its black population lazy, its planter class decadent and archaic. The riot in Morant Bay, following in the wake of the Indian Mutiny, was further evidence for the Colonial Office and the Liberal government of the day of the rebellious nature of "native" populations and the need for strong government.

The government's initial support for Eyre soon came under attack, however, from abolitionist and dissenting groups. . . . The government was forced to establish a Royal Commission to inquire into the events in Jamaica.

The Royal Commission report, based on evidence collected from witnesses in Jamaica, was published in April, 1866. It claimed that the initial violence had presented a genuine danger and that Eyre had been right to react vigorously in order to prevent the spread of the disturbance. . . . This official leniency provoked . . . a private prosecution on Eyre, . . . led . . . by the doyen of liberal intellectuals, John Stuart Mill. The threatened prosecution of Eyre caused a backlash and led to popular mobilization in his defence, culminating in the formation of an Eyre Defence Committee, pledged to raise money for any necessary legal action.

For months the debate over the Eyre case raged in Britain. On either side were leading intellectuals and public men. Behind John Stuart Mill were the cream of the liberal intelligentsia—Charles Darwin, Charles Lyall, Herbert Spencer, Thomas Huxley, John Bright, and Frederick Harrison. They believed that martial law had been misused and British subjects, regardless of colour, denied their ancient right to the rule of law. Spearheading the defence of Eyre was Thomas Carlyle, the prophetic voice of mid-nineteenth-century England, backed by Charles Dickens, John Ruskin, Charles Kingsley, and Alfred Lord Tennyson. Carlyle argued that Eyre's actions had been heroic, that he had saved the whites from massacre and that, more fundamentally, blacks were in any case born to be mastered. Between the summer of 1866 and 1867 respectable public opinion swung away from the Jamaica Committee to the supporters of Eyre. By the time the third, last and still unsuccessful attempt was made to prosecute Eyre it was clear that the defence of black Jamaican rights was no longer a popular cause. Only a small core of middle-class radicals was left, led by a disillusioned and disheartened Mill and relying for support on working-class radicalism. The respectable middle class had arrived at the view that blacks were, essentially, different from whites and thus could not expect the same rights.

At stake in this debate were issues about the relations between the "mother country" and "her" colonies, the place of martial law and the rule of law, and the very nature of black people. But also at issue were questions about the nature of Englishness itself. Ethnic identities depend on an "imagined community," a sense of self rooted in a collective consciousness of "us" compared to "them." Neither the "us" nor the "them" are fixed but rather constantly negotiated and re-worked. The debate over Eyre marked a moment when two different conceptions of "us," constructed through two different notions of "them," were publicly contested. Mill's imagined community was one of potential equality, in which "us," white Anglo-Saxon men and women, believed in the potential of Jamaican blacks to become like "us" through a process of civilization. Carlyle's imagined community was an hierarchically ordered one in which "we" would always master "them."

In each of these imagined communities the identities constructed for men and women, for blacks and whites, were distinctively different. Mill and Carlyle were particularly preoccupied with contesting each other's notions of white, male middle-class identity—for Mill, Eyre was the villain, for Carlyle, the hero. In constructing their villain and hero they demonstrated their commitment to certain definitions of "good" manliness, the kind of man they could or could not identify with, the kind of man they wanted to be themselves and wanted others to be.

For identities are historically specific, not essentially given; they are never completed but constantly in flux. Identities are the fictions, the representations, the stories that we tell ourselves about who we are. The process of forming cultural and social identities, as Stuart Hall argues, is "the construction of a sense of belonging which draws people together into an 'imagined community' and the construction of symbolic boundaries which define who does *not* belong or is excluded from it." But that imagined community is historically specific too and who is defined as belonging shifts and turns. Since self is not so much a core as a process, the varied fragments of self are in play in different ways at different historical moments. But particular identities will be structured in dominance: politically validated and institutionally legitimated. In 1866–1867 it was the discourse of the white middle-class man as master, as superior in essence and for all time, to inferior blacks which eventually emerged as the dominant discourse. . . .

Australia

In the 1830s respectable English middle-class men supported the anti-slavery movement and emancipation. To be a supporter of the weak and the dependent—women, children, slaves and animals—constituted precisely the "independence" of middle-class masculinity. True manliness was derived not from property and inheritance but from "real religion"—the faith born from religious conversion and a determination to make life anew. True manliness also encompassed a belief in individual integrity and freedom from subjection to the will of another. . . . True manhood was defined by the capacity to work for oneself in the world, to trust in the dignity of labour, and to make money rather than to live off an existing fortune. Such a definition rested on fragile foundations in a society in which economic crises were frequent—when banks collapsed and bankruptcy constantly threatened—and when for many men the activities of the market brought not sturdy independence but fearful anxieties. The very vulnerability of manhood was repressed in the ideological fictions of integrity and independence—whether in the marketplace, the political arena or the home, but arguably it was this unspoken vulnerability which gave ideologies of masculinity in this period their dynamic intensity.

In the troubled decade of the 1830s, when opportunities for young men with only a modest capital were limited, the empire beckoned as a source of riches, opportunities, and adventure. . . .

. . . The time was ripe for . . . white European man, the powerful and phallic "fire-pillar," bursting forth from "swelling, simmering, never-resting Europe" and planting his seed which would bring forth new men from painful labour. Here indeed was conquering, imperial man at work. . . .

Edward Eyre was destined to be one of these "proper men." . . .

Eyre himself had originally been intended for the army but his father was seized with the notion that his son could go to Australia, which "was then just beginning to be known . . . [as] a desirable field for a young man commencing life." . . .

On arrival in Sydney he found no lucrative government post opening to him despite his letters of introduction. Taking advice from a colonist who befriended him he decided to become a farmer. He entered into an agreement with a gentleman settler, Mr Bell, for a year to learn the trade. During that year he bought sheep and land, and was assigned convict labour under the government scheme. Setting up his own farm (which he named "Woodlands") together with his work with Mr Bell required continuous, intensive labour and Eyre soon discovered the worries which came with the ownership of property. . . .

Eyre's later narration of these years is structured through a powerful sense of the proprieties of English middle-class gentility, which for him included both a commitment to hard work and a recognition of the need for the deferral of gratification. "A man must act" if a small capital is to be converted into an income. A colonist must look to his farm first and the comforts of his home second; but he must also struggle to maintain the civilities of English life, to hold on to English notions of respectability which served to distinguish him from those convicts and "natives" who were his daily companions. . . .

Thus Eyre separated himself from those men on whom he had to rely in daily life, underpinning his own self-esteem by denigrating the lack of self-control, the base impulses, of those around him. . . .

After a year Eyre . . . decided to try his hand as an overlander, taking sheep and cattle across the country to the new settlements in South Australia. . . .

By 1839 Eyre had made a considerable amount of money from overlanding and he decided to devote his energies to an exploration of parts of the north and west of South Australia, impelled by "an innate feeling of ambition and a desire to distinguish myself in a more honourable and disinterested way than the mere acquisition of wealth." . . .

Both overlanding and exploration were quintessentially male activities—indeed, exploration can be interpreted as the ultimate expression of frontier masculinity, the extension in the European mind of man's conquest over "virgin" territory. . . .

As a farmer Eyre had been glad to employ casual Aborigine labour, making use, for example, of traditional Aborigine skills in stripping bark which could then be used for building sheep pens. As an overlander he again had need of Aborigine skills and was dependent on their knowledge of the countryside. As an explorer this knowledge was even more essential and on his expeditions into the heartlands of South Australia Eyre would not have survived without Aborigine help. At numerous points on his ill-fated exploration of the Great Bight it was Aborigine knowledge of the water holes which saved at least some of the party. "In how strong a light does such simple kindness of the inhabitants of the wilds to Europeans travelling through his country (when his fears are not excited or his prejudices violated) stand contrasted," he noted, "with the treatment he experiences from them when they occupy his country, and dispossess him of his all." . . .

. . . Eyre did not doubt that the Aborigine were "savages" in that, for example, they treated their wives as slaves (always a key index for the Victorian Englishman as to the scale of a civilization). He was also quite ready to denounce them as "silent and cunning in all they do," needing to be watched all the time. He doubted, however, that they were cannibals. They had, he was sure, no thought of the morrow, a natural taste for a rambling and indolent life, and no idea of temperance and prudence. In other words they lacked those characteristics which the middle-class Englishman valued, the belief in the deferral of gratification, the commitment to the values of labour and discipline. In his writings Eyre described with amazement and disapproval the capacity of the Aborigine, having caught a kangaroo, to eat vast quantities of meat, just like his white, male working-class companions who drank gallons of water having been deprived of it, while he, ever prudent, ate only a modest amount of his share keeping the rest for another day, content with his usual pot of tea. Nevertheless, he recognized that contrary to many European assumptions the Aborigine had their own relation to the land, their own feelings, their own value system, their own legal code, their own marriage customs, their own religious ideas, their own language. In Eyre's view their culture was different from and inferior to that of the English; the proper response to this was to make it genuinely possible for them to become "like us." . . .

English men must act to protect the savages from their own savagery and make them anew as men and women in their own —

English—image. Co-existence meant that blacks could be like brothers as long as the brothers were in their brothers' image. Once they were not, the seeds of other ways of perceiving the native were already contained in the interstices of the philanthropic mind. . . .

St. Vincent

Eyre left Australia in 1845 hoping he would find employment in the colonial service. He returned to England taking with him the two Aborigine boys that he was educating and "civilising," his personal experiment in the construction of "new men." . . .

. . . The England he encountered was changing. The respectable, emancipationist orthodoxy about blacks as brothers and sisters was breaking up and ideas about "race" and racial inferiority more openly discussed. The great experiment of emancipation in the West Indies had not been entirely successful from the British point of view. Anxieties focused around the collapse, as it was seen in Britain, of the plantation economy. While the planters' lobby loudly bemoaned their ruin at the indolent hands of lazy blacks, abolitionists were increasingly defensive in their accounts of the West Indies. Reflecting the signs of the times and articulating new thoughts on the relations between black and white Carlyle published his "Occasional Discourse on the Negro Question" in 1849, re-published as a pamphlet and re-titled in 1853 an *Occasional Discourse on the Nigger Question.* This piece, instantly repudiated by the abolitionist press, marked the moment when it became legitimate for respectable, influential men publicly to profess a belief in the essential inferiority of black people, and to claim that blacks were born to be mastered and could never attain the level of European civilization. By mid-century, it had become the fashion within scientific discourse to aver that distinct and fixed racial types provided the key to human history. . . .

It was in this climate that Eyre . . . arrived at the end of 1854 in St Vincent, one of the tiny islands of the Caribbean, with his wife, his two small children, a private secretary, a manservant and three women servants—a profoundly English middle-class party. He was shocked by the contrast between the settler colonies of Australia and New Zealand and the tropical world of the plantation economy with its long established white population and its black freed slaves. He found the financial state of the colony "deplorable," with a large debt and the annual expenditure exceeding the revenue. Public services were "most unsound and unsatisfactory" with the hospital closed, the jail dilapidated, no aid being given to schools, no refuges for the destitute or orphans, no mental institution, indeed, the island lacked "the most essential laws and the most necessary institutions." . . .

The missionaries and their allies in England had long been preoccupied with building a black middle class which would be capable, in their eyes, of conducting responsible government. Given Eyre's historic attachment to the protection of native races it might have been expected that he would have aligned himself to just such a policy; but this was not to be. Just as the presence of coloured merchants, tradesmen, and newspaper editors troubled him, so the blacks that he encountered in St Vincent were disturbingly different from the indigenous natives he was familiar with, those "children of the wilds" or "strangers in their own lands" who were to be pitied as victims and made into dependents. The blacks of the British Caribbean were freed slaves, still riven with the memory of slavery and ever watchful of any attempt to reimpose that hated institution, whether in the guise of new penal codes or the importation of indentured labourers from Asia. They had been brought forcibly from Africa but were now independent peoples with property, skills, and aspirations. On Spanish territory, all too close, slavery still flourished. Their children had never experienced slavery, but had been raised in its shadow. Numerically the blacks outnumbered the whites on St Vincent by twenty to one and had the potential, if they achieved the vote, to provide the electoral majority. Thousands of acres were being cultivated by small independent black proprietors, enjoying unparalleled prosperity. Eyre's first encounters with blacks left him disappointed with the extent to which, for him, they were "so little improved a race." The promise of emancipation had not been realized; and far from considering any extension in the franchise to raise the degree of representation he was convinced that the executive should increase its powers at the expense of the elected bodies, a conviction which he was able to translate into new constitutional legislation. . . .

At Christmas and New Year there were riots in the capital of St Vincent again. . . . Eyre did not hesitate to interpret the dangers in racial terms. . . . "It was evident," he reported to his superior, "that in the event of any collision taking place it would become one of race—the coloured against the white man." He concluded that without white troops there could be no security. . . .

Jamaica

In 1860 Eyre returned once more to England and had to wait eighteen months before he was appointed Deputy Governor of Jamaica. . . .

As the intensity of discourses of racial difference deepened, so the connotation of "native" with "irredeemable savage" became more common and immovable. . . . This was the kind of English common-sense which Eyre increasingly had recourse to from his early days in Jamaica. The language of brotherhood had disappeared. The fear now articulated was that blacks would sink back into the barbarism from which they had been briefly lifted, by their enforced enslavement and encounter with Europe. The confidence and enthusiasm which had permeated Eyre's account of his young manhood and his successful years with the Aborigine was gone. Public and private disappointments, the responsibility of supporting a growing family of five, his wife's ill-health and his separation from her and his children, all combined with the new racial discourses of the 1850s and 1860s to construct a more threatened, defensive, disturbed identity, one which depended on an assertion of established white authority. . . .

In May, 1864 Eyre was finally made Governor. . . .

Having in his own mind constructed the population of the island as "absolute savages," the shift to a highly coercive regime appeared quite logical. Theft, for example, had become a serious problem. The culprits, it appeared, were not the old and the needy but the young and able-bodied of both sexes, "those who are well able to work." "I fear," argued Eyre, moving towards the logic of Carlyle and the planters, "it is rather an indisposition to labour than an inability to procure work" which led them to steal. Far from feeling shamed by imprisonment such offenders, Eyre believed, returned home to "their people" with no stigma attached to them. From June, 1864 Eyre began to inquire of the Colonial Office whether the treadmill had ever been officially banned; and after his tour of the country he pressed for the re-introduction of the whip, together with a system of enforced apprenticeship. The proposed number of stripes was well in excess of those allowed within the British army or under the old apprenticeship system. Given "the peculiar state of things" in the West Indies, Eyre maintained flogging had become a necessary remedy, though not one that he had expected to have to resort to in his younger days. He insisted that propertied blacks, indeed all classes of the community, were in favour of such action, a view with which Gordon, for one, dissented. . . .

For Eyre, utterly convinced as he was and always had been of white superiority, the notion contained in his early memorandum on the Aborigine, the respectful recognition of their separate, and different culture with its own rituals, laws, and institutions, was no longer possible. West Indian negroes were "savages" and "barbarians" without culture, unable to adapt to the requirements of civilization. Mastery and control were the only solutions.

Given this construction of "them" as essentially, utterly different from "us," of the Caribbean islands as mine-fields, and whites as beleaguered and in great jeopardy, it became inevitable that Eyre could see the rising in Morant Bay only as the preordained fulfilment of his worst fantasies, in which the whites of Jamaica faced extinction and all manner of torment. His first despatch recounted horrific brutalities committed by the black rioters—later proven by the Royal Commission never to have occurred—which "could only be paralleled by the atrocities of the Indian mutiny." The women, he asserted, "as usual on such occasions, were even more brutal and barbarous than the men," a clear signifier for the English middle class that the last remnants of civilization had been torn away. . . .

By the time that Eyre left Jamaica in 1866, suspended from duty, he was immensely popular with the whites on the island; his departure provided an opportunity for grateful addresses, thanking him for saving the colony from anarchy. The shared commonsense of the white population was clearly adopted and articulated by Eyre in his despatches to the Colonial Office, and in his subsequent evidence to the Royal Commission. Negroes, in this view, were not black Anglo-Saxons; indeed, "there are feelings of race within the black man's breast impenetrable to those without," preventing many in England from understanding the true "character and tone of thinking of the negro population." . . . There was an unresolved tension in the thinking here, as there had been in the Indian Mutiny, between the notion of blacks as incapable of acting for themselves, puppets on strings, and blacks as a source of conspiracy and evil, awaiting only white surveillance to be lifted to explode into the light of day. Blacks at one and the same time were objects of contempt—effeminized and made dependent—and objects of terror and fear—rapists, torturers, and murderers. . . .

For the supporters of Eyre in England, shocked at the unrelenting persecution of him, . . . it was vital to make the British public understand the true character of the negro as it had been revealed all too clearly by the events at Morant Bay. . . .

It was time for real men to speak out, to end the fantasy of racial equality, to accept reality, and govern with a strong hand. This was what Eyre had done, and it was this which deserved their support and celebration. In narrating Eyre as hero—"one of the very finest types of English manhood," who had "preserved the lives of 7,000 British men, and the honour of 7,000 British women, from the murder and the lust of black savages," who "put to proof some of the very highest qualities that ever in a man . . . have been considered meritorious,"—Carlyle and his acolytes were determined to destroy earlier visions of equality, whether of the races, the classes, or the sexes. And in large part they were successful. In his defence of Eyre Carlyle poured scorn on the humanitarians, effeminizing them just as he had done in his *Occasional Discourse*. He celebrated Eyre as the manly hero, the silent doer, who had responded to threat and acted with strength, saving the whites from "black unutterabilities." The constant struggle over the meanings of English male identity took another turn: "we" must be seen to assert proper forms of hierarchy and power, "we" must defend "our own." The magazine *Punch*, which actively supported Eyre, greeted the first failed prosecution against him, which took place in Market Drayton, Shropshire, with immense glee. "FREE AS EYRE!" they trumpeted. "Well done, old Shropshire! Well done, Market Drayton . . . English good sense is seldom appealed to in vain. We really cannot murder a man for saving a colony." "We" could no longer be one people with those of the colonies. "We" had returned to a much narrower definition of the imagined community—one that was exclusively white.

Frances Gouda

Dutch Women in the East Indies

> *In Batavia, Dutch matrons sport immense bellies stuffed to the gills with food; their stomachs are bloated, too, because they take too many siestas and refuse to engage in any kind of physical exercise. In the Dutch East Indies, in fact, activity and work comprise an exclusive attribute of men. Forever in a feverish hurry, men overwork themselves to get rich within a few years in order to retire to a green old age on the borders of the river Maas or along the Frisian polders near the Wadden Sea. With only an occasional exception, their wives, in contrast, allow themselves to be lived with the indolence of chained beasts. They walk around on bare feet and wrap their bodies in only a simple sarong, without a corset; they spend their idle days surrounded by their children as well as a cumbersome, whining crowd of lazy, cheating, or foolish Malay servants.*
>
> Robert Chauvelot, *Un roman d'amour à Java*, 1919

This was the unflattering portrait of Dutch East Indies' matrons (*njonjas*) and their servants painted by the French writer Robert Chauvelot in 1919 in one of his pulp novels. The reality of European women's existence in *Indië*, however, was infinitely more varied and complex than this disconcerting picture of gluttony and idleness. In the course of the twentieth century, a growing number of Dutch and Eurasian women held paying jobs and worked as teachers, nurses, or social workers. In the public transportation sector of the Indies, for example, female employees made up a large and actually favored share of its administrative personnel.

In fact, in a late-colonial anthology about life in the Indies, *Zóó leven wij in Indië* (Such is Our Life in the Indies), a chapter on "The Working Woman" proudly announced that European women, whether they had been born in Holland or in the Indies, were employed as "lawyers, physicians, and dentists, as managers of branches of government, customs officials, clerks, secretaries, bookkeepers, directors of normal schools, [and] inspectors of education . . . Many among these vivacious and independent women pursued productive lives in a colonial culture that still measured their private conduct with a more censorious "moral yardstick" than the sexual behavior of confirmed bachelors or temporarily unmarried men. However, among a total paid labor force of approximately 85,000 Europeans in 1930, only 15 percent consisted of women.

Despite his crude caricature of Dutch *njonjas*, Robert Chouvelot did touch upon an essential theme that affected the lives of many white women in the Indies who were not single, autonomous, or gainfully employed. A kind of gnawing emptiness, or the absense of a clearly defined purpose, enveloped many married women's tropical existence. Above and beyond the supervision of household servants—whom they tended "to command while slouching in their rocking chairs or *krossi malas* (chaise longue)," the solitary, hard-working female member of the Indies *Volksraad* wrote somewhat contemptuously—daily life in the Indies did not pose serious challenges to most Dutch wives, because servants were the ones to buy food, prepare meals, clean, tend to the garden, and watch over fair-skinned Dutch children as eagle-eyed, if indulgent, nannies.

In certain ways the day-to-day existence of Chauvelot's plump Batavia matrons did not differ much from the lives of middle-class women in the European metropole. After all, a gendered, if permeable, separation between a private domain that tended to enclose bourgeois women within family life and a masculine public sphere of industry and politics prevailed in Europe as it did in the colonies. But housewives in the Netherlands itself possessed more leeway in endowing their ordinary routines with a satisfying content. If they wanted to do so, middle-class wives in Holland could engage in charitable activities or take part in church circles or book clubs. Middle-class women could attend an array of concerts and visit museums and the theater or, if they lived in large cities and were bold enough, might participate in suffragist politics. Besides, fewer wives in the Netherlands could rely on nannies to supervise their children. The average bourgeois family in Holland also hired fewer household servants to cook, wash, and scrub, because employing a retinue of domestics constituted a prerogative of only the truly well-to-do. In Europe, in other words, women's lives revolved around some real tasks, which they accomplished either cheerfully or with sullen resentment, but which nevertheless gave them a clearer sense of purpose.

In Batavia, Semarang, Surabaya and elsewhere in the Indies, however a bevy of Indonesian servants took care of most of the mundane requirements of daily life. Hence, Chauvelot's distressing depiction of female passivity and languor contained at least some truths. There were, of course, various Dutch women who used their newly found leisure in extremely fruitful ways; being liberated from the relentless daily grind of household tasks enabled them to explore their residual creativity. Especially if they lived in outlying regions, some among them became skilled botanists and designed luxuriant tropical gardens. Others developed a serious interest in medicine and treated the physical ailments of local people with empathy and expertise, while more artistically gifted or intellectually inclined Dutch women cultivated their talent as painters, gratified their desire to write fiction, or nurtured their ethnographic curiosity about local culture.

But it was infinitely more difficult for white women to pursue such creative avocations if they resided in an obsessively status-conscious colonial city, surrounded not by Chauvelot's fictional chubby matrons but by real-life counterparts, who were probably not as obese as *Un roman d'amour à Java* insinuated. In the major urban communities of the Indies, social frictions tended to arouse European women's passions and a never-ending cycle of rumor and idle chatter provided the diversions typical of the "tropical gothic." It was a society "filled with distrust, jealousy, and malice," in which even the most trivial event among white residents was "examined with a fine tooth comb, until every silly detail was exposed." . . .

. . . [W]hether they inhabited skinny or pudgy bodies, were hyperactive or lazy, or whether they had blushing pink cheeks or skins with a pale auburn tinge, few European women in Batavia ambled around on bare feet or went about in an Indonesian sarong and kebaya. It was likely, though, that the stifling heat and humidity of Java's north coast emboldened many among them to shed their suffocating corsets. Besides, the sultry climate rendered an afternoon siesta a dire necessity, not only for lethargic white women but also for their more ambitious husbands, fathers, or sons, who routinely went to work at the crack of dawn. But the only Dutch women in the twentieth century who continued to wrap a batik sarong nonchalantly around their hips during the morning hours tended to live in rustic outposts, far away from the madding crowd of Europeans in Batavia, Surabaya, Semarang, or Medan. The *totokization* or "Europeanization" of Indies social life outside the central axis of Java and the east coast of Sumatra was often an incomplete process; in some remote, outlying regions, in fact, it may not have occurred at all.

Nonetheless, domestic advice manuals in the twentieth century gently urged newly arrived Dutch women to become more engrossed in the day-to-day running of their households rather than leave it to a "whining crowd" of deceitful Indonesian servants, as Chauvelot intimated. . . .

In most European households, servants constituted an integral element of both "the white-washed manor house with its open verandahs" as well as the surrounding Indies landscape: they "belong to us" just as much as they belonged to the palm trees swaying in the wind or to "the bamboo forest, the bottomless ravine, the glimmering *sawah* and the sacred *waringin* tree." But the ambiguity of advice manuals resided in the portrayal of servants as passing their daily lives in a fundamentally different world on the other side of a disinfected, neutral middle zone—a *"cordon sanitaire"*—despite their indispensable roles in European households and their intimate involvement in the family circle. "The compound behind the house is their exclusive domain," wrote a Dutch woman who was also active in the suffragist movement in the Indies in 1926. "The two boundary markers at the end of the driveway, with their widely extending low fences, serve as watchtowers and look-out posts" from which the servants observed the happenings of white-skinned family life, which often remained a bewildering spectacle to them.

In the hearts and minds of many *totok* European women, servants' physical proximity provoked eerie feelings of discomfort. As a result, white women's handbooks frequently depicted them, too, as mysterious and untrustworthy, or as unhygienic and dirty, even perverse, in their private habits. Not only domestic advice manuals but also Dutch novels for adolescent girls equated the possession of brown skin with "human fallibility, if not danger." White-skinned people, in contrast, personified competence and safety. If the human failures of Indonesian servants were not too grievous, white women should "rescue and save" them from making their inevitable mistakes and expect everlasting gratitude in exchange. These strains and contradictions were barely hidden beneath the surface; in fact, they absorbed the average Dutch woman's life. Often, however, she was forced to negotiate such tensions in solitude, because many a husband tended to be too tired after a long day's work to listen to the "petty" concerns of his wife and simply wished to drink his jenever and bitters in peace.

Most Dutch men working in private industry and commercial agriculture lived hectic lives. Chauvelot, in his vapid *Un roman d'amour à Java*, was no more charitable toward Dutch colonial men than he was to Indies matrons. He invented a comparable burlesque of dumb, grinning "Batavian giants with bulging muscles," who performed the most physically exhausting work all day but possessed "the mentality of laboring brutes: they rarely talk and think even less." Other men resembled "ambulatory cash registers" and were in a frenzied rush to get rich. But even a considerable number of Indies-born men—those who had no desire whatsoever to return to the Netherlands with a hefty bank account in order to retire in The Hague or a pretty spot "in the polder near the Waddenzee"—worked excruciatingly long hours. Civil servants, too, dedicated seemingly endless days to the strenuous task of colonial governance.

Whether they were blue-eyed newcomers from northern Europe with a reddish, freckled complexion—which made many Indonesians suspect they suffered from ringworm—or mixed-blood, "Indies" characters with olive-colored skins, European men engaged in a concerted effort to forge solidarity across the wide social spectrum of the European community. They incorporated their wives and daughters, too, in a herculean effort to make the white colonial enclave speak with a unanimous voice. However hard they tried, though, Europeans in the baroque social setting of colonial societies could not simply abandon their sensitivity to internal class distinctions. Despite their valiant efforts to pretend that social background did not matter in the Indies, perceptions of class differences, indeed, may have been magnified.

Within the European metropole, members of the upper or middle class rarely met "the other ranks" on a tennis court, across a dinner table, or in social clubs. Women who had to shop for food themselves because their foothold in the middle class was precarious, might view the butchers, greengrocers, or milkmen they faced each day as their social inferiors. If their husbands were rich enough, they engaged "common" folk as servants, who were thus in a clearly circumscribed subservient position. It was true, of course, that in Europe—in the Netherlands or in any other European country—the signs and symbols of class were subtly articulated in sartorial display, style, and speech. But it was particularly the social geography of daily life that delineated class distinctions and imposed a palpable segregation between rich, poor, and people of the middling sort—or rather, between those Europeans who defined themselves as superior to any "other" fellow citizen they might look down upon. In Holland itself, the sensibilities of Dutch men and women were not habitually rankled by encounters with people they perceived as hailing from a dubious class background.

In the Indies, in stark contrast, such social interactions occurred on a daily basis. In big cities on Java or in Medan in northern Sumatra, humble women who had worked as seamstresses in Holland shared a bridge table or the dance floor with pretentious Dutch matrons of upper-class provenance. A middle-class woman with academic training and a lively intellectual imagination could face a dull, barely literate military wife as her only white female counterpart in a remote civil service post. Or in the fiercely competitive world of the plantation belt of Deli on the east coast of Sumatra, a Dutch lady with an impeccable patrician lineage or a wealthy family background might have to defer to a former shop girl she secretly despised as cheap and vulgar, simply because the latter's husband had ascended more rapidly up the administrative ladder of a rubber plantation. As Marie van Zeggelen posed the question, with both anger and despair, about her previous experience as a military wife in a remote and rugged mountain district of Sulawesi in 1910: "why are women in the Indies always restricted only to each other's company and then, for Pete's sake, only on the basis of their rank . . . not rank based on their respective ages, no, rank derived from the status of their husbands?"

In their daily lives, "incorporated" European wives were saddled with the role of enforcing subtle hierarchical distinctions, making them protectors of the ontological wholeness of the colonial system, even if they had little to do with its political or economic construction. As such, Dutch women served as foot soldiers—either willingly or with moral qualms—who were in charge of defending an elaborate colonial pecking order that placed indigenous women at the bottom and classified white men at the top. Hence, in their quotidian routines most *njonjas* in colonial Indonesia—as was the case with *memsahibs* in British India—gave concrete expression to a male-defined imperial agenda and knowingly contributed to "the ideological work of gender."

Gwendolyn Wright

Residential Segregation and Colonial Architecture in Morocco

When the Parisian art critic Léandre Vaillat visited Morocco in the 1920s, he was enraptured with what he saw. Casablanca and especially Rabat seemed to represent the convergence of two diametrically opposed paths for twentieth-century cities: a modern vision of wide, orderly streets coexisted, apparently peacefully, with the picturesque charm of the indigenous North Africa madina, a setting adapted to a more traditional way of life. Morocco, Vaillat wrote, is "a laboratory of Western life and conservatory of Oriental life."

Like other astute European visitors, Vaillat recognized that this cultural imagery constituted an essential element of the French colonial presence. For historians today the strategies become even more clear: urban design—sometimes used in radically different ways within the same city—assumed a major role in efforts to make colonialism more popular among Europeans and more tolerable to the colonized peoples. Administrators of three French colonies of the early twentieth century—Indochina, Madagascar, and, most notably, Morocco—consciously used urban culture as a cornerstone of their political endeavors. Their notion of culture, by no means monolithic, emphasized variety and simultaneity. . . . [There was] a new appreciation of different

Excerpted from *Tensions of Empire: Colonial Cultures in a Bourgeois World*, edited by Ann Laura Stoler and Frederick Cooper. Copyright © 1996 by The Regents of the University of California. Reprinted by permission of the University of California Press.

Translations in brackets are the editors.'

aesthetics, both vernacular and refined, traditional and contemporary, indigenous and European; . . . [and] a recognition of culture in a more anthropological sense, as values, as ways of living that varied from one group to another, even within a city. Administrators brought in professional advisers to interpret these various cultural meanings and then applied the research to their political goals.

For colonial officials, each aspect of culture had definite references to power. If social conventions acted out in public and private spaces formed a complex ritual of order, then upholding certain conventions seemed a way to prevent resistance to colonial authority— seen as a breakdown of social order. In Morocco, for example, when the French took power in 1912, Sultan Moulay-Hafid was forced to abdicate in favor of his more conciliatory brother, Moulay-Youssef; this required, the French resident-general then explained, "reviving around the [new] sultan the ancient traditions and old ceremonies of the court," as well as building and maintaining opulent palaces for the ruler. Such officials hoped to preserve an established sense of hierarchy and propriety, buttressing it with what they perceived to be traditional rituals, spatial patterns, and architectural ornament, believing that this would reinforce their own superimposed order.

Simultaneously, however, officials also experimented with settings and policies conducive to a technologically advanced, economically diversified urban world. This was most evident in the streamlined office buildings and apartment buildings of the European sections of colonial cities, but it also appeared in the public health dispensaries, the public works, and the industrial expansion that involved the entire colonial population. The modernist imagery of buildings paralleled efforts to stimulate more investment and train more productive workers, in keeping with the budgetary requirements of 1900 that all French colonies become economically self-sufficient. The goal, in sum, was to protect certain aspects of cultural traditions while sponsoring other aspects of modernization.

Because of its rich complexity and the extreme milieu of power in which it was carried out, this colonial urbanism helps orient us to the possible uses and inequities of various urban policies. As Vaillat made clear, the proposals and achievements of Morocco in the 1910s and 1920s, like those of Indochina and Madagascar, represent a particular version of modern urbanism, an approach . . . responsive to local history and culture.... The cities of these three colonies, especially their European districts, exemplified many of the principles espoused by ... modernists: more standardized construction, more rationalized organization of public services and industry, efficient circulation routes, and greater attention to the hygienic aspects of design, such as the need for ample fresh air and sunlight.... [T]his ... model, by the absolutist and authoritarian ways in which it was implemented, actually brings into focus some of the underlying problems of the modernist vision as a whole. Unequal access to the benefits of modern urbanism, while more visible in colonial cities, affected other metropolises as well; so, too, with the loss of autonomy and even livelihood for many handicraft workers, an uneconomical commitment to inappropriate materials and techniques, the tendency toward class and ethnic segregation implicit in zoning policies, and overreliance on expertise....

Indochina, Madagascar, and, above all, Morocco were much talked and written about throughout the French-speaking world and beyond during these years. They were seen as "laboratories"; again and again they were called *champs d'expérience*, or experimental terrains....

The very word "laboratory" resounded in many different circumstances in the early twentieth century, of course, but the colonial context gave it a very definite meaning. Here one could appraise firsthand the actual conditions of quite diverse settings and, simultaneously, distill general principles, whether about the nature of cities or the influence of religion; moreover, it was possible to consider and even act on the political ramifications of various ideas. In particular, two professions just emerging in France at the turn of the century but as yet unable to find official support for their expertise—urbanism and the social sciences—discovered in the colonies the opportunities denied them at home. Many French social scientists, including the anthropologist Lucien Lévy-Bruhl and the geographer Augustin Bernard, found the chance there to explore their theories about social structure or residential environments, among other topics. They discussed ideas in prestigious research centers like the Institut des Hautes Études Marocaines, the École Française d'Extrême-Orient, or the Académie Malgache and often evolved their speculations into directives for the colonial governments. And it was in the colonies that would-be urban planners like Prost and Hébrard were given their first opportunities to plan and build on a genuinely metropolitan scale, for their predilections, too, fit in with the political strategies of a new generation of colonial administrators.

Indeed, at the turn of the century, the social and aesthetic issues championed by these social scientists and urbanists quickly became key aspects of a new French colonial policy called "association." To most observers, the underlying premises of the earlier nineteenth-century approach, called "assimilation," were twofold: French cultural predominance in language, laws, and even architectural style—the famous *mission civilisatrice*—and French military prowess demonstrated through destruction of indigenous cities and towns and embodied in a continuing, visible military presence. In contrast, most advocates of association called for the preservation of distinctive local cultures, including tribal councils and historic monuments, and they believed that this respect, when combined with social services like schools and hospitals, could counter resistance far more effectively than military strength. Precisely at the moment that the nineteenth-century policy of assimilation was coming under attack—partly for moral reasons, but as much on the pragmatic grounds that it had proved to be politically and economically inefficient—colonial opportunities for the new generation of French urbanists and social scientists opened up. The policy of association that they implemented thus tended to have a strong basis in cultural sensibility and urban planning, ranging from issues of historic preservation and building style to the distribution of public services.

Let us now follow the basic principles of this phase of colonial urbanism into actual practice. Morocco, Indochina, and Madagascar each represent archetypical and distinct examples of an urbanistic association policy. In each case political problems were defined in cultural terms that gave urban planning and architectural design a central importance in consolidating political power. These problems—residential and commercial development, administrative centralization and industrial expansion, and the creation of a healthy, trained labor force—were familiar in France as well as in the colonies, articulating clearly the colonies' potential role as laboratories for metropolitan cities. In each instance, as part of their experimental mode, administrators and their consultants sought specifically to mitigate the disruption caused by modernist urban reforms by actively engaging traditional architectural forms and attuning themselves to the ways in which various cultural groups typically responded to the city.

The first example is also the best known. As resident-general of the new protectorate of Morocco between 1912 and 1925, Hubert Lyautey refined his concept of the "dual city," which we would call a form of geographic "association." This entailed, first, the strict preservation of ancient artifacts, mosques, street fronts, and other kinds of ordinary cultural forms in the Arab cities. The Service des Antiquités, Beaux-Arts, et Monuments Historiques, established during the early months of the protectorate, gave its director, a former Beaux-Arts student by the name of Maurice Tranchant de Lunel, unprecedented powers to regulate new construction and protect existing buildings in the old Moroccan madinas. The policies of this office even show a certain awareness of the dangers of speculation in historic districts. The staff was advised that "the beauty and historic interest of Moroccan architecture resides not only in the important monuments but also — even especially — in the ensemble of constructions." Administrative measures to protect a single monument could not prevent its being surrounded by new buildings as land values increased, thereby losing its historic character even if the structure itself remained untouched. Accordingly, Tranchant de Lunel promulgated a detailed set of aesthetic requirements for all new buildings and renovations in the major Moroccan madinas.

Prost's Service d'Architecture et des Plans des Villes, established in 1914 (making it the first such governmental agency in the French world), was then charged with overseeing all forms of building in the *villes nouvelles* [new cities] alongside the existing Moroccan cities. The two settlements were always separated by a zone of *non aedificandi* where construction was forbidden, although the method and scale varied from one city to another. Fez, Marrakesh, and Meknes exemplify Prost's vision, with greenbelts ranging from two to three kilometers surrounding the walls of the old city, reinforced by geological barriers like the ravines of Meknes or the steep hills of Fez. In Rabat and Casablanca, European construction before Prost's arrival precluded this strategy, and he resigned himself to thoroughfares, two hundred fifty meters wide, augmented by large public parks. These barriers marked the distinctions between two parts of a city, setting off two scales of construction, two periods of history, and often two races. The term "sanitary corridor" suggests the health precautions also inherent in this familiar colonial policy. In an off-guard moment, Prost later acknowledged that the zone existed as well "for military reasons," allowing the rapid mobilization of French troops—yet we should not reduce all his intentions to any single motive.

Sizable extensions beyond the existing Arab cities—from two to (in the case of Casablanca) twenty times larger than the madinas—served the minority population of French *colons* [settlers]. This land, while sometimes purchased from previous Moroccan owners, was more often opened to development through changes in title or outright expropriation "in the public interest," using justifications from French and Quranic law. The French *villes nouvelles* proudly displayed the tenets of modern urban design. Yet in these colonial settings, the urban imagery involved a self-conscious cultural synthesis that stressed its particular locale: from the West came the clean lines and strict design guidelines for buildings, the spacious thoroughfares and zoning regulations; from Morocco, local ornamental motifs in porcelain mosaics and cedar, together with architectural adaptations to the climate such as the *menzeh* (a pavilion with courtyard), *mashribiya* (interlaced screen), and walls of white *naqsh nadida* (stucco).

French administrators disputed charges that they were segregating the different races. They even claimed that their urban policies liberated Moroccan Jews by offering them greater economic and residential mobility since Arabs and Jews alike were allowed to live in the European districts—if they agreed to abide by its urbanistic principles and thereby adopt modern Western culture. Lyautey claimed that his dual-city approach to urban design could clearly distinguish between the two districts and give each its particular form of expression. "Touch the indigenous cities as little as possible," he explained. "Instead, improve their surroundings where, on the vast terrain that is still free, the European city rises, following a plan that realizes the most modern conceptions of large boulevards, water and electrical supplies, squares and gardens, buses and tramways, and also foresees future extensions." The system, while radical, drew on certain urban precedents in the area, for segregation of foreigners had ancient roots in North Africa, reaching back to Greek and Egyptian towns, to medieval Muslim *funduq* (hotel-warehouses) for Christians, and *mellahs* [quarters] for the Jews. The French innovation extended such geographic divisions to an elaborate interplay of spatial and architectural distinctions, all the while paying homage to the indigenous culture they had isolated.

However, Lyautey's assertion that improvements and extensions could be limited to the European districts and still benefit the Moroccans did not anticipate the rapid growth of the Arab populations in the expanding cities. By the time of World War I, overcrowding and the growth of bidonvilles had become inescapable problems, especially in Casablanca and Rabat, where the French villes nouvelles effectively walled in the older madinas; for reasons of health, political unrest, and cultural image, the French now had to consider new urban settlements for the Moroccans.

Claiming land from Islamic religious foundations called habous *(hubus)* — land known even now as habous districts (*Derb el-Hubus*, in Arabic) — colonial urbanists in Prost's service undertook the design of streets, houses, and public buildings that would harmonize, though not be continuous, with those in the old madinas. These sites featured services that had been lacking or grossly inadequate in the older Arab cities, even under French occupation, including better drainage and public water supplies, wider commercial streets for cars (side streets were kept narrow and cars prohibited there), and some municipal upkeep. In site plan and detail the referents were not modern but, rather, the traditional principles of Moroccan architecture and the established mores of Moroccan urban life. In the smaller habous district of Rabat, overseen by Pierre Michaud, one finds an appreciation of the basic tenets of local urban design: the plain facades of private houses, relieved by distinctive doorways that never faced the entry across the street, contrast strikingly with the elaborate complexity of the market areas. The principal architect of Casablanca's habous district, Albert Laprade, had filled sketchbooks with watercolors and measured drawings of "the poor dwellings of Rabat and Salé" in preparation for the project. "Every house was designed with love," he wrote of the new designs. "We taxed our ingenuity to create the maximum impression of serendipity, so dear to the Muslim."

Laprade's oversimplified generalization about Islamic aesthetics suggests a darker side to the apparent cultural sensitivity, quite similar to the academic prejudices and policies Edward Said has labeled "Orientalism." The habous districts are Western stage settings for Moroccan life, evoking the supposed harmonies of a traditional way of life that, in the Westerner's eyes, did not change over time. These architects fell prey to the desire for stopping time and history that is always implicit in a preservation campaign, yet the rationale goes deeper than their own tendency to romanticize. Colonialism did not provide for innovation or progress in the Moroccan districts; this prospect the French had reserved for themselves. Aesthetic predilections therefore had a definite political aspect, freezing Moroccan economic and political development at an archaic level of the picturesque, in sharp contrast to the visible advances and opportunities available to Europeans. Lyautey once again explained the matter straightforwardly when he told a gathering in Paris, "Since the recent, intense development of large-scale tourism, the presentation of a country's beauty has taken on an economic importance of the first order. To attract a large tourist population is to gain everything for both the public and the private budgets."

This dual urban agenda therefore sought to control the cultural vitality of colonial cities, even as it assiduously studied the local culture. The villes nouvelles exhibited both European and Moroccan themes in their urban design, suggesting there was no inherent conflict. Similarly, the French promoted modernity for the Arabs through the exploitation of indigenous people and natural resources by French commercial interests, while at the same time they sustained the past, both for political reasons and for exploitation by French tourists who wanted to see charm and authenticity.

Ann Laura Stoler

Gender, Race, and Class Boundaries in Southeast Asia

Colonial Oxymorons: On Bourgeois Civility and Racial Categories

If there is anything shared among historians about the nature of French, Dutch, and British colonial communities in the nineteenth

From Ann Laura Stoler, *Race and the Education of Desire: Foucault's History of Sexuality and the Colonial Order of Things*, pp. 101, 102–109. Copyright © 1995 by Duke University Press. Excerpted by permission of the publisher.

See page 232 for selection notes.

century, it is the assumed fact that they were largely peopled by what Ben Anderson has called a "bourgeois aristocracy"; those of petty bourgeois and bourgeois origins, who saw their privileges and profits as racially bestowed.[1] But this picture of European colonial communities is deeply flawed. . . . In the nineteenth century Indies, it is impossible to talk about a European bourgeois order that was not racially problematic at the outset.

What is striking is both how self-evident *and* tentative the joinings of middle-class respectabilities and membership in European colonial communities actually were. If colonial enterprises were such secure bourgeois ventures, then why were European colonials so often viewed disparagingly from the metropole as *parvenus*, cultural incompetents, morally suspect, and indeed "fictive" Europeans, somehow distinct from the real thing? While many historians would agree that colonized European-educated intellectuals and those of mixed-racial origin were seen as "white but not quite," this was also true of a large segment of those classified as "fully" European.[2] If colonialism was indeed a class levelling project that produced a clear consensus about European superiority—a consoling narrative that novels, newspapers, and official documents were wont to rehearse—we are still left to explain the pervasive anxiety about white degeneration in the colonies, the insistent policing of those Europeans who fell from middle-class grace, the vast compendium of health manuals and housekeeping guides that threatened ill-health, ruin, and even death, if certain moral prescriptions and modes of conduct were not met.

The question is whether those who made up these European colonial communities in fact saw themselves as part of a firmly entrenched ruling class, and if so on what basis? Eric Hobsbawm's definition of Europe's nineteenth-century bourgeoisie offers a useful contrast:

> [It was] . . . *a body of persons of power and influence, independent of the power and influence of traditional birth and status. To belong to it a man had to be "someone"; a person who counted as an individual, because of his wealth, his capacity to command other men, or otherwise to influence them.*[3]

Some European colonial men would have numbered themselves within that class but not others. Some may have characterized themselves as having "power and influence" over the native population, but not over other Europeans. Still others, as George Orwell's subdistrict officer in "Shooting an Elephant" attests, were only too well aware of their dubious command over "the natives," and their limited mastery over themselves.[4] While the colonial right to command was allegedly independent of "traditional birth and status," the rosters of high government officials in India and the Indies suggest otherwise. In the nineteenth century, these positions were increasingly delimited to those who could afford to send their sons to law school in Leiden or to an Oxbridge public school, to those of the "cultivated classes," and to those of "full-blooded" Dutch or British birth. If "everyone [European] in India was, more or less, somebody" as the British novelist Maud Diver professed in 1916, how do we explain the sustained presence of a subterranean colonial discourse that anxiously debated who was truly European and whether those who were both poor and white should be included among them?[5] Contra Diver's claim, we know from a range of colonial contexts that class distinctions within these European colonial communities were not increasingly attenuated but sharpened over time, lending credence to Robert Hughes's contention for another colonial context that "the question of class was all pervasive and pathological."[6]

In fact, it is not clear how many "Europeans" in the colonies ever enjoyed the privileges of belonging to a "bourgeois aristocracy" at all.[7] This is not to suggest that there was not a large segment of the European population that made up a social and economic elite. Those of the Indies' stolid *burgerstand* (middle-class/bourgeois citizenry) recruited from Holland included plantation and trading company management, upper-level civil servants, professional personnel in the fields of education, health, and agriculture. But while colonial sources bespeak a European colonial elite comprised of those from "good" families, birth in the Indies could exclude well-heeled creole families from membership. In 1856, W. Ritter observed:

> We count as European all those with white faces, who are not born in the Indies, all Dutch, English, French, Germans . . . even North Americans. Our readers will repeat: A European is a European and will remain so wherever he finds himself. . . . We know him well. But you are greatly mistaken, Readers, for a European . . . in the Indies is an entirely different being than in his country. . . . There, he identifies himself so much with all that surrounds him that he no longer can be

> *considered as a European, at least for the duration of his stay in the Indies, but rather as belonging to a specific caste of the Indische population . . . whose morals, customs and habits are certainly worthy of close examination.*[8]

While Ritter's exclusion of all those born in the Indies from the category "European" was unusual, it belies an anxiety that was much more widely shared: that even for the European-born, the Indies was transformative of cultural essence, social disposition, and personhood itself. His Lamarckian distinction was rarely so explicitly expressed; namely, that "Europeanness" was not a fixed attribute, but one altered by environment, class contingent, and not secured by birth.[9] Thus the Dutch doctor Kohlbrugge would write fifty years later that Europeans born and bred in the Indies lived in surroundings that stripped them of their European sensibilities to such an extent that they "could easily . . . metamorphize into Javanese."[10] What is at issue here is not a shared conviction of the fixity of European identity but the protean nature of it. In both cases, as we shall see, what sustained racial membership was a middle-class morality, nationalist sentiments, bourgeois sensibilities, normalized sexuality, and a carefully circumscribed "milieu" in school and home.

Ritter counted three major divisions among Europeans in the Indies: the military, civil servants, and merchants for whom the lines of class distinction [were] "not clearly drawn." By his account, the Indies had no "so-called lower [European] classes."[11] But such lower classes did exist and in increasing numbers throughout the nineteenth century as a burgeoning archive of government investigations on the problem of destitute Europeans in the Indies can attest. For the category "European" also included an ill-defined population of poor whites, subaltern soldiers, minor clerks, abandoned children of European men and Asian women, as well as creole Europeans whose economic and social circumstances made their ties to metropolitan bourgeois civilities often tenuous at best.[12] At later moments it was to include Japanese, Africans, and Chinese.[13] Being "European" was supposed to be self-evident but was also a quality that only the qualified were equipped to define.

Complicated local folk taxonomies registered these internal distinctions. Thus, the term *indischen menschen* might refer, as did Ritter, to those hybrid offspring of Dutch men and native women "whose blood was not unmixed European," but it could also connote those with lasting ties in the Indies, marking cultural and not biological affiliations. Creole whites born in the Indies were distinguished from those who were not. Those who came from and returned to Holland when their contracts expired *(trekkers)* were distinguished from those for whom the Indies was a permanent residence for generations *(blijvers)*. "Pure-blooded *(zuiver)* Dutch were distinguished from those *mestizen*, "Indo-European," *métis*, of mixed-blood origin.

But perhaps the most telling term in this racial grammar was that which prevailed throughout the nineteenth century for those who were white but impoverished, and usually, but not always, of mixed-blood origin. Firmly dissociated from the European born, the term *inlandsche kinderen* neither referred to "natives" nor "children" as a literal translation might lead us to expect. It identified an ambiguous, hybrid population of those who were neither native nor endowed with the class background nor cultural accoutrements that could count them as truly European and fit to rule (accounting perhaps for Ritter's categorical exclusion of them). In the 1860s, some officials estimated thousands of such impoverished whites in the Indies; by the turn of the century, others calculated as many as sixty thousand.[14]

The enormous administrative energy levelled at the destitute living conditions of the *inlandsche kinderen* and proposals for their amelioration joined the policing of individuals with the defense of Dutch rule in specific ways. It was this group that confused the equation of whiteness and middle-class sensibilities in a discourse that legitimated the state's interventions in how all Europeans raised their children and managed their domestic and sexual arrangements. The discourse on destitute and degenerate whites whose "Dutchness" was suspect underscored what could happen to European colonials who did not know "how to live." Debates about the moral degradation of the *inlandsche kinderen* did more than produce narratives about maternal vigilance, child rearing, and appropriate milieu. It prompted new institutional initiatives and government policies that made claims to racial superiority *dependent* on middle-class respectability for the entire European population. It made linguistic competence in Dutch the marker of cultural "suitability" for European middle-class norms. It implicitly tied the quality of maternal sentiment and parental care to racial affiliation and nationality.

Architects of colonial policy worked off a set of contradictory premises. If the legitimation of European privilege and profit rested on a social taxonomy that equated Europeanness and bourgeois civilities, were those legally classified Europeans who fell short of these economic and cultural standards to be pulled back into these communities or banished from them? Was being poor and white politically untenable, a veritable colonial oxymoron? Were the unacknowledged children of European men and their native concubines to be reclaimed and redeemed by the state as Dutch, French, and British citizens or categorically barred?

These questions of racial identity and class distinctions pervaded the colonial discourses in the Dutch East Indies, French Indochina, British Malaya, and India in the nineteenth and early twentieth centuries at different moments but in patterned ways. Mixed bloods were seen as one problem, poor whites as another, but in practice these persons were often treated as indistinguishable, one and the same. In each of these contexts, it called into question the very criteria by which Europeanness could be identified, how citizenship would be accorded and nationality assigned. In the Indies, the problem of "European pauperism," debated and scrutinized in government commissions throughout the late second half of the nineteenth century, was about indigent whites and their mixed-blood progeny, mixed-blood European men and their native wives whose life styles indicated not always a failed effort to live up to the standards of bourgeois civility but sometimes an outright rejection of them.[15]

But subaltern and economically marginal whites were not the only challenge to the taxonomic colonial state. The equation of middle-class dispositions and European membership were threatened by creole Europeans as well, not by those impoverished but as strongly by the well-heeled and well-to-do. Thus, it was this group of respectable "city fathers" of creole origin who petitioned the Dutch authorities in 1848 for the establishment of equivalent schools of higher education in the Indies and protested policies requiring their sons be sent for training to Holland to meet civil service entry requirements. It was their children who conversed more easily in Malay than Dutch, whose fatherland was more the Indies than the Netherlands, who were feared to see themselves as "world citizens," not faithful partisans of continued Dutch rule.[16]

It is striking, for example, that in the 1850s Indo-Europeans born in the Indies were barred from posts in the civil service that would put them in direct contact with the native population at precisely the time when new administrative attention was focused on the inadequate training in native languages displayed by the Indies' colonial civil servants. At issue was obviously not whether civil servants knew local languages, but how those languages were learned and used and whether that knowledge was appropriately classified and controlled. While enormous funds were dispensed on teaching Javanese at the Delft Academy in Holland to students with a proper "Dutch rearing," those *inlandsche kinderen* who already knew Javanese or Malay but lacked the proprieties and cultural knowledge that a Dutch rearing provided, were categorically barred. What was being taught to future officers in the colonial civil service at Delft was not only language but a more general set of disciplines that included distancing postures of comportment and imperious forms of address to inferiors that were crucial to appropriate language use.[17] Given the emphasis placed on "character" and conduct, the sustained attention of the colonial state to the importance of home environments is not surprising. The increasing attention given to a moral "upbringing" (*opvoeding*) as a prerequisite for the proper use of a formal education (*onderwijs*) turned on a basic assumption: that it was in the domestic domain, not the public sphere, where essential dispositions of manliness, bourgeois morality, and racial attribute could be dangerously undone or securely made.

While we could read these debates on the "so-called *inlandsche kinderen*" and the philanthropic moralizing impulses directed toward them as discourses prompted by threats to white prestige, these discourses spoke to other concerns as well. The "civilizing mission" of the nineteenth century was a bourgeois impulse directed not only at the colonized as often assumed, but at recalcitrant and ambiguous participants in imperial culture at home and abroad.[18] But these bourgeois initiatives were as strongly directed at "reform of themselves."[19] As a new generation of Dutch social historians now argue, the "civilizing offensive" was not only about the "poor and their needs, but the rich and their motives."[20] In Indies perspective, the validity of these observations is well borne out. To abide by *burgerlijk* values was crucial to the racial rhetoric of rule, but that rhetoric often diverged from the messier realities of culturally hybrid urban wards where persons of varied class origin, in a range of domestic and sexual arrangements lived side by side—where the moral highground of middle-class prescripts was seen under threat in how the "European village population" *(Europeesche kampongbevolking)* lived—on colonial ground. . . .[21]

Owen White

Miscegenation and Identity in French West Africa

One image of métis [person of mixed race], propagated by a variety of French individuals and organisations, was of a passive social group, the mute beneficiary of French largesse. This image, however, increasingly failed to reflect reality as growing numbers of métis reached maturity across French West Africa. Both individually and collectively, people of mixed race adopted a number of different strategies for making sense of the society in which they lived. Some of these strategies, of course, were more successful than others; the quest for some viable form of social identity was undoubtedly fraught with difficulties, and it was easy for individual[s] . . . to feel socially marginalised. Gradually, however, métis began to address some of the ambiguities and complexities which appeared to be part of their inheritance. From the 1930s in particular, when they began to organise themselves in mutual self-help groups [known as *mutualités de métis*], West African métis set about defining the boundaries of their own community, and the relationship of this community *vis-à-vis* the French and other Africans. . . .

. . . From the 1930s, French West African métis increasingly sought to create a mutually protective space which would enable them to emerge as a social group with shared interests, mediating the ambigui-

From Owen White, "Miscegenation and Colonial Society of French West Africa, c. 1900–1960." Copyright © 1996 by Owen White. Used by permission.

ties of social identity through collective action. The most conspicuous examples of this tendency are provided by the *mutualités de métis.* . . .

Voluntary associations set up by Africans played an important role in colonial French West Africa. On one level, these associations served a valuable integrative function for migrants to the rapidly expanding urban centres of the federation, particularly after the First World War. More importantly, Michael Crowder has observed that in such associations can be found "the origins of modern political organisations in French West Africa." Strict controls imposed by the colonial authorities ensured, however, that until March, 1937, when the Popular Front government introduced limited freedom of association, such organisations had to avoid any suspicion of political activity to survive. Before 1937, therefore, most were cultural or sporting associations, or represented the interests of a particular ethnic group.

In such a climate, the colonial government in Guinea authorised in 1933 the foundation of the Society for Mutual Aid of the Métis of French Guinea. By the end of the decade, similar societies had been officially authorised in the Ivory Coast, the French Soudan, Niger and Togo, the security services having first checked up on those involved.

These associations were at once social groups, charities, pressure groups, and insurance societies. The statutes of the Society for Mutual Aid of the Métis of French Guinea illustrate some of the functions served by these organisations. From 1944, when the fees in the founding statutes were revised, it cost 100 francs to join the society, followed by a monthly payment of 25 francs. Each member was then entitled to a range of benefits. Members who were unemployed or hospitalised could call upon the society to help pay their upkeep for a period of three or four months respectively. If a member died, the society would contribute to the cost of the funeral; a smaller sum of money was payable on the death of a member's child, "ascendant" or wife — which suggests that the Guinean *mutualité* at least consisted mainly of men.

In addition to these benefits, the society promised to meet the burial costs when an indigent métis who was not a member of the society died. As such, all métis, whether rich or poor, were deemed to be "deserving." In this way, the society was formalising an inclusive definition of the métis community in Guinea. The philanthropic aspect of the society's work further enabled its members to feel a greater sense of control over their own destinies.

Philanthropy was similarly to the fore in the activities of the Mutual Aid Society of the Métis of the French Soudan. From the time it was founded in 1937, the society took a special interest in the "orphanages" for métis children in the French Soudan. Having been brought up in such institutions themselves—the society's first president, Paul Leroux, had attended the "orphanage" in Ségou—members knew that boredom was one of the worst aspects of life there. In an effort to tackle the problem of idleness, the society supplied the Orphelinat des Métisses de Bamako ["orphanage" for métis girls] with skipping-ropes, balls and various other games, along with a grant for the creation of a small library. . . .

These small-scale charitable acts helped to create new opportunities for the emergent métis community in the French Soudan. By behaving in a manner which visibly conformed to norms of social responsibility valorised by the French, the Mutual Aid Society of the Métis of the French Soudan was quickly able to forge links with the colonial authorities, the beneficial effects of which almost as rapidly became apparent. In November, 1937, for example, Governor Rougier of the French Soudan praised the assistance of the society in finding an acceptable solution to the scandal caused when two métisses became pregnant in the girls' "orphanage" in Bamako. That same month, as a result of the society's lobbying, the allowance due to the mother of each infant métis too young to be admitted to an "orphanage" was approximately doubled, from between fifteen and thirty francs per month to fifty francs. In addition, the president of the society was placed on a par with district administrators in being able to recommend people for this allowance.

The Soudanese government, indeed, was sufficiently impressed with the conduct of the society that when the Commission Guernut sent out its survey on the "métis problem," the Mutual Aid Society of the Métis of the French Soudan was given the task of completing the colony's response to the commission's questionnaire. In February, 1938, moreover, a delegation from the society (whose membership had risen to eighty-six by 1939) met with Governor-General de Coppet to discuss matters relating to the treatment of métis. There, they were able to express the desire, for example, to be able to reach levels of the civil service . . . normally reserved for Europeans. Philanthropy, therefore, can be seen both as an expression and a further cause of the growing social autonomy and sense of empowerment of the métis community in French West Africa. . . .

. . . The Charitable Association of the French Métis of French West Africa, based in Dakar, was authorised in July, 1944, . . .

In 1949, . . . the organisation was revived under a new name, the Union of the Eurafricans of French West Africa. . . . The driving force behind this development was Nicolas Rigonaux, a métis in his mid-thirties who had moved to Dakar from Cotonou in Dahomey. The Union of the Eurafricans was representative of a much greater number of West African métis. . . . The Union of the Eurafricans created regional sections across French West Africa, and cultivated (with the assistance of the French authorities) links with similar organisations in French Equatorial Africa, Indochina, and Madagascar.

. . . [T]he sense of métis identity *vis-à-vis* black Africans in the 1930s and early 1940s was characterised by a certain unease. By the time of the foundation of the Union of the Eurafricans, however, some of these tensions were beginning to be resolved; similarly, the burgeoning social identity among the urbanised, comparatively well-educated métis who typically joined the association was more fully developed. Most obviously, the society's decision to refer to métis as "Eurafricans," a term appearing for the first time, is significant, suggesting a conjoining of identities, and, in the process, the creation of something new. Moreover, while those involved in the society tended to emphasise the primacy of French civilisation and culture, this did not in itself involve a denial of "Africanness." In a letter sent in May, 1949 to all members of the new society, Rigonaux wrote that "Our cause will be that of any assimilable African," thereby identifying métis primarily with the aspirations of other educated Africans; in any case, as he observed in the same letter, as a scattered minority, métis could not hope to separate their fate from the fate of what he called the "native populations." Later that year, Rigonaux wrote that

> *A human being cannot belong simultaneously to two races and two civilizations; he must opt for one or the other or sink into the anonymous despair of an individual without social ties.*

Rigonaux was admitting, therefore, that there was a choice to be made; the choice, however, was as much between social alienation and some viable form of social identity as it was between "two civilisations." Elsewhere, he insisted that "The métis . . . is not in the least embarrassed by the lack of sophistication of his native kin." . . .

One of the statutes of the Union of the Eurafricans stated that the society would combat all forms of racial prejudice. The remaining statutes, however, suggest that this was understood in a particular way. The society aimed to ensure that "Eurafricains français" were treated on equal terms with French people from the *métropole*. It would counsel the African mothers of métis children, to help them raise and educate their children "à la française." . . . Moreover, it would work to maintain among West African métis "the secular feelings of loyalty to France which they have always held." For Rigonaux, métis were the "vanguard of the French civilizing influence."

In effect, Rigonaux was asking the members of his association to abide by the "civilising" ideals of French colonialism more faithfully than had the French themselves. The conduct of métis should, he felt, be "above all criticism, the more so because we are claiming to act as links between two races." . . . The demonstration of social virtues idealised by the French helped to create links to the real sources of power in French West Africa, legitimising the claims of métis to an identity in elite society.

Rigonaux envisaged métis moving towards "a complete Gallicization" but in saying this he was not denying the possibility that black Africans could do likewise. Nor did this mean that the French were beyond criticism: French men were regularly condemned for their failings (especially as fathers) in the pages of *L'Eurafricain*, the society's journal. In 1957, *L'Eurafricain* reported a complaint from the Mutual Aid Society of Eurafricans of the Ivory Coast that "French West Africa is overflowing with poor whites *(petits blancs)* who tarnish the true civilizing face of France." . . . This was typical of the kind of criticism made by educated Africans of the influx of European workers to post-war French West Africa, but it was the principles by which the French claimed to operate that continued to matter most of all; these principles had been taught in the schools and "orphanages" attended by métis, and were now taken up as a set of values which helped to structure their lives. . . .

. . . [A] coherent sense of identity among métis in colonial society took time to emerge . . . [and] was beset with problems. . . . [I]t was all too easy for métis to feel socially marginal or even persecuted. . . .

At times, métis despaired of ever finding the sense of identity they desired. In 1937, for example, a group of métis from the French

Soudan offered, in a letter to the journal *Le Monde Colonial Illustré*, the following "solution" to their predicament as they saw it:

> It is pointless . . . to continue to delude ourselves any longer. Therefore, to satisfy the wishes and desires of métis, since all the evidence suggests that nothing of value can be done for them, a decree should be passed formally prohibiting any amorous or conjugal relations between the two races.

Other métis, however, did not accept that marginality was their unavoidable destiny. By acting collectively in voluntary associations, they were able to mediate some of the problems of métis identity. Indeed, Paul Leroux, first president of the Mutual Aid Society of the Métis of the French Soudan, strongly criticised the authors of the letter cited above in a later issue of *Le Monde Colonial Illustré*, making it clear that they were not members of his organisation.

Significantly, Leroux also made a point of contradicting their suggestion that métis were poorly treated by "the natives." The relationship between métis and other Africans perhaps held the key to the development by métis of a more satisfactory social identity. The racial "intermediacy" of métis had been all but pathologised, the mixture of races thought by the French and even, apparently, by Africans such as Abdoulaye Sadji, to create unstable "hybrids." Gradually, however, métis began to see this mixture as a positive strength, as symbolised, for example, in the growing use of the term "Eurafricain."

The *mutualités de métis* did more than define the boundaries of the métis community. Through their charitable activities, they began to appropriate the ideals which the French themselves had used to legitimise their presence in Africa. This enabled them to create links with the colonial authorities which proved to be advantageous, allowing métis to claim a role in elite society.

The success of this strategy can perhaps be seen most clearly in the account given in *L'Eurafricain* of the ball held by the Union of the Eurafricans of French West Africa in Dakar in April 1950. At this function, the president of the society, Nicolas Rigonaux, spoke proudly of "notre action humanitaire et éminemment française" before an assembly of dignitaries, both French and African. High Commissioner Béchard was unable to attend, but a number of high-ranking colonial officials were present, along with several other important people including the American consul in Dakar and Seydou Nourou Tall,

Grand Marabout of the Tijaniyya, the largest Muslim brotherhood in Senegal. One [society ... member] wrote of the evening in *L'Eurafricain* that

> [*Those who attended the ball*] *were not whites, blacks and métis; they were simply friends from every part of black Africa and France. For in the Union of the Eurafricans, there is one word the meaning of which we will never understand. That word is "RACISM."*

The ball of 1950 symbolised the kind of social relations desired by métis in colonial society. Though West African métis were still as likely to be in need of charity as in a position to supply it, and while the members of the Union des Eurafricains could in no way be said to have held any true power in French West Africa, on this evening, to members of the association, it seemed that métis had made their début in society.

The Universal Exposition of 1900 in Paris, with the Algerian palace (center foreground) and the Tunisian palace (right foreground). The "exotic" colonial world was a familiar sight in metropolitan popular culture. (Archive Photos, New York)

The Empire in Europe

Imperialism was not an exclusively "overseas" phenomenon. It played a constitutive role in European economics, politics, and culture. For example, as suppliers of raw materials and agricultural commodities to the metropole and consumers of manufactured goods in return, the colonies underpinned industries that employed millions of workers and generated profits for owners and investors in Europe. The material evidence of this relationship was visible on the docks of Barcelona, Genoa, Hamburg, Lisbon, London, Marseilles, Rotterdam, and many other ports. It was evident in factories, stores, streets, and homes. Empire was also the stuff of politics, with movements and parties frequently mobilizing or manipulating support by connecting the "colonial" and "domestic" spheres in issues like war and peace, social reform, and trade. It is difficult to say with any certainty how ordinary Europeans felt about specific questions of policy, like the suppression of anticolonial revolts, but it is safe to assume that the imperialism of cheap imported food from the colonies, of overseas opportunities for emigration and employment, of national prestige and humanitarian endeavor had at least the passive consent of most people.

This imperial context and presence could take spectacular forms. As Zeynep Çelik shows, the architecture and material culture of Muslim countries and colonies were accorded a prominent place in the great expositions and fairs of the nineteenth century. She argues that such representations of foreign and colonial cultures educated spectators in the "difference" of Islam and the Orient, to the point where the supposedly exotic became quite familiar to generations of Europeans. Indeed, empire was part and parcel of everyday life, from the geography lessons in school textbooks to the lyrics of music hall songs to the headlines of daily newspapers. As Anne McClintock shows, the use of colonial imagery in commercial advertising meant that the empire was never out of sight. Paradoxically, these highly racialized and gendered signs of empire effaced the labor of plantation workers in the colonies and of domestic servants or female family members in the metropole. Moreover, such advertising was bound up in the enlargement of mass markets and the creation of modern consumer society. These manifestations of the culture of empire in Europe suggest that imperialism influenced people's identities in myriad ways, as men and women, as workers and consumers, and as citizens of imperial nation-states.

Although we don't know the precise numbers of the men and women involved, people as well as products came to Europe. Building on a presence already established by people of color during the early modern centuries of Atlantic slavery and Asian commerce, colonial subjects from virtually every corner of the European empires made their way to the metropole. Some were visiting notables from the indigenous elites who collaborated with colonial European officials and merchants. Others were students and travelers from the new middle classes, intent on gaining an education, lobbying for reforms, or simply seeing how the other half lived. Antoinette Burton explores the experience of Indian visitors as they encountered the British "at home," and produced accounts of their travels for compatriots "back home." Their observations and investigations dramatically reversed the ethnographic relationship between Europeans and their colonial and racial "others."

Not all colonial subjects were from relatively privileged positions. For example, the shipping industry used large numbers of colonial workers, and some settled permanently in European cities. Other workers were recruited for seasonal agricultural or construction labor or became part of the regular industrial work-force. The crisis of World War I produced an enormous demand for colonial workers as well as soldiers. As Tyler Stovall shows, the regimentation of these laborers by the French authorities was much harsher than the restrictions placed on foreign European workers. The inspiration for such discrimination seems to have de-rived from colonial attitudes and policies, and their importation contributed to the growth of popular racism.

The recollections of Doris Reiprich and Erika Ngambi ul Kuo of growing up Afro-German in the 1920s and 1930s offer a rich and remarkable testimony to the lives and struggles of colonial subjects and people of color in Europe. They remind us of the connections between the "new imperialism" at the end of the nine-teenth century, which advanced such far-reaching claims of a civi-lizing mission for Europe, and the rise of fascism, which drew upon fantasies of racial supremacy and colonial reconquest in both Italy and Germany. Equally important, they point to the complexities of human behavior. Even under the Nazi dictatorship, people sur-vived, cared for each other, and resisted the pressure to conform.

Zeynep Çelik

Displaying the Orient

The second half of the nineteenth century was the time of universal expositions in the Western world. Beginning in 1851 in London, the exhibitions, held in many cities of Europe and North America, be-came, in the words of the historian Eric Hobsbawm, "great new rituals of self-congratulation," celebrating economic and industrial triumphs. These "new rituals" were directly linked to the dramatic transforma-tion of the economic order. During the first half of the century, indus-trialization had developed more rapidly than the market for industrial products. With the advancement of modern communication systems, however, the capitalist economy grew to encompass the globe.

Imperialism and colonialism played crucial roles in this growth, redefining the global power structure and stimulating widespread interest in the non-Western world—now part of the universal economy. Aside from offering a market and rich sources of raw materials, the non-Western world also provided a supply of labor crucial to the new economic order. The advance of Western capitalism thus led to a much smaller world, one that was unified, if not equal. Simultaneously, the desire to maintain economic and political dominance called for better knowledge of subaltern peoples. While the Western world exported its industrial revolution to the rest of the globe, it also began to import information about other cultures.

Universal expositions represented this "single expanded world" in a microcosm, celebrating the products of industry and technological progress and displaying the entire human experience. Other cultures were brought piecemeal to European and American cities and exhibited as artifacts in pavilions that were themselves summaries of cultures. The experiential qualities of architecture—personal, intimate, and accessible to all—made it possible for exhibition buildings to offer a quick and seemingly realistic impression of the culture and society represented.

As early as the Great Exhibition of 1851 in London, replicas of parts of well-known buildings (such as the Alhambra) were displayed inside the main structure, the Crystal Palace; separate pavilions for different nations outside the main exhibition hall were first built for the Paris Universal Exposition of 1867. By gathering architectural pieces from all over the world, the fair grounds introduced the notion of an imaginary journey and created a new type of tourism, *en place*. Architectural displays became indispensable at every fair, setting the precedent for the "period room" and the "outdoor architectural museum."

The architectural representation of cultures at the world's fairs was double-sided, making a claim to scientific authority and accuracy while nourishing fantasy and illusion. The architectural critic Montgomery Schuyler argued on the occasion of the 1893 World's Columbian Exposition in Chicago that the buildings erected for the fairs belonged to a "festal" world and formed the "stage-setting for an unexampled spectacle." This was, he claimed, a world of dreams, and "in the world of dreams, illusion is all that we require.". . .

. . . The displays of non-Western peoples at the nineteenth-century world's fairs were organized around the anthropologist's concept of distance. "Natives" were placed in "authentic" settings, dressed in "authentic" costumes, and made to perform "authentic" activities, which seemed to belong to another age. They formed *tableaux vivants,* spectacles that fixed societies in history. Mixing entertainment with education, these spectacles painted the world at large in microcosm, with an emphasis on the "strangeness" of the unfamiliar. . . . Such spectacles also served the politics of colonialism. The display of both subject peoples and products from foreign possessions made colonialism concrete to those at home and reaffirmed the colonizing society's "racial superiority," manifest in its technical, scientific, and moral development—as the French prime minister Jules Ferry argued in the 1880s. . . .

In colonial displays people were frequently displayed as trophies. Artisans working in traditional crafts in small settings that re-created the "authenticity" of their place of origin were "trophies in special enclosures." "Colonial soldiers" were presented similarly in 1889 and in 1900, when armed Algerians in their local costumes, in a setting designed to evoke the colony, "gave legitimate satisfaction to [French] patriotic feelings."

People were presented as subjects of research more often than in any other guise at the fairs. The aura of these displays was "scientific," as was the language used to describe them. In 1867 a certain Docteur Warnier compared the physiology and character of the Arab and the Berber. The Arab was tall and thin, with a "pyriform" skull, a narrow forehead, an arched and bony nose, and black eyes, hair, and beard; the Berber was of medium height, with a large round skull, broad straight forehead, fleshy nose, square jaw, and eyes, hair, and beard varying from black to red. Whereas the Arab was a fighter who enjoyed war but was otherwise undisciplined, a "born enemy of work," the Berber was the opposite: he was docile, worked hard, and because of his intelligence could "become a devoted auxiliary of European and Christian colonization." The Arab looked Asiatic, the Berber European.

The Tunisian musicians in Paris in 1878, of a "type bien africain," displayed the traits of a "beautiful race, indolent, sleepy, but with features not lacking nobility or energy"; the "Arabesque races" on the fairgrounds in 1889 were of the "Israelite type"; the Arabs of the

Algerian theater were "generally handsome, having preserved the nervous grace and the pride of nomadic races." Behavioral attitudes were also displayed. The Arabs of the Camp of Damascus in the Turkish village in Chicago "squatted about as at home. They had little occupation, except the smoking of the narghile, without which [they] would consider [their] hours of leisure devoid of any pleasure."

The "scientific" display of indigenous peoples seemed to require that all the races from a specific region be included to give fairgoers as complete a picture as possible. The Cairo Street in Chicago had "Jews, Franks, Greeks, Armenians, Nubians, Sudanese, Arabs, and Turks . . . representing faithfully the population of the old city of Egypt." The Tunisian section in 1900 had 140 Jews and Muslims (Moors and Berbers), "representing the different types one encounters in Tunisia." The contemporary press, echoing the notion of a microcosm, commonly published images of all the racial types to be seen on the fairgrounds. The caption for a photographic collage from the Columbian Exposition dwelt on the diversity of the thirteen racial types depicted:

> To say that all these characters were taken from a street less than a mile long, would seem to indicate a most heterogeneous massing of nations, but when is added the thought that they are but types, and that each one represented from twenty to fifty more, the idea becomes quite overpowering. These individuals represented Europe, Asia, Africa, North America, South America, and the islands of the South Pacific.

The hierarchy of races in the world's fair displays made the premises of nineteenth-century anthropology and ethnography constituents of mass culture in Europe and America. . . .

Universal Exposition of 1867, Paris

As representatives of Islamic urban settings, Ottoman and Egyptian quarters were placed adjacent to each other in 1867 in Paris, and, despite their independent designs, they formed an ensemble: visitors could meander through the Egyptian street into the Turkish square. Both quarters were deliberately made irregular to reflect the tortuous streets with many dead ends of Islamic cities. The choice of an irregular urban fabric to represent Istanbul and Cairo at the fairs reflects one of the dilemmas of Ottoman and Egyptian officials and their European advisors. Even though in both Istanbul and Cairo the 1860s were marked by an intense campaign to regularize the network of streets, to create monumental avenues and vistas, and to establish large urban squares, . . . the exposition planners turned to the past, to an image that they considered outdated but that the West associated with Islam. . . .

The Egyptian quarter at the 1867 fair consisted of three buildings on a street: a temple, a *selamlik* (a small palace), and an *okel* (a covered market, or caravansary). The temple, a replica of the temple of Philae, was a museum where antiquities were exhibited; an avenue lined with sphinxes led to its entrance. Together, the temple, *selamlik*, and *okel* were intended to convey the complete history of Egypt. The temple stood for Egyptian antiquity, the *selamlik* for the nation's Arab civilization, and the *okel* for contemporary industrial and commercial life. Between the *okel* and the temple was a copy of Bartholdi's statue of the famous Egyptologist Jean-François Champollion, who seemed to meditate on a future when "the veil covering forty centuries of history would be torn." A pavilion called the Isthme de Suez displayed documents and models of Ferdinand de Lesseps's work on the Suez Canal, then under construction, as well as the geography and the natural history of the site.

In 6,000 square meters, a "condensed and miniature Egypt" was presented to the world, a "brilliant, splendid" achievement, in the eyes of the general commissary to the Egyptian exposition, and one that "revealed [Egypt's] past grandeur and its present richness." The effort was applauded by the West. One French journalist, for example, argued that no other country had understood the idea of a universal exhibition as well as Egypt, which displayed its past and its present. Hippolyte Gautier praised the Egyptian quarter as "not only one of the most sumptuous, but also the most complete and the most instructive."

The Egyptian exhibition had attempted to encapsulate Egypt's history. The Ottoman Empire, in contrast, condensed its cultural and social life in a selection of building types. The Ottoman section, designed by Léon Parvillée, was composed of three buildings—a mosque, a residential structure called the Pavillon du Bosphore, and a bath—around a loosely defined open space. In the center of this space was a fountain. The mosque represented the religious sphere; the Pavillon du Bosphore, the homefront; the bath, social and cultural ritual; and the fountain, the public sphere. On the occasion of Sultan Abdülaziz's visit, a triumphal gate to the quarter was erected; with its formal references to the gates leading to the different courts of the Topkapi Palace and its imperial *tuğra*, "sultan's seal," it symbolized the imperial presence.

Like that of the Egyptian section, the layout of the Turkish quarter was deliberately irregular, even though the basic premise—a square open space with a fountain in the center, surrounded by buildings with symmetrical facades—did not call for it. This arrangement was derived not from Turkish precedent but from French academicism. The idea was to create by irregularity an "authentic" and "picturesque appearance."

Not far from the Egyptian-Ottoman complex was another Islamic section, composed of the Tunisian and Moroccan exhibitions. Perhaps because of their associations with bedouin culture, both had tents for the display of products. Tunisia also had a residential structure, called the Palace of the Bey because the bey of Tunisia had stopped there briefly during his visit to Paris. The two domes of this palace and the tents created an Islamic skyline. Strolling from the Quai d'Orsay toward the main exhibition hall, a visitor would see first these domes and tents and then the domes and minarets of the Egyptian and Ottoman parks. Hippolyte Gautier called the entire section the Quartier Oriental:

> The entire Orient is before you; do not look for machines here, or for the practical inventions of the human mind; you are in the domain of contemplative life: the agreeable precedes the utilitarian, and poetry is intricately mixed into the smallest detail of existence.

People dressed in colorful local costumes, Middle Eastern music coming from the pavilions, and the aromas of local cuisines from the cafés gave the quarter the real flavor of the Orient. According to one observer, "the illusion was complete. . . . To see the Orient . . . it is enough to get on the omnibus.". . .

The Universal Exposition of 1900, Paris

The 1900 "exposition of the century,". . . had a street of nations but at a more visible location. The Street of Nations now occupied the Quai d'Orsay between the Pont des Invalides and the Pont de l'Alma, the bridges connecting the two principal sections of the exhibition, the Champ de Mars—Trocadéro and the Esplanade des Invalides—Avenue Nicolas II along the waterfront. Nations considered more important were given larger sites facing both the river and the street.

The allocation of space to Islamic countries in the 1900 exposition made evident a hierarchical classification. The Ottoman Empire and Persia, both sovereign nations, had their pavilions on the Rue des Nations. The Ottoman Empire, perceived as more important politically, also faced the embankment and was located between the pavilions of Italy and the United States, whereas Persia's much smaller pavilion sat on the back row, between Peru and Luxembourg. Egypt, now accepted as a British colony, was with the other colonies in the Trocadéro Park.

The displays of the Ottoman Empire and Persia were confined each to a single building. Egypt still had its temple, bazaar, and theater, but this time in a single three-part structure. Now it was the French colonies of North Africa that represented the full exotica of the Muslim world. The palaces of the two important colonies, Algeria and Tunisia, were in the Trocadéro Park, on the main avenue bisecting the park itself and the Champ de Mars and connecting the Trocadéro Palace to the Eiffel Tower via the Iéna Bridge. Viewed from the Iéna Bridge, with the Trocadéro Palace behind them, they helped to define the axis of the exposition grounds and complemented the larger palace stylistically with their Islamic references. Seen from the palace, with the Eiffel Tower in the background, their white stucco masses and their facades abstracted from various precolonial monuments contrasted with the engineering aesthetics of the tower, thus juxtaposing the industrial progress of the empire and the timelessness of its colonies. The juxtaposition offered a visual symbol of the French colonial tactics of assimilation and contrast.

The Algerian Palace, given the "place of honor" in the Trocadéro Park, was a "symmetrical and coherent" building. Inside, however, was an entire Rue d'Alger, winding picturesquely, replete with two-story houses with projecting second stories, *musharabiyyas*, decorated doorways, and shops on the street level. It was considered "a faithful reproduction of one of those tortuous streets."

The Tunisian exposition was next to the Algerian village, and the entire complex was called the Ville Arabe. It was an agglomeration of architecture from Tunisia: a replica of a fountain from the Rue Sadun in Tunis, a minaret from the Great Mosque of Sfax, a copy of the Mosque of Sidi-Maklouf from Kef, a *zawiya* (Sufi convent) from the Casbah Square in Tunis, the Bab al-Jadid gate from the walls of Tunis, and another old town gate from Soussa — all surrounding a large court. The main pavilion was a model of the Mosque of Sidi Mahres in Tunis. In sum, this village represented "all the towns of Tunisia."

The pieces were integrated by vaulted picturesque passageways and irregular streets, all designed "as though by chance." One observer remarked:

> *One could swear that these buildings are inhabited; the angles are rounded, the rough-cast broken, the tiles frosted — this imperceptible steam which represents time — and the stones, skillfully made up, display the superb reddish color of limestone in the countries loved by the sun.*

The appeal to the senses was complete. Even the smells were authentic. Here one could "breathe the smell of Africa," one Frenchman noted, "and for us, the colonizers, the smell of Africa is delicious."

Although a concern for authenticity continued to inform the architectural representation of the French colonies, a new interest in symmetry emerged in 1900, with the result that the picturesqueness was hidden behind uniform screens or regularized along an axis. The enclosing of the Rue d'Alger clearly manifested the first tendency; the site plan of the Tunisian quarter revealed the second: the pavilions of the "village" were placed axially and symmetrically around a central open space. Furthermore, the entire Tunisian section was neatly hidden behind "regular facades, meeting at right angles.". . .

After four decades, the Islamic world no longer seemed exotic. Islamic nations' displays at the international fairs had entertained Westerners and had taken them to distant lands, nurturing their imaginations by offering them unknown sights, images, foods, drinks, music, and dance. At the fairs, the Orient that European writers, scholars, and artists had defined and described (in Edward Said's word, "constructed") since at least the beginning of the nineteenth century was presented as a three-dimensional living model. Thus it was brought to the West and incorporated into Western culture. Moreover, with the expansion of colonial territories, the exotic increasingly belonged to the Western powers.

Anne McClintock

Advertising the Empire

At the beginning of the nineteenth century, soap was a scarce and humdrum item and washing a cursory activity at best. A few decades later, the manufacture of soap had burgeoned into an imperial commerce; Victorian cleaning rituals were peddled globally as the God-given sign of Britain's evolutionary superiority, and soap was invested with magical, fetish powers. The soap saga captured the hidden affinity between domesticity and empire and embodied a triangulated crisis in value: the *undervaluation* of women's work in the domestic realm, the *overvaluation* of the commodity in the industrial market and the *disavowal* of colonized economies in the arena of empire. Soap entered the realm of Victorian fetishism with spectacular effect, notwithstanding the fact that male Victorians promoted soap as the icon of nonfetishistic rationality.

Both the cult of domesticity and the new imperialism found in soap an exemplary mediating form. The emergent middle-class values—monogamy ("clean" sex, which has value), industrial capital ("clean" money, which has value), Christianity ("being washed in the blood of the lamb"), class control ("cleansing the great unwashed") and the imperial civilizing mission ("washing and clothing the savage")—could all be marvelously embodied in a single household commodity. Soap advertising, in particular the Pears soap campaign, took its place at the vanguard of Britain's new commodity culture and its civilizing mission. . . .

Victorian advertising reveals a paradox, however, for, as the cultural form that was entrusted with upholding and marketing abroad those founding middle-class distinctions—between private and public, paid work and unpaid work—advertising also from the outset began to confound those distinctions. Advertising took the intimate signs of domesticity (children bathing, men shaving, women laced into corsets, maids delivering nightcaps) into the public realm, plastering scenes of domesticity on walls, buses, shopfronts, and billboards. At the same time, advertising took scenes of empire into every corner of the home, stamping images of colonial conquest on soap boxes, matchboxes, biscuit tins, whiskey bottles, tea tins, and chocolate bars. By trafficking promiscuously across the threshold of private and public, advertising began to subvert one of the fundamental distinctions of commodity capital, even as it was coming into being.

From the outset, moreover, Victorian advertising took explicit shape around the reinvention of racial difference. Commodity kitsch made possible, as never before, the mass marketing of empire as an organized system of images and attitudes. Soap flourished not only because it created and filled a spectacular gap in the domestic market but also because, as a cheap and portable domestic commodity, it could persuasively mediate the Victorian poetics of racial hygiene and imperial progress.

Commodity racism became distinct from scientific racism in its capacity to expand beyond the literate, propertied elite through the marketing of commodity spectacle. If, after the 1850s, scientific racism saturated anthropological, scientific and medical journals, travel writing and novels, these cultural forms were still relatively class-bound and inaccessible to most Victorians, who had neither the means nor the education to read such material. Imperial kitsch as consumer spectacle, by contrast, could package, market, and distribute evolutionary racism on a hitherto unimagined scale. No preexisting form of organized racism had ever before been able to reach so large and so differentiated a mass of the populace. Thus, as domestic commodities were mass marketed through their appeal to imperial jingoism, commodity jingoism itself helped reinvent and maintain British national unity in the face of deepening imperial competition and colonial resistance. The cult of domesticity became indispensable to the consolidation of British national identity, and at the center of the domestic cult stood the simple bar of soap.

Yet soap has no social history. Since it purportedly belongs in the female realm of domesticity, soap is figured as beyond history and beyond politics proper. To begin a social history of soap, then, is to refuse, in part, to accept the erasure of women's domestic value under imperial capitalism. It cannot be forgotten, moreover, that the history of European attempts to impose a commodity economy on African cultures was also the history of diverse African attempts either to refuse or to transform European commodity fetishism to suit their own needs. The story of soap reveals that fetishism, far from being a quintessentially African propensity, as nineteenth-century anthropology maintained, was central to industrial modernity, inhabiting and mediating the uncertain threshold zones between domesticity and industry, metropolis and empire. . . .

The initial impetus for soap advertising came from the realm of empire. With the burgeoning of imperial cotton on the slave plantations came the surplus of cheap cotton goods, alongside the growing buying power of a middle class that could afford for the first time to consume such goods in large quantities. Similarly, the sources for cheap palm oil, coconut oil, and cottonseed oil flourished in the imperial plantations of West Africa, Malay, Ceylon, Fiji, and New Guinea. As rapid changes in the technology of soapmaking took place in Britain after midcentury, the prospect dawned of a large domestic market for soft body soaps, which had previously been a luxury that only the upper class could afford.

Economic competition with the United States and Germany created the need for a more aggressive promotion of British products and led to the first real innovations in advertising. In 1884, the year of the Berlin Conference, the first wrapped soap was sold under a brand name. This small event signified a major transformation in capitalism, as imperial competition gave rise to the creation of monopolies. Henceforth, items formerly indistinguishable from each other (soap sold simply as soap) would be marketed by their corporate signature (Pears, Monkey Brand, etc). Soap became one of the first commodities to register the historic shift from myriad small businesses to the great imperial monopolies. In the 1870s, hundreds of small soap companies plied the new trade in hygiene, but by the end of the century, the trade was monopolized by ten large companies.

In order to manage the great soap show, an aggressively entrepreneurial breed of advertisers emerged, dedicated to gracing each homely product with a radiant halo of imperial glamour and racial potency. The advertising agent, like the bureaucrat, played a vital role in the imperial expansion of foreign trade. Advertisers billed themselves as "empire builders" and flattered themselves with "the responsibility of the historic imperial mission." Said one: "Commerce even more than sentiment binds the ocean sundered portions of empire together.

Anyone who increases these commercial interests strengthens the whole fabric of the empire." Soap was credited not only with bringing moral and economic salvation to Britain's "great unwashed" but also with magically embodying the spiritual ingredient of the imperial mission itself.

In an ad for Pears, for example, a black and implicitly racialized coalsweeper holds in his hands a glowing, occult object. Luminous with its own inner radiance, the simple soap bar glows like a fetish, pulsating magically with spiritual enlightenment and imperial grandeur, promising to warm the hands and hearts of working people across the globe. Pears, in particular, became intimately associated with a purified nature magically cleansed of polluting industry (tumbling kittens, faithful dogs, children festooned with flowers) and a purified working class magically cleansed of polluting labor (smiling servants in crisp white aprons, rosy-cheeked match girls, and scrubbed scullions).

Nonetheless, the Victorian obsession with cotton and cleanliness was not simply a mechanical reflex of economic surplus. If imperialism garnered a bounty of cheap cotton and soap oils from coerced colonial labor, the middle-class Victorian fascination with clean, white bodies and clean, white clothing stemmed not only from the rampant profiteering of the imperial economy but also from the realms of ritual and fetish.

Soap did not flourish when imperial ebullience was at its peak. It emerged commercially during an era of impending crisis and social calamity, serving to preserve, through fetish ritual, the uncertain boundaries of class, gender and race identity in a social order felt to be threatened by the fetid effluvia of the slums, the belching smoke of industry, social agitation, economic upheaval, imperial competition, and anticolonial resistance. Soap offered the promise of spiritual salvation and regeneration through commodity consumption, a regime of domestic hygiene that could restore the threatened potency of the imperial body politic and the race. . . .

Four fetishes recur ritualistically in soap advertising: soap itself, white clothing (especially aprons), mirrors, and monkeys. A typical Pears' advertisement figures a black child and a white child together in a bathroom. The Victorian bathroom is the innermost sanctuary of domestic hygiene and by extension the private temple of public regeneration. The sacrament of soap offers a reformation allegory whereby the purification of the domestic body becomes a metaphor for the regeneration of the body politic. In this particular ad, a black boy sits in the bath, gazing wide-eyed into the water as if into a foreign element. A white boy, clothed in a white apron—the familiar fetish of domestic purity—bends benevolently over his "lesser" brother, bestowing upon him the precious talisman of racial progress. The magical fetish of soap promises that the commodity can regenerate the Family of Man by washing from the skin the very stigma of racial and class degeneration.

Soap advertising offers an allegory of imperial progress as spectacle. In this ad, the imperial topos that I call panoptical time (progress consumed as a spectacle from a point of privileged invisibility) enters the domain of the commodity. In the second frame of the ad, the black child is out of the bath and the white boy shows him his startled visage in the mirror. The black boy's body has become magically white, but his face—for Victorians the seat of rational individuality and self-consciousness—remains stubbornly black. The white child is thereby figured as the agent of history and the male heir to progress, reflecting his lesser brother in the European mirror of self-consciousness. In the Victorian mirror, the black child witnesses the predetermined destiny of imperial metamorphosis but remains a passive racial hybrid, part black, part white, brought to the brink of civilization by the twin commodity fetishes of soap and mirror. The advertisement discloses a crucial element of late Victorian commodity culture: the metaphoric transformation of imperial *time* into consumer *space*—imperial progress consumed at a glance as domestic spectacle. . . .

The metamorphosis of imperial time into domestic space is captured most vividly by the advertising campaign for Monkey Brand Soap. During the 1880s, the urban landscape of Victorian Britain teemed with the fetish monkeys of this soap. The monkey with its frying pan and bar of soap perched everywhere, on grimy hoardings and buses, on walls and shop fronts, promoting the soap that promised magically to do away with domestic labor: "No dust, no dirt, no labor." Monkey Brand Soap promised not only to regenerate the race but also to magically erase the unseemly spectacle of women's manual labor.

In an exemplary ad, the fetish soap-monkey sits cross-legged on a doorstep, the threshold boundary between private domesticity and public commerce—the embodiment of anachronistic space. Dressed like an organ grinder's minion in a gentleman's ragged suit, white shirt, and tie, but with improbably human hands and feet, the monkey extends a frying pan to catch the surplus cash of passersby. On the doormat before him, a great bar of soap is displayed, accompanied by a placard that reads: "My Own Work." In every respect the soap-monkey is a hybrid: not entirely ape, not entirely human; part street beggar, part gentleman; part artist, part advertiser. The creature inhabits the ambivalent border of jungle and city, private and public, the domestic and the commercial, and offers as its handiwork a fetish that is both art and commodity.

Monkeys inhabit Western discourse on the borders of social limit, marking the place of a contradiction in social value. As Donna Haraway has argued: "the primate body, as part of the body of nature, may be read as a map of power." Primatology, Haraway insists, "is a Western discourse . . . a political order that works by the negotiation of boundaries achieved through ordering differences." In Victorian iconography, the ritual recurrence of the monkey figure is eloquent of a crisis in value and hence anxiety at possible boundary breakdown. The primate body became a symbolic space for reordering and policing boundaries between humans and nature, women and men, family and politics, empire and metropolis.

Simian imperialism is also centrally concerned with the problem of representing *social change*. By projecting history (rather than fate, or God's will) onto the theater of nature, primatology made nature the alibi of political violence and placed in the hands of "rational science" the authority to sanction and legitimize social change. Here, "the scene of origins," Haraway argues, "is not the cradle of civilization, but the cradle of culture . . . the origin of sociality itself, especially in the densely meaning-laden icon of the family." Primatology emerges as a theater for negotiating the perilous boundaries between the family (as natural and female) and power (as political and male).

The appearance of monkeys in soap advertising signals a dilemma: *how to represent domesticity without representing women at work*. The Victorian middle-class house was structured round the fundamental contradiction between women's paid and unpaid domestic work. As women were driven from paid work in mines, factories, shops, and trades to private, unpaid work in the home, domestic work became economically undervalued and the middle-class definition of femininity figured the "proper" woman as one who did not work for profit. At the same time, a *cordon sanitaire* of racial degeneration was thrown around those women who did work publicly and visibly for money. What could not be incorporated into the industrial formation (women's domestic economic value) was displaced onto the invented domain of the primitive, and thereby disciplined and contained.

Monkeys, in particular, were deployed to legitimize social boundaries as edicts of nature. Fetishes straddling nature and culture, monkeys were seen as allied with the dangerous classes: the "apelike" wandering poor, the hungry Irish, Jews, prostitutes, impoverished black people, the ragged working class, criminals, the insane, and female miners and servants, who were collectively seen to inhabit the threshold of racial degeneration. When Charles Kingsley visited Ireland, for example, he lamented: "I am haunted by the human chimpanzees I saw along that hundred miles of horrible country. . . . But to see white chimpanzees is dreadful; if they were black, one would not feel it so much, but their skins, except where tanned by exposure, are as white as ours."

In the Monkey Brand advertisement, the monkey's signature of labor ("My Own Work") signals a double disavowal. Soap is masculinized, figured as a male product, while the (mostly female) labor of the workers in the huge, unhealthy soap factories is disavowed. At the same time, the labor of social transformation in the daily scrubbing and scouring of the sinks, pans, and dishes, labyrinthine floors and corridors of Victorian domestic space vanishes—refigured as anachronistic space, primitive and bestial. Female servants disappear and in their place crouches a phantasmic male hybrid. Thus, domesticity—seen as the sphere most separate from the marketplace and the masculine hurly-burly of empire—takes shape around the invented ideas of the primitive and the commodity fetish.

In Victorian culture, the monkey was an icon of metamorphosis, perfectly serving soap's liminal role in mediating the transformations of nature (dirt, waste, and disorder) into culture (cleanliness, rationality, and industry). Like all fetishes, the monkey is a contradictory image, embodying the hope of imperial progress through commerce while at the same time rendering visible deepening Victorian fears of urban militancy and colonial misrule. The soap-monkey became the emblem of industrial progress and imperial evolution, embodying the double promise that nature could be redeemed by consumer capital and that consumer capital could be guaranteed by natural law. At the same time, however, the soap-monkey was eloquent of the degree to which fetishism structures industrial rationality. . . .

In most Monkey Brand advertisements, the monkey holds a frying pan, which is also a mirror. In a similar Brooke's Soap ad, a classical female beauty with bare white arms stands draped in white, her skin and clothes epitomizing the exhibition value of sexual purity and domestic leisure, while from the cornucopia she holds flows a grotesque effluvium of hobgoblin angels. Each hybrid fetish embodies the doubled Victorian image of woman as "angel in the drawing room, monkey in the bedroom," as well as the racial iconography of evolutionary progress from ape to angel. Historical time, again, is captured as domestic spectacle, eerily reflected in the frying pan/mirror fetish.

In this ad, the Brooke's Soap offers an alchemy of economic progress, promising to make "copper like gold." At the same time, the Enlightenment idea of linear, rational time leading to angelic perfection finds its antithesis in the other time of housework, ruled by the hobgoblins of dirt, disorder, and fetishistic, nonprogressive time. Erupting on the margins of the rational frame, the ad displays the irrational consequences of the idea of progress. The mirror/frying pan, like all fetishes, visibly expresses a crisis in value but cannot resolve it. It can only embody the contradiction, frozen as commodity spectacle, luring the spectator deeper and deeper into consumerism.

Mirrors glint and gleam in soap advertising, as they do in the culture of imperial kitsch at large. In Victorian middle-class households, servants scoured and polished every metal and wooden surface until it shone like a mirror. Doorknobs, lamp stands and banisters, tables and chairs, mirrors and clocks, knives and forks, kettles and pans, shoes and boots were polished until they shimmered, reflecting in their gleaming surfaces other object-mirrors, an infinity of crystalline mirrors within mirrors, until the interior of the house was all shining surfaces, a labyrinth of reflection. The mirror became the epitome of commodity fetishism: erasing both the signs of domestic labor and the industrial origins of domestic commodities. In the domestic world of mirrors, objects multiply without apparent human intervention in a promiscuous economy of self-generation.

Why the attention to surface and reflection? The polishing was dedicated, in part, to policing the boundaries between private and public, removing every trace of labor, replacing the disorderly evidence of working women with the exhibition of domesticity as veneer, the commodity spectacle as surface, the house arranged as a theater of clean surfaces for commodity display. The mirror/commodity renders the value of the object as an exhibit, a spectacle to be consumed, admired, and displayed for its capacity to embody a twofold value: the man's market worth and the wife's exhibition status. The house existed to display femininity as bearing exhibition value only, beyond the marketplace and therefore, by natural decree, beyond political power.

An ad for Stephenson's Furniture Cream figures a spotless maid on all fours, smiling up from a floor so clean that it mirrors her reflection. The cream is "warranted not to fingermark." A superior soap should leave no telltale smear, no fingerprint of female labor. As Victorian servants lost individuality in the generic names their employers imposed on them, so soaps erased the imprint of women's work on middle-class history.

Antoinette Burton

Indian Travellers in Victorian Britain

On the 4th of May, 1886 the Colonial and Indian Exhibition opened in London to rave reviews from the metropolitan press. The *Pall Mall Gazette* called the exhibition at South Kensington a "revelation of Empire," praised the "jungle realism" of its displays, and trumpeted the wares, ingenuity and industry of Britain's Indian "fellow-subjects." Between May and September of that year, over five million visitors passed through the Indian courts, which were designated individually as Rajputana, Central India, Bombay, Bengal, Nepal, North-west Provinces and Oudh, the Punjab, Kashmir, the Central Provinces and Madras, among others. According to the exhibition catalogue, the

Excerpted from Antoinette Burton, "Making a Spectacle of Empire: Indian Travellers in Fin-de-Siècle London," *History Workshop Journal* 42 (1996): 127–146. Copyright © 1996 History Workshop Journal. Reprinted by permission of Oxford University Press Journals division and the author.

courts were laid out in this sequence in order to indicate "with considerable clearness the changing complexion and character of Art manufacture as we pass from one part of India to another." The staff's hopes were realized for one visitor at least, who declared approvingly that the exhibition brought the nation of India "right up to us here in London without the bother of going there.". . .

While the organizers of the Colonial and Indian Exhibition were busy manufacturing this particular spectacle of empire, colonial subjects in London were engaged in some map-making of their own. 1886 marked the beginning of a spate of travelogues written in English by Indian men, many of whom had either travelled to London to visit the exhibition or used it as a pretext for writing a guidebook of the imperial metropolis. Although Indians had travelled to Britain since the eighteenth century, and had written accounts of their metropolitan experiences since at least the 1830s, the 1880s witnessed a flourishing of guidebooks that detailed the urban experiences of colonial men exploring the heart of the empire for the first time. . . . These displays of cosmopolitanism were a contemporaneous response to William Booth and other English social investigators who were mapping parts of the capital city as a world apart—as colonial spaces evocative, for example, of the African jungle. Indians travelling to the heart of the empire revealed that the privilege accorded the rambler, the stroller, or the flaneur was open to appropriation, and that London itself could be represented as a site open to colonization in the process.

. . . If, as Anne McClintock has argued, commodity capitalism helped to reorder metropolitan culture for the display of imperial power, London was one of the primary spaces in which and through which this refiguration occurred. . . . [C]olonial subjects were among those historical actors who worked to manage—and to challenge—the terms upon which the spectacle of empire was produced in the late-Victorian imperial metropolis. Like other eastern travellers who produced Europe itself as an exhibitionary site, Indians in Britain made London into a theatre where the drama of the colonial citizen-subject was played out for the benefit of rulers and ruled alike. Their narratives provide historical evidence of how imperial power was staged at home, and how it could be interrogated by "natives" in the "mother-city of the kingdom and the Empire" itself. Thus they did not simply return the gaze, but demonstrated how readily available its disciplinary regimes were for contest and refiguration—especially by Indian men, whose pretensions to nationhood and its cultural corollary, Victorian masculinity, were under scrutiny at this particular historical moment.

"London," wrote A. L. Roy in his *Reminiscences English and American (1890)*, "means the centre of a world-wide empire . . . a repository of wealth and a reservoir of energy . . . a whirlpool of activity and a deep sea of thought, a point where the ends of the world may be said to meet.". . . As did many westerners travelling to Victorian London for the first time, Indians got caught up in the vitality and ceaseless motion of "the world's greatest metropolis," "the most remarkable city on the face of the globe," "this ocean of human life called London." A generic feature of these texts is astonishment at the "surging traffic," the "bustling crowd," and the endless crush of people, buses, and animals. T. N. Mukharji, who came to London in 1886 as an employee of the Government of India and oversaw a section of the Colonial and Indian Exhibition, was preoccupied with the density of the crowds, the likes of which he claimed never to have seen in his home town of Calcutta. Jhinda Ram, who came from Lahore, concurred. What impressed him, in addition to the multitude of "hansoms, cabs, landaulets, traps, dogcarts, and . . . conveyances of all sizes," was the fact that the streets were full of people "neatly dressed with faces beaming with gladness and hilarity." If the people in the crowded thoroughfares were well-behaved, this was often attributed to the efficacy of the metropolitan police force, for whom most if not all well-heeled Indian travellers, at any rate, professed respect and admiration. Behramji Malabari, who came to London in 1890 from Bombay on a social reform mission, echoed the opinion of many of his countrymen when he remarked: "Dear old Bobby; roughly tender in your attentions to all in need, seldom losing your temper, though distracted by a score of tongues at a time, or your presence of mind amid the confusion and clatter of a hundred feet!" Unlike Mayhew, the mid-Victorian urban ethnographer who disliked policemen because they kept him moving, Indians were gratified by their friendliness. And Malabari was not the only one who contrasted the probity of the Peelers — "the most conspicuous and commanding figures in every London crowd" — with the corruption of their counterparts in India. . . .

Accounts of London life suggest that in fact, Indians on the streets were as keenly observed as they were observing, if not more so — for almost all Indian travellers who left memoirs of their experiences there reported that they had been made to feel conspicuous as they wandered round the city. So common was it to be stared at that N. Dasa, author of *Reminiscences English and Australasian* observed "that I need not mention that I was noticed by almost everyone on the streets. My dark complexion and my chupkan, which I retained throughout the whole of my travels . . . attracted everybody's notice. They looked at me, and it was quite natural for them to do so." It was a pre-occupying, if not always unpleasant, experience to be the object of attention from curious passers-by. . . . Such intense public scrutiny was at its height at the Colonial and Indian Exhibition where, according to Mukharji, "we were pierced through and through by stares from eyes of all colours—green, gray, blue, and black—and every movement and act of ours, walking, sitting, eating, reading, received its full share of 'O, I never!' " Although he was good-natured about it all, Mukharji hinted at some of the intrusiveness of such publicity when he asked: "would they discuss us so freely if they knew that we understood their language?"

Clothing was what appeared to distinguish Indians, to make them the objects of ridicule and fun on London streets, though headgear was also a factor. . . .

The spectacular effect of Indians in the public eye cannot, of course, be attributed to their distinctive garments alone. As a number of Indian men were quick to remark, it was their "dark visages" and apparently self-evident Indianness which drew strangers to them, especially women. Some of these took an innocent interest in the Indian men they approached, as for example the elderly matron who came up to Mukharji at the Colonial and Indian Exhibition and inquired as to whether he knew her nephew, a soldier in one of the Indian regiments. Other encounters were less disinterested. A number of travel writers related stories of being solicited by English girls and women for drinks, favours, and presumably the possibility of sex as well. Behramji Malabari was particularly agitated by this kind of urban experience, and though he described one such instance at some length in his book *The Indian Eye on English Life,* he preferred to dismiss the sordid possibilities as "an evil dream," rather than confront the precariousness of his position as a gentleman stroller. Even young Gandhi, who left a wife in India when he came to study for the bar in London in the late 1880s, recorded evidence of the sexual temptations of metropolitan streets. When such encounters occurred, they invariably drew a po-

liceman's attention and intervention—a recurrent theme which suggests that although the bobby may have been viewed as a friend by the
colonial flaneur, he may actually have been attempting to patrol the
boundaries between brown men and white women in public.

It was partly in order to compensate for being made into spectacle
that Indian visitors produced the kind of spectacle of London that they
did for Indian readers in India. . . . The maps of London that men like
Ram, Malabari, Dutt, Dasa, and others produced in the course of their
travelogues were not just guides to the city or even simply ethnogra-
phies of late-Victorian urban life. They were visual evidence that despite the assaults and mockery that Indians experienced on the streets
of the empire's capital city, London could be possessed by its colonial
subjects, who proclaimed themselves free to wander its avenues and
hence to claim its grandeur and its power as their own. By making
themselves into seeing subjects at the heart of the empire, Indians par-
ried the "spectacular gestures" characteristic of Victorian imperial
culture and made Britain itself the subject of surveillance and critique. . . .

Not all travellers were laudatory in their accounts of London land-
marks or of the most available signifier of imperial power, London itself. Bhagvat Sinh Gee professed to be "overjoyed at setting my foot in
the renowned country which it was my long cherished desire to see."
But he was quickly disillusioned by the city, which he found "smoky
and sooty. Wipe your face or furniture now and again and in a couple
of hours you will see your kerchief tinged with soot.". . . And there
were few who did not remark on the poverty, the homelessness and the
contrasts between rich and poor that were to be found all across the
city. Indian travel writers took little relish in describing the conditions
of the poor, but they often used these circumstances as a way of criti-
cising the much-vaunted discourse of progress to which they as colonials were particularly subject. "Poor as India is," wrote Malabari, "I
thank God she knows not much of the poverty to which parts of
Britain have become accustomed—[take] the East End of London, for
instance . . . [where there are] men and women living in a chronic
state of emaciation, till they can hardly be recognized as human." As a
newspaper man himself (he was the editor of the *Indian Spectator* in
Bombay) Malabari, like other colonial travellers, appropriated the hy-
perbole of newspaper commentary and sensationalist social investigation partly to display his worldliness. But he also made an implicit

critique of imperial civilization as well, one which revealed poverty and distress as the daily condition of the lower classes at the heart of the world's largest empire. For he was quick to add: "this is not a picture of occasional misery . . . it represents the every-day life of the victims of misfortune.". . .

. . . [D]espite the attraction of parks and public buildings, it was museums which structured the map of the imperial capital produced by late-Victorian Indian travellers. A. L. Roy, whose 1890 text has already been referred to, begins his *Reminiscences* by describing London's museums and is so caught up in detailing their contents and explaining their significance that he scarcely ever leaves them. Indeed, it is not too much of an exaggeration to say that his memoir is an extended reflection on metropolitan life and by extension, English civilization, that is both prompted and sustained by a discussion of the British Museum. Malabari, who was "seldom drawn to art galleries and shows" because he didn't like the crowds, was an exception. The Royal Academy, the National Gallery, the Natural History Museum, Madame Tussaud's, the Crystal Palace—each of these repositories was routinely represented as an important landmark on the cultural map of the metropolis which Indian travellers laid out and laid claim to in the process. Of all these it was the British Museum which loomed largest and occupied pride of place. For some, especially those who had been students in London at one time or another, the British Museum was primarily a library—a place where, in Roy's words, "the encyclopedic book of entire London was spread before me to study as closely as I pleased." For others, it was a site of homage, and "no foreigner coming to London should go without paying a visit" there. The British Museum represented all that was superior about English civilization and culture for many Indians who visited its galleries; it also provided an opportunity to look at, and interpret, some of the most famous collectables in the world for the benefit of their countrymen at home. Readers following closely could visualize the vastness of the British Museum's collection even as they saw Egyptian mummies, ancient Greek vases, and renaissance manuscripts put on display before their eyes. Most importantly perhaps, they saw Indians acting as spectators rather than as objects of spectacle. They were able to watch colonial observers turning an educated and, in the case of someone like Mukharji, an expert eye on the empire's treasures.

The Indian traveller's role as interpreter of museum display worked in interesting ways. Jhinda Ram waxed eloquent about the Egyptian galleries in the British Museum in his 1893 travelogue, *My Trip to Europe*, identifying apparently quite effortlessly with the orientalist presentations of Egypt as a classical but finally primitive culture ripe for collection at the imperial centre. Differentiating India as not just any colony, but a special and culturally superior British possession, was constitutive of the late-Victorian exhibitionary impulse, and it was a message appreciated by a number of Indian visitors to Britain. Distinguishing tribal peoples like the Naga from high-caste Hindus—as Mukharji did in his account of the 1886 exhibition—was yet another way of laying claim to the taxonomic impulse of imperial collecting and of identifying with the imperial project as a whole. Even so, such distinctions were neither uniform nor predictable: India was at times displayed in "ethnological galleries" alongside African materials, and "*West*" Indian performers could be read by naive Britons as "*South Asian*" *Indians*, as Mukharji discovered to his distress when talking to some English visitors to the 1886 exhibition. He did his best to correct his readers and to explain that he was in fact neither African nor black. For Indian travellers as for Britons of many classes, ranking people of colour was a way of displaying not just knowledge of colonial hierarchies, but a certain claim to civilization on the basis of distinction (especially distinction from Africans) as well. The curatorial displays on offer in London's museums were not, in other words, passively consumed. They were quite purposefully re-produced both as critiques of how the British saw India as well as evidence of Indians' capacity to discover "India" at the heart of the empire and to consume British (imperial) culture like other "native" Britons. Lala Baijnath declared the materials in the "Indian section" of the British Museum even more interesting than the European art, and announced with an air of proprietorship that "one could learn much about India even in London, if one wanted to." The fact that a number of late-nineteenth century travel books used the technology of the eye (*The Indian Eye on English Life, London and Paris Through Indian Spectacles, England to an Indian Eye*) in their titles suggests that the desire to make a spectacle of London, its streets and particularly its imperial treasures, was one of the chief motivations behind the production of these colonial travel narratives. . . .

The desire to manage the spectacle of empire exhibited by many Indian travel writers was no doubt especially acute in the wake of the Colonial and Indian Exhibition where, as has been indicated, all manner of Indian goods and Indian people were on display. Mukharji's account of the 1886 event is particularly instructive here because it effectively reduces the spectacular effects of the exhibition to the rather parochial viewpoint of Londoners and other native Britons. . . .

. . . [T]he section of his travelogue devoted to the exhibition (entitled "The Exhibition and its Visitors") did not simply guide readers through the courts, but focused on the spectators' reactions to them as well. Referring no doubt to his countrymen, a Mr. Gupte and Mr. U. C. Mukharji, who were also officially connected with the Exhibition, Mukharji recounted that

> *we . . . constantly watched with pleasure the anxious acquisitive scrutiny to which the various raw products of India were daily subjected by thousands of visitors. . . . Merchants, manufacturers and scientists flocked there to see what new sources of wealth and human comfort had been brought within their reach from Her Majesty's distant dominions. Even the natives who came from villages took an unusual interest in the most trivial objects, such as leaves and bark, and exhibited intelligence of a superior order in mastering the details of the various uses to which they are put in India and other parts of the world. Parents explained to their children, and young men to their sweethearts, the various points of interest found in the innumerable products and manufactures which India sent to that Exhibition from her different provinces . . . they were as much astonished to see the Indians produce works of art with the aid of rude apparatus they themselves had discarded long ago as a Hindu would be to see a chimpanzee officiating as a priest in a funeral ceremony and reading out Sanskrit texts from a palm leaf book spread out before him.*

On display in this passage are the arts and crafts, the raw materials, and the cultural artifacts which represent England's commercial power in the Indian empire. Also on view are Britons themselves—those "natives" streaming into London from villages all over the British Isles, who could be seen gawking at the colonial spectacle produced for their delectation by the British government. Mukharji was not alone among his contemporaries, European or Indian, in contrasting the Exhibition's wealth with the poverty of "real" colonial peoples. That he intended to criticize the thirst for commodity capitalism displayed by the exhibition and its visitors—and in so doing to return the metropolitan gaze—there can be little doubt. He made it clear that 1886 was not just a "revelation of Empire," but the unmasking of its exploitative commercial interests as well. Indeed, nothing less than British colonialism itself was turned into an object of public scrutiny in his travelogue, together with its vividly unjust effects. As Mukharji tersely noted, while Britons avidly consumed Indian jewels, cloth, and wares on display at South Kensington, "half of India goes half-naked for want of means to purchase the necessary clothing." In one brief, graphic moment, the "spectacular gesture" of 1886 was reduced to the realities of colonial poverty, and the grandeur of imperial power was shown to rest on the backs of the indigenous colonial poor.

Tyler Stovall

Colonial Workers in France during the Great War

. . . In January, 1916, . . . the War Ministry took over this function [of recruitment] creating the Colonial Labour Organisation Service (SOTC) to bring in colonial subjects. Thus, most colonial workers came to France under the aegis of the military and, unlike Europeans, were subject to military conditions and discipline. SOTC also directed the recruitment of workers from China. . . .

. . . The largest single group came from Algeria (78,566); other large contingents came from Indochina, principally Annam and Tonkin (48,995), China (36,941), and Morocco (35,506), followed by Tunisia (18,249) and Madagascar (4,546). Only token numbers of workers came from France's sub-Saharan African possessions. . . .

From Tyler Stovall, "Colour-blind France? Colonial Workers During the First World War," from *Race and Class* 35, 2 (University of California, Santa Cruz, 1993): 35–55. Copyright © 1993. Excerpted by permission of the author.

The French use of forced colonial labour led to both individual and collective acts of resistance. The reluctance of North Africans and Indochinese to volunteer arose both from the widespread belief that those recruited as workers would actually be used as soldiers, and from negative descriptions of life in France sent back by those already there. One type of resistance was the attempt to find substitutes for those requisitioned by the authorities. In Indochina, families would substitute elderly or infirm members, in the hopes that they would be rejected on medical grounds and the family as a whole would be spared. In Tunisia, where one could legally purchase replacements for the draft, families mobilised their resources towards this end. One Tunisian worker writing from south-western France in 1918 stressed the importance of doing so:

> *Give us information on the draft lottery. Have operations begun or not? Insofar as you are concerned, my dear brother, if God decrees that you are taken, do not allow yourself to come to this country. Sell everything you possess and buy a replacement. Here, we are suffering from famine.*

Resistance to conscription also took the form of large-scale revolts in both Indochina and North Africa. In Cambodia, recruitment led to an insurrection in 1916, and both there and in Cochin China recruiters failed to overcome widespread hostility, consequently signing up few people. In November, 1916, conscription led to an uprising of over 1,000 people in the Kabyle province of Algeria. In both cases, resistance seems to have been directed against both military and labour conscription. . . .

. . . The government's basic approach was termed *encadrement*, or regimentation. All aspects of the lives of non-white workers in France were set by SOTC, with an eye to keeping them as isolated from the French population as possible. . . . In contrast to European immigrant workers, who led their own private lives and had some scope to participate in the wider society, non-whites lived and worked in rigorously segregated conditions similar to those experienced by prisoners of war. *Encadrement* reinforced the constrained character of their labour. Moreover, since it applied to the Chinese as well as those from the French empire, it emphasised the salience of skin colour in differentiating between foreign workers. . . .

Officials . . . advanced several reasons for the regimentation of colonial and Chinese labour. One was the need to guarantee greater productivity; many employers complained that non-white workers were lazy and/or inefficient and would only give a decent output if strictly controlled. This was alleged especially about the Chinese, for whom regimentation was not implemented initially but developed gradually. Language differences and the need for interpreters also underlay arguments for this system. However, fears of contacts between non-whites and French society constituted the basic justification for *encadrement*. This concern had at least two aspects. One was a paternalistic desire to avoid "corrupting" the natives with European practices. . . . Officials frequently mentioned the dangers posed by alcoholism and prostitution to colonial workers. However, colonial authorities in particular feared contamination by such social "dangers" as high wages, unions, strikes, and political activism, which such workers might bring back home with them.

Perhaps more important to SOTC was the desire to preserve French society from contact with a large non-white population. One report on importing Chinese labour alleged the social problems its introduction had created in the United States and other countries. In particular, public authorities noted the possibility of conflicts with French workers. Such a possibility was real but, in some ways, intensified by regimentation. In addition, SOTC hoped to prevent contacts between non-white labourers and French women.

. . . In spite of the paternalist platitudes offered by French authorities, the regimentation of colonial and Chinese labour made their working and living conditions in France worse, not better. For example, the tight control exercised over these workers had the effect of keeping their wages artificially low. . . .

In addition to keeping the wages of non-white workers at the bottom of the pay scale, regimentation also worked to concentrate them in the least desirable occupations. Most immigrants in France during the war, both European and non-European, lacked appreciable industrial skills. Although both groups were brought to France to work for the war effort, colonial workers more often ended up in munitions plants, whereas most of the Spaniards spent the war on French farms, and many Portuguese worked either there, in construction, or on the railroads. . . .

The munitions plants paid high wages, but often at the cost of difficult work and unsafe conditions. Colonial and Chinese workers, however, could not benefit from the former because of their contracts and regimented status, but they experienced the latter in full measure. . . .

Regimentation also adversely affected the living conditions of colonial and Chinese workers, especially the quality of housing and food. . . .

Finally, regimentation meant that colonial and Chinese workers experienced much more direct supervision than European immigrants, and came into conflict with them more often. . . .

Government officials carefully censored the letters sent by immigrant workers to friends and family at home, in order to monitor their general state of mind and guard against disloyal thoughts and actions. These letters reveal that non-white workers were well aware of their low status and had a lot to say about it. . . . In general, the image that emerges is of people caught in a harsh, bewildering situation:

> *Oh my eye, let the tears flow! My heart is grieved by the separation from Zalah and from Senaim. Oh my heart, cry for my separation from my father! The infidels have taken me by force . . . now I wander with a shovel or a pickaxe in my hand . . . I work like a condemned man in coal mines and limestone quarries . . . I work from morning to night with infidels who have no pity on us; they are the enemies of religion.*

Colonial and Chinese workers did more to protest against their conditions than write letters. There were numerous instances of brief work stoppages, and some more organised strikes, at factories employing non-white labour. In February, 1918, about thirty Moroccans employed at a laundry near Epinal struck for several days to protest their insufficient food rations. Chinese workers, in particular, had a reputation for militancy. The thousand employees of the Holtzer munitions plant in Unieux engaged in several strikes during the summer of 1917. At times, such movements scored small and temporary successes, but, on the whole, they did little to alter the poor conditions under which workers of colour lived and worked in France during the first world war.

Any analysis of the regimentation system would be incomplete, however, without a consideration of French racism as manifested towards non-white workers. Such racist attitudes both motivated and were reinforced by the regimentation system, and cannot be separated from it. . . .

Hostility to foreign workers and foreigners in general was nothing new in France. French workers, in particular, had often reacted antagonistically, even violently, to outsiders in their midst during the late nineteenth and early twentieth centuries. Although one can find instances of prejudice against non-white workers in France in this period, since there were so few of them, most anti-foreign sentiment was directed against Italians, Belgians, Germans, and other European immigrants. This antagonism ranged from name-calling to full-scale riots. . . .

On the surface, such a history supports the view that xenophobia is the root cause of French hostility to both white and non-white immigrant workers. However, when one looks at both official attitudes and the views of French workers and the French people as a whole, it is hard to escape the conclusion that colonial and Chinese workers experienced far greater levels of antagonism than did their European equivalents. . . .

A few dominant stereotypes permeate the official literature. First, the conception of non-whites as physically weak was very common. This applied especially to Indochinese and, to a lesser extent, to North Africans. One report, for example, said that the Indochinese had no more strength than women, while another emphasised their suitability for work requiring dexterity as opposed to physical force. Increasingly during the war, officials translated this alleged physical deficiency into a moral one, speaking less of weakness and more of laziness. Officials and employers accused all groups of this from time to time, but the Chinese were a prime target. The Chinese also had a reputation for insubordination, being considered the non-white workers most likely to protest, refuse to work, and get into conflict with the civilian population. In addition, officials often viewed colonial and Chinese workers as morally weak and corruptible. Without strict supervision, it was believed, these people would quickly fall prey to gambling, drink and, most shocking of all, white women.

Underlying these different stereotypes was the tendency of French officials to view Asian and African workers as children: essentially good-natured, yet wayward and sneaky. These infants not only needed but, at bottom, desired firm, paternal discipline from their betters.

The Madagascan easily lets himself be guided by the European, whose superiority he implicitly recognises. Conducted with firmness and

> *goodwill at the same time, one can get good work from him. . . . Although intelligent, the Madagascan has little initiative, which explains the small number of industries he has created.*
>
> *The Madagascan rarely reaches an advanced age. The taste for promiscuity which he often abuses, even from childhood, is for him a cause of degeneracy and abbreviates his days.*

The striking similarity of these stereotypes to those formulated by French officials in the empire is no accident. Because of language skills or a more general familiarity with the "natives," colonial officers often found positions working with colonial and Chinese workers in France. In evaluating these workers, they and SOTC as a whole drew upon ideas already formulated in the colonial context. Experiences in France were interpreted in the context of such preconceptions. For example, inspectors and interpreters would view high rates of illness among these workers as proof of their physical weakness, or see acts of resistance like absenteeism or work stoppages as laziness. They responded to most problems with a call for more discipline and regimentation, rather than questioning the abusive and patronising nature of the system. Within the context of a racist perspective, experiences in both the empire and metropolitan France interacted to produce a view of Africans and Asians as substandard. . . .

The first world war represented the first time French working people came into contact with large numbers of non-Europeans on their own territory. Their reactions were not always hostile. Labour inspectors reported instances of French and colonial workers socialising together at cafes after work, or of members of both groups raising money to support an injured co-worker. Several letters written by colonial workers mention friendly treatment by French labourers in their factories. Yet, in general, the two groups had little direct contact with each other, kept apart by the regimentation system as well as by French prejudice.

The French labour movement disapproved of the introduction of all foreign labour into France during the war, only reluctantly accepting it for the sake of the national effort but trying to limit it as much as possible. French unions feared that immigrants would be used to lower wages and worsen working conditions, as well as taking the jobs of French workers and returning veterans. . . . [C]omplaints about colonial and Chinese workers at times dealt with issues unrelated to wages and working conditions, as the objections considered in a CIMO meeting reveal:

> *The Pas-de-Calais miners union protests . . . to the Ministry of Public Works against the use of foreign workers, especially Kabyles, in the mines. . . . The union raises two objections: one concerning questions of morality, given the close proximity of North Africans to working-class families whose heads are absent; one concerning sanitation inspired by the fear of the possible contamination of the local population. On this last point, it seems that a rigorous medical examination of the North Africans would reassure the local population.*

In February 1918, the Bourges metal workers union sent a letter of protest to the Munitions Ministry complaining about the prospect of a future France peopled by foreigners, including what they termed promiscuous peoples of manifestly inferior levels of civilisation.

Reports by various government officials indicate that such sentiments were shared widely by French workers. Many believed that colonial and Chinese workers were used as strikebreakers, and that their introduction made it possible for the government to send more Frenchmen to the front. For example, in June 1917, a colonial worker, Chaouch Ali, was sweeping the Boulevard Saint-Michel in Paris when he was surrounded by French civilians who accused him of performing women's work and of being a shirker. At times, the expression of these feelings went beyond hostile words and gestures, resulting in violent attacks on workers of colour. There were several cases of non-white workers who left their camps to visit local villages and towns at night being beaten up, often by gangs of youths or French soldiers on leave.

Such individual incidents sometimes escalated into full-scale collective violence. One finds indications of numerous scattered race riots from 1916 to the end of the war, but the greatest concentration seems to have taken place during the spring and summer of 1917. During this period, war weariness among the French population suddenly surfaced in dramatic fashion, with mutinies in the French army and massive strikes in war industries. There were frequent rumours in the spring that colonial soldiers had fired upon striking French workers. Moreover, although strikers made little or no effort to appeal to or include non-whites, many resented their continuing to work.

Rioting took place in Saint-Medard after a strike at the major gunpowder factory there had been broken by the use of Indochinese labour. On June 19, 1917, a quarrel erupted in a Dijon cafe between a French soldier and a Moroccan worker over the latter's mandolin playing; a fight developed, leading French workers to join the fray and attack any Moroccans they could find in the streets of the city, wounding several. By that evening, a crowd of 500–1,500 had surrounded the camp where the Moroccans lived, wildly threatening to tear down its walls and massacre all its inhabitants. Letters from colonial workers during this period are full of allusions to tension and violent conflicts with the French. These tensions relaxed somewhat after October, but racial incidents did not completely disappear.

Economic competition was not the only factor in such conflicts; there was also an important undercurrent of sexual hostility. Both French officials and the French population as a whole reacted strongly to the possibility of sexual relations between non-white workers and French women. Postal censors kept a close look-out for letters from colonial workers mentioning sexual exploits and/or projected engagements to French women, as well as pornographic postcards; their monthly reports often included specific sections devoted to these issues alone. These and other displays of interest in local women could bring disciplinary action. One Indochinese worker at the Saint-Medard gunpowder factory found himself condemned to eight days in prison for the "crime" of "having, by gestures, failed to show respect for a young girl." Complaints about the colonials and Chinese by French workers often alleged promiscuity and the "danger" posed to local women. An incident related by a Madagascan in Toulouse at the beginning of 1918 shows that non-white workers were well aware of such rivalries.

> Emmanuel Rasafimanjary relates how, upon being stopped by a soldier and two civilians who called him a "sale nègre" [dirty black] while he was enjoying a peaceful stroll in the company of two women friends, he and a comrade boxed the ears of the Europeans, setting them to flight. He adds that such incidents occur frequently, the French being very jealous of the favours shown to Madagascans by women.

Regimentation tended to promote French working-class racism against colonial and Chinese labour. By keeping the wages of the latter especially low, it reinforced French fears about the impact of these new workers on their own incomes. These fears were not without grounds; some French officials wanted to use colonial labour precisely to prevent wage increases. In asking for 100 colonial workers in March 1918, an administrator of the port of Bordeaux noted that "this native labour will help to regulate the price of civilian labour, and act as a brake upon the underhanded but continual agitation of the dockers, who are always trying to impose their will by using the threat of strikes."

Racism occupied a central position in French attitudes towards colonial and Chinese workers during the first world war, in contrast to attitudes towards European immigrants. . . . [I]t seems that the wartime experience remoulded traditional French xenophobia into racism and directed it almost exclusively against non-white workers. In this instance, economic rivalries and cultural prejudices combined to entrench the colour line as a salient division of working-class life.

The French experiment with the use of non-white labour came to a screeching halt with the end of the war. After the Armistice, North Africans, in particular, were rounded up in police raids in Paris and Marseille and quickly repatriated. By 1921, only about 25,000 colonial and Chinese workers remained in France, often illegally. During the inter-war years, many North Africans continued to work in France, but usually as seasonal labour and only in the worst jobs, when white workers could not be found. Asian immigration was almost entirely terminated. In contrast, both individual French employers and the state recruited Europeans heavily, bringing to France large populations of Polish and Italian immigrants in the 1920s. While France's foreign population was larger than ever in the inter-war years, public and private authorities successfully purged it of the most "troublesome" elements and restored a semblance of European homogeneity.

The conclusion of France's wartime use of foreign labour reinforces the observation that it was fundamentally shaped by distinctions based upon race and colour, and underlines the need to take both race and class into account in any analysis of the condition of immigrant workers. The racism that confronted colonial and Chinese workers suggests that something more than xenophobia was at work and contradicts the myth that France was ever a colour-blind nation.

Doris Reiprich and Erika Ngambi ul Kuo

An Afro-German Family

[Sisters Doris Reiprich and Erika Ngambi ul Kuo were the daughters of a Cameroonian father and a Prussian mother, and grew up in the city of Danzig, today Gdansk.]

DORIS: We had a sheltered childhood and never felt we were different. When children called us "Negro" or "Negerbabbi," that didn't annoy me. I simply called them something back: one boy named Gabriel, I called "Archangel Gabriel"; one with a round head, "balloonhead"; the boy named Gabriel ran after me, caught me at my front door, and beat the stuffing out of me. I didn't bother him again.

I still remember, once, my blond girlfriend and I—we were around five years old—compared our hands and were amazed that mine were so brown and hers so light. We couldn't explain it. The grown-ups didn't say anything about it either, for them it was obvious. Yes, we grew up just like other children.

At school we were given very preferential treatment. When the school doctor came to our class, we were supposed to undress. I wouldn't, so the teacher picked me up, put a piece of chocolate in my mouth, and carried me up and down the room because I cried so much. I can still see her white lace handkerchief turning all brown from wiping my mouth. I got a kick out of that.

ERIKA: Our mother was aware that boys and men were always after colored girls, just to try them out. That's why she always told us: "Don't let them fool you; you're just like white girls! They think you're something special, and when they've had their fun with you—boom. Watch out!" I went unkissed for a long time out of absolute fear.

DORIS: Me, too [laughing]. My friends and I still believed in the stork at thirteen or fourteen, and wondered where babies came from.

ERIKA: Our father was well liked and well known in Danzig, and so were we.

Reprinted from May Opitz, et al., eds., *Showing Our Colors: Afro-German Women Speak Out* (Amherst: University of Massachusetts Press, 1991). English translation copyright © 1992 by the University of Massachusetts Press.

DORIS: There weren't any other Africans besides us. Once in a while a freighter would come through or a circus with a colored person. My father would bring them all home, and Mother would have to cook a huge pot of rice and stew. We used to love that, especially that babble of voices when they talked to each other in their African languages.

ERIKA: Father came to Hamburg in 1891 as a twenty-year-old with two other Cameroonians, on the Wohrmann Line [a German freight and cruise ship company]. The three of them came from prominent families in Cameroon and, at the suggestion of Kaiser Wilhelm II, were supposed to be educated here.

DORIS: Father was to study medicine, but fainted at the first dissection of a corpse. Then a shoemaker offered to train him. But he put Father in the shop window to have him work. A black man was a sensation at that time; everyone would run and press his nose up against the window. Father never went back there again and became a merchant.

He got married, and in 1895 his first daughter was born; she's twenty years older than we. In 1896 Father purchased German citizenship for fifty gold marks. And when Danzig became a Free State in 1918, his citizenship was changed over to the Free State. Father was loyal to the kaiser and more German than many native-born Germans.

Our mother met Father at the home of mutual friends in Danzig. He was divorced, and in 1914 they got married. Mother's family had quite varied reactions: it didn't make any difference to her brother; he was very nice and later spoiled us children. Her sister took it all right at first, but during the Nazi period she would say: "It's fine for you to come, but I don't want to see your husband and your kids in my home." Of course Mother didn't go there anymore.

Our grandmother lived in a tiny village in East Prussia and was absolutely mortified over her daughter's marriage plans. She didn't come to the wedding either. She had never seen a black person in her life, not even from a distance. After Erika was born, mother sent her mother a picture, in which Erika was posing the way babies do in such photos—her little slip unbuttoned on one side, legs drawn up, she holding one toe bent way back. Grandmother showed up immediately, scared to death that the baby was crippled with a deformed leg. With Father she was very distant at first, but she stayed with us until she died and became bosom buddies with her black son-in-law.

Father was a good family man. He used to romp and play with us. To his way of thinking we were to go first to boarding school and then get married. But we had our own ideas: I wanted to be a fashion designer, because I had a talent for drawing. . . .

ERIKA: . . . and I wanted to be a pediatrician. . . .

ERIKA: In the fall of 1932 Father was summoned to our school — a private high school for girls — and was asked to take us out of the school. Father was so shocked that he complied immediately. I was almost finished at the time. In looking for a training position afterward, I heard at every turn: "What, you want to work for us? We only hire 'Aryans.' " One good friend who I had been close to from the first day of school dropped me like a hot potato. Later, in Berlin people spat on us in the street and taunted us with "bastard," and "mulatto." It was awful.

Finally, I found a job that I really liked, in a Danzig art shop. However, after four weeks I had to leave, because business associates had threatened my boss that they would stop doing business with him if he kept me on. He was very satisfied with me, and he was really sorry.

Actually, it had already started in 1927–1928 . . .

DORIS: But not for us; for the Jews. Two neighborhood boys were already going around in SA uniforms, chasing Jews off the streets and pulling their beards. There were a lot of Jews living in our neighborhood, from Galicia and elsewhere. A lot of them wore pajes [characteristic hair locks worn by devout Jewish men].

Our mother became terribly upset over this and asked the boys' mother if she couldn't train her boys better. But it got worse and worse; for us the troubles really started in 1932. All of a sudden many folks — particularly recent arrivals from the so-called Reich — saw that we were different. As Erika mentioned, they started instigating dissent, thereby hindering Father in his work as a salesman. Merchants were urged not to order from him anymore.

A little while later we received an eviction notice for our five-room apartment. We probably would not have been able to afford the rent any longer anyway, because Father's business had gone broke by then.

ERIKA: After that Father worked for a Jewish firm that had been dispossessed. An SS man took over the business in trust and was decent enough to pay our father the weekly commission for re-orders from some of his old customers. That's something he didn't have to do. Besides that, our mother carted a lot of good stuff to the pawnshop. That's how we lived.

DORIS: Times were getting hard. Mother had to look for a new apartment, because as a Black man Father wouldn't have gotten one. We moved into a shabby three-room flat at the edge of town, and even one of those rooms we rented out. I was signed up at a middle school, where I was well received in the beginning. Some teachers remained neutral and friendly, but others made life very hard for me from 1933 on.

Often when I came home from school my mother would notice right away that something was wrong: "What's happened?" And then I would cry, she would cry, we'd hold each other tight. "Oh, people are so crude, to do that to a fourteen-year-old child!"

I had to take part in the course on "Race" and had to listen to statements like "God made all whites and Blacks, half-breeds come from the Devil" or: "Half-breeds can only inherit the bad characteristics of both races."

The teacher made me go with them to the exhibit "Race and Folk." When my mother wrote asking that I be excused from classes like that, the answer came that this was a schoolday like any other and it was the same for all schools. At the exhibit they showed, among other things, retouched photos of colored people in Munich whom I knew, with filed down teeth and weird facial expressions.

They also made me go along on a trip to see a ship, even though I didn't want to. After the trolley ride we had to march behind the flag; of course, I walked with my head down. We had barely gotten there when the teacher called me over, stuck carfare in my hand, and said that I had to go home. "As a non-Aryan you can't march with us behind the flag!"

. . . Mother also suffered a lot back then; the authorities even asked her to get a divorce. Most of our friends and neighbors suddenly didn't know us anymore. I don't know how they could bring themselves to just drop us like that. It was really terrible for me when I ran into my best girlfriend, with whom I used to do everything—answer marriage ads and I don't know what other silly things—and she suddenly got red in the face, turned, and walked away. I ran after her asking, "Why, what's wrong?" But she didn't know me anymore. Once when I dropped off some photography work at the shop where she was working, she had to wait on me. She acted as though she had never seen me before in her life.

I was also kicked out of the German Gymnastics League. At some point I received a note from the team leader—a pretty nice fellow, actually—saying that I wouldn't be allowed to come anymore. I was put out of Girls' Bible Circle, too.

In 1936 I finished middle school. From 1936 to 1939 I tried to find work. It was simply impossible. On the basis of my applications I did get a lot of replies, but as soon as I presented myself, it was: "No." I started working in a little one-horse town as a nanny, just to have something to do and so that there would be one less mouth to feed at home. After three days I had to leave because the mayor had seen me. I enrolled in a typing course at the *Arbeitsfront* ("work front"). Once there, I was asked in writing not to show up anymore—although they had allowed me to pay for the course. At home I learned to type on our old typewriter, practiced shorthand I knew from school, and my sister drilled me thoroughly. . . .

The "Adolf period" was the worst that anyone can imagine. You can't just suddenly label people as having a "life not worth living." They couldn't really liquidate us, but neither did they want to tolerate us. . . .

ERIKA: In 1938 I married a countryman of Father's in Danzig and moved with him to Berlin. My husband was a wrestler on tour at the time, and I met him when he was visiting in Danzig. . . .

DORIS: In 1939, just at the beginning of the war, Danzig became German, in keeping with the motto: "Home to the Empire." Accordingly, we had to surrender our Free State passports. . . .

ERIKA: My husband was stripped of his German citizenship then. Since Cameroon was still a French colony, he turned to the French consulate and got French citizenship with no trouble. Thus I became a French citizen through marriage. We had to check in with the police every week.

In Berlin we had to put up with a lot. During my pregnancy I had to hear: "Our führer places no value in that kind of children." When our daughter was four years old, I registered her in nursery school, since I was working during the day. After a week I couldn't take her there anymore, because they argued they couldn't subject the other children to having to play with a "nigger child.". . .

Father was very well liked in Danzig and was an honorary member of the Citizens' Army. Even today the old Danzigers still speak of him with the highest respect. This also no doubt worked in his favor when the *Gauleiter* came to visit. In order to get to our house near the old town hall he had to pass through two SS barriers. Father, a tall, imposing person, went up to them and said: "Excuse me, please, gentlemen." The SS immediately let him through, and then again on the other side, too.

Mother and I had been watching the whole time from behind the curtains; our neighbor came running over, white as a sheet: "For God's sake, what's going to happen now?"

Later we were told that the *Gauleiter* had asked what was going on and was told: "Oh, that's an old African from our colony. We all know him." That was all.

Father was sixty-seven when our passports were taken away. He was determined to get out of Germany and go back to Cameroon. Everything seemed to be in order; he was examined and declared "fit for use in the tropics." He just had to go to the colonial office one more time; there they informed him: "You may go if you'll make propaganda for us." His answer was, we were told later: "But, gentlemen, how can you suggest such a thing? I can't promote a country that despises my color."

What happened then, I don't know. Anyhow, after he left the office, he had a heart attack on the street. That was in May, 1943.

He never recovered; but we got a lot of assistance from people. Someone brought two eggs, someone else, a piece of bacon or whatever they could spare. Everyone thought that Father had fainted from hunger. The word had gone around that we were getting Polish ration cards, which had practically nothing on them. Trolley cars and other such facilities were also forbidden to dogs, Jews, and Poles.

When Father died in June 1943, the gravediggers took off their hats in dismay, mumbling "the old gentleman." The funeral procession was endless, despite the Nazis.

Veiled women taking part in an anti-British demonstration in Cairo in 1919. The anticolonial struggle involved women and men, and encouraged the development of feminism as well as nationalism. (UPI/Corbis-Bettmann)

V Anticolonial Resistance

Anticolonial resistance among the colonized was an ongoing fact of empire. An earlier generation of scholarship focused on the most spectacular revolts against foreign rule and the early organized manifestations of political nationalism. The new interest in culture and colonialism has now shifted attention to the less visible but more prevalent practices of resistance, and the politics of cultural survival among a complex variety of groups, from peasants and ex-slaves, to traditional notables and educated elites. These scholars have also redefined what we mean by resistance and uncovered new sites of colonial contestation. Regardless of the status or tactics of the colonized groups, their challenges to European authority decisively shaped the colonial encounter. Blinded by their own prejudices and anxious to keep costs down through the use of local intermediaries, the colonizers were often manipulated or stymied by the populations they sought to coerce and transform.

The majority of the peoples colonized, James Scott reminds us, were peasants. Although peasants under colonialism have not typically been seen as rebellious or politically active, like all relatively powerless groups, they had "weapons of the weak" that could be and were mobilized against the colonizer. European rulers demanded labor, food, taxes, cash crops, and rents from the rural masses; the latter responded less with open confrontation than with evasive measures. These tactics were not designed to end colonial rule per se, but rather to work the colonial system to the peasants' minimal disadvantage.

Frederick Cooper also takes up the question of peasant resistance, this time among former slaves in colonial Kenya in the early twentieth century. Europeans sought to abolish slavery as part of their civilizing mission. But what labor form did they think should replace it? Officials expected ex-slaves to voluntarily go to work on European-owned plantations, for a fixed time period, with set wages and work conditions carefully regulated by the employer. However, ex-slaves refused, preferring to work on more informal terms for indigenous landowners. At issue, Cooper argues, were two different concepts of time and work discipline. In this instance, the African concept triumphed.

Julia Clancy-Smith maintains that the behavior of male and female religious notables provides another neglected locus of cultural anticolonial resistance. She focuses on a network of Muslim lodges—centers of learning, pilgrimage, and social welfare for the surrounding communities—that dotted the desert margins of French Algeria and Tunisia in the nineteenth century. These Islamic elites neither revolted against nor accommodated colonial rule; rather, they adopted a more nuanced strategy that ranged from risk avoidance to collaboration. Their principal objective was to keep their lodges—and thus their peoples' cultural patrimony—intact. In the complicated world of French gender and Orientalist stereotypes, Clancy-Smith shows that even an exceptional female saint could wield the anticolonial politics of cultural survival successfully.

The most studied aspect of resistance has been the emergence of nationalist political parties, particularly among the "new native elite" educated by the colonial state. The need for local collaborators as well as European civilizing ideals led missionaries and governments to send a minority of their subjects to school. Benedict Anderson argues that, once fluent in the language of the colonizer, it was only a matter of time before this generation in the Dutch East Indies began to ask why Dutch men and women who were free at home were suppressing political liberty overseas. From here it was but a short step for them to organize politically for a sovereign nation state of their own, "Indonesia," and to embark on an anticolonial war of national liberation.

For Anderson, all nations are "imagined communities;" Europeans imagined their modern nation-states first, and colonial elites educated by Europeans then imitated them by organizing politically for national independence. Partha Chatterjee who, like Clancy-Smith, focuses on cultural forms of resistance to the colonial state, agrees that the educated elite in Bengal, India, pioneered a new nationalism that challenged Western rule. However, Chatterjee believes that Anderson is wrong in assuming that anticolonial nationalists in India imagined their new nations in political terms borrowed from the West. Rather, they produced their own sovereign cultural domain within colonial society well before beginning their political battle with the imperial power. This domain was the spiritual sphere, represented by religion, caste, women, and the family.

These five essays, while barely scratching the surface of the literature on indigenous responses to colonialism, raise a number of important issues encountered elsewhere in this volume. Resistance of some kind is presumably a universal response to oppression, but there is no single universal form this resistance will take. Successful resistance of any kind presupposes that the system of rule was not as powerful, paradoxically, as those wielding authority liked to suggest. Last but not least, empire was as much a war of cultures as it was a system of economic exploitation and political conquest. Indeed, given the technological superiority of Europe, cultural weapons were perhaps the most powerful ones available to the colonized, regardless of class or gender.

James C. Scott

Peasant Weapons of the Weak

The Unwritten History of Resistance

The idea for this study, its concerns and its methods, originated in a growing dissatisfaction with much recent work—my own as well as that of others—on the subject of peasant rebellions and revolution. It is only too apparent that the inordinate attention accorded to large-scale peasant insurrection was, in North America at least, stimulated by the Vietnam war and something of a left-wing academic romance with wars of national liberation. In this case interest and source material were mutually reinforcing. For the historical and archival records were richest at precisely those moments when the peasantry came to pose a threat to the state and to the existing international order. At other times, which is to say most of the time, the peasantry appeared in the historical record not so much as historical actors but as more or less anonymous contributors to statistics on conscription, taxes, labor migration, land holdings, and crop production.

The fact is that, for all their importance when they do occur, peasant rebellions, let alone peasant "revolutions," are few and far between. Not only are the circumstances that favor large scale peasant uprisings comparatively rare, but when they do appear the revolts that develop are nearly always crushed unceremoniously. To be sure, even a failed revolt may achieve something: a few concessions from the state or landlords, a brief respite from new and painful relations of production and, not least, a memory of resistance and courage that may lie in wait for the future. Such gains, however, are uncertain, while the carnage, the repression, and the demoralization of defeat are all too certain and real. It is worth recalling as well that even at those extraordinary historical moments when a peasant-backed revolution actually succeeds in taking power, the results are, at the very best, a mixed blessing for the peasantry. Whatever else the revolution may achieve, it almost always creates a more coercive and hegemonic state apparatus—one that is often able to batten itself on the rural population like no other before it. All too frequently the peasantry finds itself in the ironic position of having helped to power a ruling group whose plans for industrialization, taxation, and collectivization are very much at odds with the goals for which peasants had imagined they were fighting.

For all these reasons it occurred to me that the emphasis on peasant rebellion was misplaced. Instead, it seemed far more important to understand what we might call *everyday* forms of peasant resistance—the prosaic but constant struggle between the peasantry and those who seek to extract labor, food, taxes, rents, and interest from them. Most of the forms this struggle takes stop well short of collective outright defiance. Here I have in mind the ordinary weapons of relatively powerless groups: foot dragging, dissimulation, false compliance, pilfering, feigned ignorance, slander, arson, sabotage, and so forth. These Brechtian forms of class struggle have certain features in common. They require little or no coordination or planning; they often represent a form of individual self-help; and they typically avoid any direct symbolic confrontation with authority or with elite norms. To understand these commonplace forms of resistance is to understand what much of the peasantry does "between revolts" to defend its interests as best it can. . . .

. . . [E]vasion of taxes [has] classically curbed the ambition and reach of Third World states—whether precolonial, colonial, or independent. . . . Small wonder that a large share of the tax receipts of Third World states is collected in the form of levies on imports and exports; the pattern is in no small measure a tribute to the tax resistance capacities of their subjects. Even a casual reading of the literature on rural "development" yields a rich harvest of unpopular government schemes and programs nibbled to extinction by the passive resistance of the peasantry. The author of a rare account detailing how peasants— in this case in East Africa—have managed over several decades to undo or evade threatening state policy concludes in the following tone:

> In this situation, it is understandable if the development equation is often reduced to a zero-sum game. As this study has shown, the winners of those games are by no means always the rulers. The African peasant is hardly a hero in the light of current development thinking, but by using his deceptive skills he has often defeated the authorities.

On some occasions this resistance has become active, even violent. More often, however, it takes the form of passive noncompliance, subtle sabotage, evasion, and deception. The persistent efforts of the colonial government in Malaya to discourage the peasantry from growing and selling rubber that would compete with the plantation sector for land and markets is a case in point. Various restriction schemes and land use laws were tried from 1922 until 1928 and again in the 1930s with only modest results because of massive peasant resistance. The efforts of peasants in self-styled socialist states to prevent and then to mitigate or even undo unpopular forms of collective agriculture represent a striking example of the defensive techniques available to a beleaguered peasantry. Again the struggle is marked less by massive and defiant confrontations than by a quiet evasion that is equally massive and often far more effective.

The style of resistance in question is perhaps best described by contrasting, paired forms of resistance, each aimed more or less at the same objective. The first of each pair is "everyday" resistance, in our meaning of the term; the second represents the open defiance that dominates the study of peasant and working-class politics. In one sphere, for example, lies the quiet, piecemeal process by which peasant squatters have often encroached on plantation and state forest lands; in the other a public invasion of land that openly challenges property relations. In terms of actual occupation and use, the encroachments by squatting may accomplish more than an openly defiant land invasion, though the de jure distribution of property rights is never publicly challenged. Turning to another example, in one sphere lies a rash of military desertions that incapacitates an army and, in the other, an open mutiny aiming at eliminating or replacing officers. Desertions may, as we have noted, achieve something where mutiny may fail, precisely because it aims at self-help and withdrawal rather than institutional confrontation. And yet, the massive withdrawal of compliance is in a sense more radical in its implications for the army as an institution than the replacement of officers. As a final example, in one sphere lies the pilfering of public or private grain stores; in the other an open attack on markets or granaries aiming at an open redistribution of the food supply.

What everyday forms of resistance share with the more dramatic public confrontations is of course that they are intended to mitigate or deny claims made by superordinate classes or to advance claims vis-à-vis those superordinate classes. Such claims have ordinarily to do with the material nexus of class struggle—the appropriation of land, labor, taxes, rents, and so forth. Where everyday resistance most strikingly departs from other forms of resistance is in its implicit disavowal of public and symbolic goals. Where institutionalized politics is formal, overt, concerned with systematic, de jure change, everyday resistance is informal, often covert, and concerned largely with immediate, de facto gains.

It is reasonably clear that the success of de facto resistance is often directly proportional to the symbolic conformity with which it is masked. Open insubordination in almost any context will provoke a more rapid and ferocious response than an insubordination that may be as pervasive but never ventures to contest the formal definitions of hierarchy and power. For most subordinate classes, which, as a matter of sheer history, have had little prospect of improving their status, this form of resistance has been the only option. What may be accomplished *within* this symbolic straitjacket is nonetheless something of a testament to human persistence and inventiveness. . . .

Such techniques of resistance are well adapted to the particular characteristics of the peasantry. Being a diverse class of "low classness," scattered across the countryside, often lacking the discipline and leadership that would encourage opposition of a more organized sort, the peasantry is best suited to extended guerrilla-style campaigns of attrition that require little or no coordination. Their individual acts of foot dragging and evasion are often reinforced by a venerable popular culture of resistance. Seen in the light of a supportive subculture and the knowledge that the risk to any single resister is generally reduced to the extent that the whole community is involved, it becomes plausible to speak of a social movement. Curiously, however, this is a social movement with no formal organization, no formal leaders, no manifestoes, no dues, no name, and no banner. By virtue of their institutional invisibility, activities on anything less than a massive scale are, if they are noticed at all, rarely accorded any social significance.

Multiplied many thousandfold, such petty acts of resistance by peasants may in the end make an utter shambles of the policies dreamed up by their would-be superiors in the capital. The state may respond in a variety of ways. Policies may be recast in line with more realistic expectations. They may be retained but reinforced with positive incentives aimed at encouraging voluntary compliance. And, of course, the state may simply choose to employ more coercion. Whatever the response, we must not miss the fact that the action of the peasantry has thus changed or narrowed the policy options available to the state. It is in this fashion, and not through revolts, let alone legal political pressure, that the peasantry has classically made its political presence felt. Thus any history or theory of peasant politics that attempts to do justice to the peasantry as a historical actor must necessarily come to grips with what I have chosen to call *everyday forms of resistance*. For this reason alone it is important to both document and bring some conceptual order to this seeming welter of human activity.

Everyday forms of resistance make no headlines. Just as millions of anthozoan polyps create, willy-nilly, a coral reef, so do thousands upon thousands of individual acts of insubordination and evasion create a political or economic barrier reef of their own. There is rarely any dramatic confrontation, any moment that is particularly newsworthy. And whenever, to pursue the simile, the ship of state runs aground on such a reef, attention is typically directed to the shipwreck itself and not to the vast aggregation of petty acts that made it possible. It is only rarely that the perpetrators of these petty acts seek to call attention to themselves. Their safety lies in their anonymity. It is also extremely rarely that officials of the state wish to publicize the insubordination. To do so would be to admit that their policy is unpopular, and, above all, to expose the tenuousness of their authority in the countryside — neither of which the sovereign state finds in its interest. The nature of the acts themselves and the self-interested muteness of the antagonists thus conspire to create a kind of complicitous silence that all but expunges everyday forms of resistance from the historical record. . . .

If we were to confine our search for peasant resistance to formally organized activity, we would search largely in vain, for in Malaysia as in many other Third World countries, such organizations are either absent or the creations of officials and rural elites. We would simply miss much of what is happening. The history of Malay peasant resistance to the state, for example, has yet to be written. When, and if, it is written, however, it will not be a history in which open rebellion or formal organizations play a significant role. The account of resistance in the precolonial era would perhaps be dominated by flight and avoidance of corvée labor and a host of tolls and taxes. Resistance to colonial rule was marked far less by open confrontations than by willful and massive noncompliance with its most threatening aspects, for example, the persistent underreporting of land-holdings and crop yields to minimize taxes, the relentless disregard for all regulations designed to restrict smallholders' rubber planting and marketing, the unabated pioneer settlement of new land despite a host of laws forbidding it. Much of this continues today. There is ample evidence for this resistance in the archives, but, inasmuch as its goal was to evade the state and the legal order, not to attack them, it has received far less historical attention than the quite rare and small revolts that had far less impact on the course of colonial rule. Even in advanced capitalist nations, the "movements" of the poor take place largely outside the sphere of formal political activity. It follows that, if a persuasive case can be made for such forms of political activity among the poor in highly industrialized, urban economies with high rates of literacy and a relatively open political system, the case would be far stronger for the peasantry in agrarian economy where open political activity is sharply restricted. Formal political activity may be the norm for the elites, the intelligentsia, and the middle classes which, in the Third World as well as in the West, have a near monopoly of institutional skills and access. But it would be naive to expect that peasant resistance can or will normally take the same form.

Frederick Cooper

Wage Labor and Anticolonial Resistance in Colonial Kenya

Colonizing space was one question, colonizing time another. Britain, France, and the other colonizing powers sent their armies across the African continent at the end of the nineteenth century, concentrating

From Frederick Cooper, "Colonizing Time," *Colonialism and Culture*, ed. Nicholas Dirks. Copyright © 1995 by The University of Michigan Press. Used by permission.

forces sufficiently to subdue kingdoms and intimidate villages into acknowledging the sovereignty of a distant power. The content of that sovereignty, however, remained problematic. At the time of conquest, industrial capitalism in Europe had reached a stage of great complexity and considerable — if hardly unchallenged — self-confidence: Europeans thought they knew what kind of economic structures would lead to progress in the colonies as well as at home.

This article is about the effort of a colonial power to induce African workers to adapt to the work rhythms of industrial capitalism: to the idea that work should be steady and regular and carefully controlled. . . .

The significance of the question of time in the development of industrial capitalism was the focus of a now famous article by E. P. Thompson (1967). He argued that, at one time, European cultivators and peasants shared with people in parts of the world now described as undeveloped an attitude toward time and work discipline vastly different from that which came to dominate European society. It was not that people worked less or with less motivation, but that their notions of discipline were geared around the notion of "task time." When something had to be done, it was, and so effort varied seasonally and in other ways, while work rhythms were integrated into patterns of social life. The work rhythms of modern Europe — "clock time" — were not natural characteristics of a particular culture, but historical developments, consequences of the rise of wage labor and the imposition of discipline from above. The capitalist bought his laborer's time and insisted that he get his precise due. The notion of clock time was vigorously insinuated into daily life: from the highly visible clock to the factory bell to the commercialization of timepieces to the regular rhythms of school periods to the practice of clocking-in, as workers' arrivals and departures were coded onto a card. When workers started to demand extra payments for overtime it was a sign that they "had accepted the categories of their employers and learned to fight back within them. They had learned their lesson, that time is money, only too well." . . .

. . . [I]t is clear that the clash of different notions of time and work occurred in the context of colonization, particularly as certain colonial regimes tried to harness the labor power of the colonized. . . . Zulu workers in mid-nineteenth-century South Africa had an identifiable work culture, only it was not the work culture of the white conquerors and employers. The confrontation of alternative conceptions of work time, however, was read by white commentators as the laziness of the African.

I argue that the contestation over time was, in fact, a long one, its outcome hardly determined by the formal imposition of colonial rule; [and] that there were more than two alternative ways of organizing the working day and the working life and African workers explored, individually and collectively, a series of new forms. . . .

Time and work were contested before the advent of colonial conquerors and managers. A particularly important site of confrontation was the coast of what is now Kenya, part of a belt of fertile territory often no more than ten miles deep, with (in places) a range of hills followed by an arid region on one side, and the Indian Ocean on the other. Coastal society gazed toward the interior of Africa and out to sea. The regional language, Swahili, shared its basic structure with the largest language group in Africa, but included a substantial component of loanwords, mainly Arabic, in its vocabulary.

The seaborne commercial linkages of the coast provided the starting point for the large-scale development of export agriculture using slave labor during the nineteenth century. Arab immigrants and indigenous—Muslim, Swahili-speaking—inhabitants of coastal towns took advantage of new opportunities, buying slaves in a market that had expanded to serve export needs and selling cloves, grain, and dried coconut in an Indian Ocean-wide system of exchange. In coastal Kenya, large plantations, sometimes with hundreds of slaves, were founded by people from a variety of local and immigrant communal groups in the relatively open spaces around Malindi. In Mombasa, with a higher population, less room to expand, and a longer tradition of urban life, the expansion of agricultural production took place on a smaller and less intensive scale: aside from a small number of plantations, a few slaves supplemented the labor of their owners, or else a group of slaves was settled on a farm near the city, cultivating more or less on their own while their urban owner checked up on them occasionally and oversaw the harvest. . . .

Slavery's work week was five days: all sources agree that this was generally accepted. Slaves were given small plots on which they could build their own huts and grow their own food. Near Mombasa, owners' intervention in the agricultural labor process was often intermittent. Meanwhile, urban slaves frequently hired themselves out as port carriers, artisans, or caravan porters, paying about half of their wages to their owners. Turn-of-the-century land registers reveal that many slaves owned their own small huts: the urban master-slave relationship was not a question of the daily intimacy of power but largely a matter of cash payments. . . .

Informants of slave descent remembered that discipline on plantations was enforced with the *kiboko*, a whip made of hippopotamus hide; informants from formerly slaveholding communal groups generally claimed that planters were lenient and—in accordance with Islamic norms—benevolent, but do not deny that slaves were punished. Where coastal slaveholders differed from their Western Hemisphere counterparts was in the weakness of coercive capabilities beyond the plantation. Malindi—where work routines were the most demanding—had only a tiny garrison of mercenary soldiers under an official representing the Sultan of Zanzibar. . . .

As in all slave societies, the vulnerability of slaves followed from the fact that they had been alienated from the places and communities of birth (Patterson 1982). In coastal society, anyone without a place, however lowly, in a recognized communal group was in an anomalous and dangerous situation. The other side of this dependence was the efforts of slaves to counter it: escape took place frequently, but it had to have a collective element to it. Runaways created maroon villages in the hinterland behind the fertile coastal belt; others joined the entourages of potentates hostile to the Sultanate of Zanzibar; others, by the 1870s, fled to Christian missions, where they entered a new sort of community and a new sort of discipline. For slaves who did not escape, there is evidence that many resisted the cultural onslaught of their owners, keeping up the dances, the initiation rites, and other practices of their home societies, and maintaining—even sixty-five years after abolition—a form of self-identification that countered the idea that they could only be inferior members of coastal society: *Wanyasa*. This was a generic label, after the Lake Nyasa region from which the majority had been taken, and in its affirmation of a hinterland identification negated the dualities of slaveholder hegemony: Muslim-pagan, civilized-heathen, coast-interior. . . .

. . . The slave trade . . . provided the most vivid symbolism in European anti-slavery propaganda of the horrors associated with slavery.

David Livingstone's voyages in the 1860s in the Lake Nyasa region portrayed a large area where villages lived in constant fear of slave raiders, where people retreated in defensive isolation, and, hence, where the slave trade presented "an unsurmountable barrier to all moral and commercial progress." . . . The image of Africa as a slave-ridden continent, however exaggerated, entered European discourse as a marker of the contrast between Africa's tyranny and backwardness and Europe's capacity for benign progress. At the great conclaves in Berlin in 1884 and Brussels in 1889–1890 at which European powers agreed on the rules for competing for African territory, leaders declared themselves willing to make action against African slave trading a basic standard of morality in imperial endeavors. . . .

As conquest proceeded, emancipating slaves was thus an imperative, even as officials, learning more and more about the complexities of the societies they were taking over, came quickly to doubt their own capacity to abolish slavery while maintaining order and productivity. They realized that work discipline was embedded in a social system, and that tampering with any part of it posed risks. Even missionaries were concerned that if slaves were freed but not subjected to close control they "would tend to produce a demoralized and dangerous class of people, such as would be sure in the future to embarrass the good government and to mar the prosperity of the country." An official worried that "if a large number of slaves are liberated at one time, they are apt to break loose, loot shops and shambas [farms] and commit all sorts of excesses."

The Kenya government—having taken power in 1895 after a British chartered company had ineffectually administered the coastal zone since 1888—hesitated. A rebellion by one of the dissident coastal communal groups (with its entourage of clients, ex-slaves, and slaves) made officials even more uncertain that the colonial state was strong enough to superintend abolition. So it was not until 1907—ten years after slavery was abolished in the closely connected British colony on Zanzibar—that slavery was finally abolished. . . .

. . . By 1907, however, the slaves [in Kenya] had already gone a long way to free themselves. They took advantage of the British presence to undermine the subtle relations of dependency of a slave society. The end of the slave trade meant that the slave population could no longer be reproduced; the Pax Britannica meant that people could leave plantations without fear for their lives; railway construction and other colonial projects created alternative employment. The slow but steady exodus of slave labor meant a readjustment of labor conditions for those who stayed: slaves devoted more time (and space) to their own cultivation and less to the landowners' fields.

When abolition came to Kenya in 1907—allowing slaveholders to claim compensation for slaves whose services they lost—it in effect ratified the freedom slaves had already effectively claimed, while legitimating the efforts of landowners to get the slaves of other landowners to squat on their land. The reality of the situation (on both sides of 1907) was that a tied labor system was giving way to competition between landowners for increasingly mobile workers, and squatters paid only a modest rent or provided vaguely specified labor services. People who lived in the hinterland behind the more fertile coastal belt—belonging to nine distinct political and communal groups later collectively known as Mijikenda (nine villages)—began to join ex-slaves as squatters on coastal estates. Near Mombasa, both ex-slaves and Mijikenda established a symbiosis between urban and rural activities, seeking casual labor, mainly on the docks, which would provide cash for a day's work but which would not compromise participation in agriculture. . . .

The planters had lost their once effective control over labor. Land was another question. In 1905, as an official Land Committee sat, the coast promised to stand alongside the Highlands as one of the twin poles of a European-dominated economy. The committee—anxious to legitimate private ownership of land—did not wish to flout Islamic law as it did African systems of land tenure, yet it feared that confusion over titles would make productive investment too risky. As a result, the government set out to establish the *legal* structure for capitalist development: it called for the systematic survey and adjudication of all claims to land ownership in the coastal belt, and it insisted that all transactions be registered. . . .

Europeans did acquire substantial tracts of land by purchase from planters who could no longer plant or as concessions from the government, but members of the old landowning groups of Arab or local origin still retained title to the largest portion. The European plantation experiment, meanwhile, proved a fiasco. . . .

. . . European plantations were unable to recruit local labor, despite numerous attempts and considerable pressure from colonial officials. Coastal people would seek to become squatters or they would work for indigenous landowners, who made no demands about length of service. European planters insisted on a contract of at least several months duration, and commitment to full-time, carefully monitored labor for that length of time would have jeopardized what was most important: acquiring long-term, secure access to land, as squatters on the coast plain or as members of a communal group in the hinterland. For labor, the plantations had to look upcountry, where denser European settlement and a higher level of intimidation was pushing labor out. . . .

What collapsed on the old plantations was not so much agriculture as the British fantasy of agricultural wage labor. Regional exchange—between different parts of the coast and between Mombasa and the rural areas around it—became more intense, more varied, more ramified. Exports were more modest, but coconut products and grain continued to be sent forth. But the people who worked had gained at the expense of the people who owned. In most cases, landowners could only extract a modest rent and a share of the harvest of coconut trees on their plantations; they could not control the production process. Squatters grew and directly sold modest surpluses of grain. . . .

Officials periodically expressed displeasure at the squatters and never recognized the contribution they were making to the regional and export agriculture. They feared their presence would compromise the system of individual land tenure and discourage new purchasers of land, particularly Europeans. Even squatters who were reviving grain production on former plantation lands were accused by the governor of leading a "useless and degenerate existence." In the government blueprint, the coastal zone was for private ownership and wage labor agriculture; the Mijikenda migrants belonged in their hinterland homeland—now labeled a "reserve"—and should only come forth when they had a definite arrangement to work. A government attempt to evict squatters from a fertile region north of Malindi—as late as 1914—resulted in a major rebellion and a famine that officials were obliged to relieve. Shortly thereafter, squatters returned to the area where their huts had been burned and fields destroyed, and this time officials gave up: the renewed presence of squatters—welcomed by the hapless Arab landlords of the area—heralded a modest revival of grain exports. . . .

The colonial regime did not face the task of transforming a pristine "precolonial concept of time." The temporality of the labor process had already been transformed by the development of plantation slavery. Work rhythms—and the limits of discipline—were a question of power, and as slaveholders' power faded in the decade before formal abolition, the limits were redefined again. As the colonial regime sought to remake time in one direction, ex-slaves sought to remake it in another, and squatting, crop production, [and] short-term agricultural labor all became part of a complex testing of new limits and defining of new expectations among ex-slaves, ex-slaveholders, and colonial officials.

Julia Clancy-Smith

Saint or Rebel?
Resistance in French
North Africa

As the nineteenth century drew to a close, an Algerian female saint and sufi, residing in a small oasis on the Sahara's upper rim, composed a letter containing gentle rebukes to local French military officials: "I beg you to display solicitude and friendship by keeping away from me people who are unjust and disturb the peace and to examine attentively my case from the legal viewpoint since you are just and equitable." Why was an Algerian woman, Lalla Zaynab, reminding colonial authorities of their duties while simultaneously characterizing France's rule as "just" and "equitable"? Are Zaynab's words and the fact that she corresponded with Algeria's foreign masters to be interpreted as evidence of collaboration or of accommodation? Were her actions unusual or was Zaynab, a Muslim woman revered for her piety and erudition, merely acting as other religious notables did in the past century? And what do letters appealing to those ostensibly monopolizing certain kinds of power betray about the nature of relations between colonizer and colonized, about the cultures of colonialism?

The present study seeks to change the way we think about North African history during the turbulent nineteenth century. This perhaps immodest objective results from a decade of painstaking inquiry into the political behavior of a group of provincial, yet regionally powerful, Muslim notables and their clienteles. The complex responses of these notables, both individual and collective, to the imposition of the French colonial regime upon Algeria after 1830 shaped, indeed altered, the course of Maghribi history. That history and that century were fashioned by a succession of encounters between the peoples of North Africa on the one hand and the twin forces of European imperialism and the larger world economy on the other. In these multiple confrontations, inconclusive skirmishes, bet hedging, implicit pacts, and prudent retreats were as important to historical process as violent clashes or heroic last stands. . . .

What follows is an investigation of the political behavior of religious notables and other figures, or more accurately, of the implicit cultural norms governing that behavior. For just as there existed a moral economy of peasant rebellion, the political behavior of Muslim notables was dictated by shared and commonly accepted norms. In addition, it is argued that even as jihad was proclaimed or the millennium predicted, implicit pacts were being tentatively worked out between some religious notables and representatives of the colonial order. These unstated agreements were crucial to modern Algerian history since they permitted the survival of her cultural patrimony in a society literally and figuratively under siege.

Political action thus is broadly defined to include not only participation in jihads or mahdist movements but also such things as moral persuasion, propaganda, *hijra* (emigration), evasion, withdrawal, and accommodation with the colonial regime. Indeed, many of these strategies were continually merged—employed together or alternatively—as North Africans, whether of notable status or humble station, sought to create a space where the impact of asymmetrical power could be attenuated. In this most failed, a few succeeded, and some achieved success in failure. . . .

One thesis is that an underground yet momentous transformation unfolded quietly sometime during the tumultuous era of Algeria's conquest (1830–1871) and the century's close. This transformation involved the establishment of unstated, although compelling, pacts between prominent religious figures, such as Muhammad b. Abi al-Qasim (c. 1823–1897) and his daughter, Lalla Zaynab (c. 1850–1904), and colonial officials. The elaboration of these unwritten contracts and their observance by both parties meant that Algerian Muslim culture survived and in some cases was able to flourish modestly under the less than favorable circumstances of the period. . . .

. . . After mid-century, sufi leaders and saintly lineages in areas under direct, or even indirect, colonial rule wavered between various forms of submission, accommodation, evasion, and resistance; survival demanded such. While emigration in the pre-1881 era was one option, it carried both penalties and rewards. If those Algerians who migrated to Tunisia, Morocco, or the Levant enjoyed the moral-religious comfort of residing in Islamic states, they faced the social adversities that all immigrants perforce suffer. After the imposition of the French protectorate upon Tunisia in 1881, even those with the will or means to emigrate found physical evasion increasingly difficult as the frontiers between the Maghribi countries were more efficiently policed. . . .

The slow hemorrhaging of human resources, which migration represented, eroded Algeria's core of learned activists, great families, and religious notables. This imposed a heavier burden upon religious leaders electing to remain, for the sociospiritual services they provided were greatly oversubscribed. Nevertheless, the passing of the conquest era opened new avenues for some religious notables, including women, to engage in low-level political maneuvering to achieve limited cultural autonomy. For those who stayed in the colony, internal evasion or interior hijra represented a means of coping and therefore of endurance—*sauve-garde*, to use Jacques Berque's felicitous term. And while safeguarding and preserving North African society demanded a measure of *inkimash* (withdrawal, retreat), this did not mean political passivity or social lassitude, far from it. . . .

. . . Nothing proves this more than the biographies of the shaykh of al-Hamil and his daughter, Zaynab, whose lives span seventy-five years of Algeria's most turbulent history, from the twilight of Turkish rule to the eve of the nationalist movement.

Shaykh Muhammad b. Abi al-Qasim's (1823–1897) strategies for survival, and those of his successor, Lalla Zaynab (c. 1850–1904), . . . resulted from a pragmatic assessment of the prospects for certain kinds of social action, based upon a reading of how and why earlier stratagems had failed. In this sense, they forged a new path. In a war of cultures, cultural weapons—and not militant opposition—proved the most formidable defense. And one of the most intrepid warriors in this bloodless battle was a woman, precisely because the colonial edifice was conceived of as an imperial man's world. While the colonial order had evolved a formidable arsenal of methods for containing unsubmissive Algerian men, it had few, if any, to repress rebellious females. Indeed, contrary to what is frequently asserted—that colonized women lost power and status—it can be argued that the contradictions of the French regime offered opportunities, under certain conditions, for women to offer nonviolent resistance. Thus, Zaynab's confrontation with French authorities indicates that women could be political agents as well as social actors even in a system of dual patriarchy. "But it is principally her audacity that renders this woman remarkable," observed Zaynab's main opponent within French officialdom.

The Zawiya of al-Hamil: Upon a Great Rose-Brown Mountain

The oasis of al-Hamil is located some twelve kilometers to the southwest of the market town of Bu Sa´ada, which, for colonial strategists, represented little else than a military station used to defend the Tell. Aside from Bu Sa´ada's garrison, few French civilians resided permanently there since the lack of cultivable land and the indigenous system of land tenure excluded settler colonialism. If Bu Sa´ada was on the margins of the colonial state, al-Hamil was even more so; no Europeans inhabited the oasis, and foreign travelers through the region were infrequent before 1897. Thus al-Hamil offered the advantage of relative isolation, a space where Muslim society, then under cultural siege, could protect itself against the noxious effects of *Algérie Française*.

Those few Europeans who visited the Rahmaniyya *zawiya* [lodge] in al-Hamil before 1897 were inevitably surprised by its appearance. The village, constructed of dun-shaded mud brick, sat upon "a great rose-brown mountain" in the barren foothills of the Saharan Atlas. The square white minaret of the mosque adjacent to the *zawiya* formed the town's highest point. Not far away the *wadi* [riverbed], which funneled water to the date-palm groves below, snaked down the side of the mountain. The sufi center was of recent construction, having been founded only in 1863; like other desert *zawiya*, it resembled a fortress. By the close of the nineteenth century, thousands of pilgrims, scholars, students, and the needy flocked to the *zawiya* from all over Algeria and the Maghrib for it provided religious, cultural, and socioeconomic services not readily available elsewhere. Moreover, the life-giving waters of the *wadi* permitted agrarian development to feed the oasis's expanding population.

Al-Hamil's popularity as a pilgrimage site and educational center was due to the Rahmaniyya *zawiya*, which boasted a prestigious *madrasa* [religious school] and a fine library, whose rich manuscript collection represented a significant portion of North Africa's cultural patrimony. The Rahmaniyya complex was the work of Sidi Muhammad b. Abi al-Qasim, one of the most powerful saints, mystics, and scholars to emerge from the Rahmaniyya movement. Because of Shaykh Muhammad's piety, *baraka* [holiness], erudition, and unstinting generosity, the *zawiya* commanded a huge popular and elite following. Moreover, the oasis attracted not only the living but also those nearing the end of their days. The village's relatively small size was accentuated by the vast burial grounds encircling it. From far away, Muslim families came to bury their dead and fulfill the deceased's last wish. Al-Hamil's cemeteries betrayed its moral importance. And the desire to retreat in death to a space untainted by the humiliations of foreign conquest produced the mass of tombs, *qubbas* [domes], and simple graves, sheltering North Africans of all social ranks and ages.

By the late nineteenth century, Sidi Muhammad claimed the single largest number of Rahmaniyya sufi clients in Algeria, which made him a spiritual power to be reckoned with by colonial authorities ever mindful of the threat of revolt. His equally pious and saintly daughter, Lalla Zaynab, inherited her father's clientele and control of the *zawiya* but only after a determined struggle with military officials to assert her rights to spiritual succession. . . .

The Shaykh's Daughter: Lalla Zaynab

Nineteenth-century Algerian historiography appears as an imperial male preserve, peopled almost exclusively by men, whether French military heroes like General Bugeaud, celebrated in colonial hagiography, or Muslim resistance figures, such as Amir Abd al-Qadir, venerated as an early nationalist leader. One of the few exceptions was the "fille insoumise," the rebellious daughter of Muhammad b. Abi al-Qasim, although her story has remained untold until now.

In some ways, Zaynab is emblematic of the social situation of indigenous females in European settler-colonial societies of Africa or Asia. In addition to class or social ranking and gender distinctions, these societies were structured according to "racial" boundaries. For North Africans, the category of race was manipulated by eighteenth- and nineteenth-century European thinkers, writers, and colonial administrators to include cultural and ethnic attributes. By virtue of their Islamic religion and Arab-Semitic language, which had consequently "retarded" sociomoral development, most North Africans were deemed "racially inferior" to their colonial masters. Nevertheless, the Berbers were at times placed a bit higher on the "racial" scale than Arabic speakers. In *Les femmes arabes en Algérie*, Hubertine Auclert stated quite bluntly the prevailing colonial estimation of the North Africans: "In Algeria, only a small minority of Frenchmen would place the Arab race in the category of humanity." As for indigenous North African women, they were part of a social order that was doubly patriarchal—colonial, on the one hand, and indigenous, on the other.

Nevertheless, saintliness, sharifian descent, piety, and the miracles attributed to her by religious clients rendered Zaynab an extraordinary person, at least in the eyes of the Muslim faithful. Sainthood and special virtue placed her outside of the normal bounds defining female public behavior and sociolegal status in Muslim society. While colonial officials obviously did not subscribe to the same cultural norms, they were reluctant to take certain kinds of action against female religious notables, like Zaynab, out of fear of offending Muslim sensibilities and provoking unrest. Perhaps more than their male counterparts, some women were strategically situated to exploit the weaker points within the colonial system of control. . . .

Shaykh Muhammad centralized the management of the sufi center's numerous properties and complex affairs within his own hands. Nevertheless, he apparently kept Zaynab informed of financial and other operations, viewing her as a confidant. After a massive heart attack in 1877, Sidi Muhammad directed the *qadi* [judge] in Bu Saʿada to draw up a *hubus* [religious foundation] document specifying the terms of inheritance under Maliki law. In this document, the shaykh's substantial possessions—land, houses, gardens, library manuscripts, valuable household items—were constituted as a family hubus "in favor of his daughter Zaynab and other children of either the male or female sex." In a departure from the usual inheritance practices, Zaynab was singled out to receive a "portion equal to male" descendants, although no sons were ever born (or survived to adulthood). All other female descendants would inherit only the customary one-half of a male share of property. But the document was more than a legal blueprint for distributing material goods; it may have been an expression of the shaykh's desire that his daughter succeed him as head of the *zawiya*. Two decades later, Zaynab relied upon the 1877 *hubus* document as part of a campaign to advance her claims to spiritual succession over and against those of her male cousin. . . .

On June 2, 1897, Sidi Muhammad b. Abi al-Qasim suffered another heart attack while returning from a visit to the governor-general, Jules Cambon, in Algiers; he died among his religious clients. . . .

No sooner had the shaykh been laid to rest and the funerary ceremonials concluded, than Zaynab's cousin belligerently affirmed his right to al-Hamil's headship. Accompanied by a band of followers, Muhammad b. al-Hajj Muhammad went to the shaykh's residence and was immediately confronted by a resolute and hostile Zaynab, who refused to acknowledge his moral and spiritual authority. She forbade the students and *zawiya* personnel from obeying her cousin's orders, denied him entry to the center's library, books, and buildings, and imposed a sort of lockout by taking possession of the keys. . . .

The conflict soon widened. Zaynab sent letters to Rahmaniyya notables all over the region denouncing her cousin; she also contacted the nearby office of the *Affaires Indigènes* [Native Affairs], demanding redress of her grievances. Accusing Muhammad b. al-Hajj Muhammad of advancing spurious claims to the post of head shaykh, she also informed French authorities of her cousin's untoward comportment toward her, insisting that they curb his "injustice and thievery" and reminding them pointedly of her father's "devotion to France and to [the maintenance] of public order." In a war of words, Zaynab's arguments were a stroke of genius—her attack on French insistence upon her cousin as a fitting successor was based entirely upon the logic of keeping order. . . .

As far as can be ascertained from the available sources, the hesitation of some Muslim Algerians to endorse Zaynab's directorship did not necessarily revolve around the issue of gender and proper gender roles. The wellspring of legitimate succession was the matter of baraka and the worthiness of an individual to inherit the defunct shaykh's blessings and charisma. Moreover, within the Rahmaniyya *tariqa* [way], precedents existed for the assumption of spiritual authority by female saints, at least temporarily. It was rather local colonial officials who argued most vehemently against Lalla Zaynab in 1897 solely because she was of the weaker sex. For French officers, Zaynab's femininity meant ipso facto that she would be a pliable instrument in the hands of anti-French forces; her very nature made her incapable of effective administration. While Sidi Muhammad's political neutrality had kept colonial interference in the zawiya's spiritual affairs at bay, once Zaynab assumed control outside meddling escalated.

While massive French intervention was in large measure due to the prospect of a woman in charge, colonial authorities had been increasingly concerned about the zawiya's educational activities even before the shaykh's death. Astute officials perceived that Islamic education posed as much of a threat—perhaps more—to France's grand design for Algeria as did insurrection. Accordingly, decrees and laws regulating Muslim "private" schools were promulgated from the 1880s seeking to better supervise, and thus suppress, the taproot of North African culture and civilization—its religious schools. . . .

The rebellious daughter's unexpected behavior provoked a great deal of bitter frustration among local military officers. Dealing with a defiant Muslim woman was somewhat of a novelty for those long accustomed to breaking the will of obstreperous Muslim males. At one point, the officers of the *Affaires Indigènes* had indeed considered coercion to evict her from the *zawiya*—an index of their sense of impotence. Yet Zaynab was a saint and venerated mystic with her own popular following, which rendered the matter all the more delicate. . . .

Evaluations of Zaynab contained in official correspondence translate the helpless rage felt by those in command, whose very careers were endangered by female recalcitrance. Not surprisingly, Captain Crochard felt compelled to characterize her as the passive, foolish victim of sinister, female intrigues within the *zawiya*. According to his reports, she was exploited by anti-French malcontents, who perceived Zaynab's cousin as inimical to their own political interests: "Among her associates, there are no good men; she is surrounded by untrust-worthy people, capable of the worst excesses . . . they know well that she can be manipulated." Thus, her strength was interpreted as the product of inherent female weakness. In addition to revealing perva-sive French male attitudes toward female nature in general, such ex-planations also unveil something much more profound: the absence of colonial mechanisms for containing small-scale, nonviolent rebel-lions, particularly by Muslim women. . . .

. . . The captain also disclosed the true source of his resentment toward her, lamenting, "Lalla Zaynab's behavior has completely de-stroyed all that I have labored so hard to effect," that is, to arrange for a politically tranquil succession after Shaykh Muhammad's death. In late nineteenth-century Algeria, small defiant acts could be as men-acing to the political order as large, militant gestures: "This affair demonstrates that Zaynab is a dangerous woman whose intrigues and activities should be closely surveyed." She had trespassed into political territory theoretically prohibited to the colonized. . . .

. . . By the end of 1897, . . . [c]onvinced that she would never yield without recourse to force, the authorities in Algiers [were] or-dered to desist. Muhammad b. al-Hajj Muhammad was relegated to the sidelines for the next seven years, although his gracious female cousin gave him managerial functions at the *zawiya*. Zaynab had de-feated the combined forces of French officialdom and her cousin. More important, she had succeeded her father. . . .

Taken together, the stories of the shaykh and his daughter provide evidence for two historical processes whose significance has gone largely unrecognized: if resistance in the post-1871 era was mainly cultural and educational, it was no less deeply patriotic or politically subversive; and women as well as men, ordinary people as well as elites, were active agents in contests for power whose outcome assured the endurance of North Africa's cultural patrimony.

Benedict Anderson

Imagined Community in Anticolonial Nationalism

. . . I propose the following definition of the *nation:* it is an imagined political community—and imagined as both inherently limited and sovereign.

It is *imagined* because the members of even the smallest nation will never know most of their fellow-members, meet them, or even hear of them, yet in the minds of each lives the image of their communion. Renan referred to this imagining in his suavely back-handed way when he wrote that "Or l'essence d'une nation est que tous les individus aient beaucoup de choses en commun, et aussi que tous aient oublié bien des choses."[*] With a certain ferocity Gellner makes a comparable point when he rules that "Nationalism is not the awakening of nations to self-consciousness: it *invents* nations where they do not exist." The drawback to this formulation, however, is that Gellner is so anxious to show that nationalism masquerades under false pretences that he assimilates "invention" to "fabrication" and "falsity," rather than to "imagining" and "creation." In this way he implies that "true" communities exist which can be advantageously juxtaposed to nations. In fact, all communities larger than primordial villages of face-to-face contact (and perhaps even these) are imagined. Communities are to be distinguished, not by their falsity/genuineness, but by the style in which they are imagined. Javanese villagers have always known that they are connected to people they have never seen, but these ties were once imagined particularistically—as indefinitely stretchable nets of kinship and clientship. Until quite recently, the Javanese language had no word meaning the abstraction "society." We may today think of the French aristocracy of the *ancien régime* as a

[*]Yet the essence of a nation is that all individuals have many things in common, and also that everyone has forgotten plenty of things. (Editors' translation)

class; but surely it was imagined this way only very late. To the question "Who is the Comte de X?" the normal answer would have been, not "a member of the aristocracy," but "the lord of X," "the uncle of the Baronne de Y," or "a client of the Duc de Z."

The nation is imagined as *limited* because even the largest of them, encompassing perhaps a billion living human beings, has finite, if elastic, boundaries, beyond which lie other nations. No nation imagines itself coterminous with mankind. The most messianic nationalists do not dream of a day when all the members of the human race will join their nation in the way that it was possible, in certain epochs, for, say, Christians to dream of a wholly Christian planet.

It is imagined as *sovereign* because the concept was born in an age in which Enlightenment and Revolution were destroying the legitimacy of the divinely-ordained, hierarchical dynastic realm. Coming to maturity at a stage of human history when even the most devout adherents of any universal religion were inescapably confronted with the living *pluralism* of such religions, and the allomorphism between each faith's ontological claims and territorial stretch, nations dream of being free, and, if under God, directly so. The gage and emblem of this freedom is the sovereign state.

Finally, it is imagined as a *community*, because, regardless of the actual inequality and exploitation that may prevail in each, the nation is always conceived as a deep, horizontal comradeship. Ultimately it is this fraternity that makes it possible, over the past two centuries, for so many millions of people, not so much to kill, as willingly to die for such limited imaginings. . . .

We can summarize the conclusions to be drawn from the argument thus far by saying that the convergence of capitalism and print technology on the fatal diversity of human language created the possibility of a new form of imagined community, which in its basic morphology set the stage for the modern nation. The potential stretch of these communities was inherently limited, and, at the same time, bore none but the most fortuitous relationship to existing political boundaries (which were, on the whole, the highwater marks of dynastic expansionisms).

Yet it is obvious that while today almost all modern self-conceived nations—and also nation-states—have "national print-languages," many of them have these languages in common, and in others only a tiny fraction of the population "uses" the national language in conversation or on paper. The nation-states of Spanish America or those of the "Anglo-Saxon family" are conspicuous examples of the first outcome; many ex-colonial states, particularly in Africa, of the second. In other words, the concrete formation of contemporary nation-states is by no means isomorphic with the determinate reach of particular print-languages. To account for the discontinuity-in-connectedness between print-languages, national consciousness, and nation-states, it is necessary to turn to the large cluster of new political entities that sprang up in the Western hemisphere between 1776 and 1838, all of which self-conciously defined themselves as nations, and, with the interesting exception of Brazil, as (non-dynastic) republics. For not only were they historically the first such states to emerge on the world stage, and therefore inevitably provided the first real models of what such states should "look like," but their numbers and contemporary births offer fruitful ground for comparative enquiry. . . .

Old Languages, New Models

The close of the era of successful national liberation movements in the Americas coincided rather closely with the onset of the age of nationalism in Europe. If we consider the character of these newer nationalisms which, between 1820 and 1920, changed the face of the Old World, two striking features mark them off from their ancestors. First, in almost all of them "national print-languages" were of central ideological and political importance, whereas Spanish and English were never issues in the revolutionary Americas. Second, all were able to work from visible models provided by their distant, and after the convulsions of the French Revolution, not so distant, predecessors. The "nation" thus became something capable of being consciously aspired to from early on, rather than a slowly sharpening frame of vision. Indeed, as we shall see, the "nation" proved an invention on which it was impossible to secure a patent. It became available for pirating by widely different, and sometimes unexpected, hands. . . .

Hobsbawm observes that "The French Revolution was not made or led by a formed party or movement in the modern sense, nor by men attempting to carry out a systematic programme. It hardly even threw up 'leaders' of the kind to which twentieth century revolutions have accustomed us, until the post-revolutionary figure of Napoléon." But once it had occurred, it entered the accumulating memory of print. The overwhelming and bewildering concatenation of events experienced by its makers and its victims became a "thing"—and with its own name: The French Revolution. Like a vast shapeless rock worn to a rounded boulder by countless drops of water, the experience was shaped by millions of printed words into a "concept" on the printed page, and, in due course, into a model. Why "it" broke out, what "it" aimed for, why "it" succeeded or failed, became subjects for endless polemics on the part of friends and foes: but of its "it-ness," as it were, no one ever after had much doubt.

In much the same way, the independence movements, in the Americas became, as soon as they were printed about, "concepts," "models," and indeed "blueprints." . . . Out of the American welter came these imagined realities: nation-states, republican institutions, common citizenships, popular sovereignty, national flags and anthems, etc., and the liquidation of their conceptual opposites: dynastic empires, monarchical institutions, absolutisms, subjecthoods, inherited nobilities, serfdoms, ghettoes, and so forth. (Nothing more stunning, in this context, than the general "elision" of massive slavery from the "modal" USA of the nineteenth century, and of the shared language of the "modal" Southern republics.) Furthermore, the validity and generalizability of the blueprint were undoubtedly confirmed by the *plurality* of the independent states.

In effect, by the second decade of the nineteenth century, if not earlier, a "model" of "the" independent national state was available for pirating. (The first groups to do so were the marginalized vernacular-based coalitions of the educated. . . .) But precisely because it was by then a known model, it imposed certain "standards" from which too-marked deviations were impermissible. Even backward and reactionary Hungarian and Polish gentries were hard put to it not to make a show of "inviting in" (if only to the pantry) their oppressed compatriots. If you like, the logic of San Martín's Peruvianization was at work. If "Hungarians" deserved a national state, then that *meant* Hungarians, all of them; it meant a state in which the ultimate locus of sovereignty had to be the collectivity of Hungarian-speakers and readers; and, in due course, the liquidation of serfdom, the promotion of popular education, the expansion of the suffrage, and so on. Thus the "populist" character of the early European nationalisms, even when led, demagogically, by the most backward social groups, was deeper than in the Americas: serfdom *had* to go, legal slavery was unimaginable—not least because the conceptual model was set in ineradicable place. . . .

The Last Wave

The First World War brought the age of high dynasticism to an end. By 1922, Habsburgs, Hohenzollerns, Romanovs and Ottomans were gone. In place of the Congress of Berlin came the League of *Nations*, from which non-Europeans were not excluded. From this time on, the legitimate international norm was the nation-state, so that in the League even the surviving imperial powers came dressed in national costume rather than imperial uniform. After the cataclysm of World War II the nation-state tide reached full flood. By the mid-1970s even the Portuguese Empire had become a thing of the past.

The new states of the post-World War II period have their own character, which nonetheless is incomprehensible except in terms of the succession of models we have been considering. One way of underlining this ancestry is to remind ourselves that a very large number of these (mainly non-European) nations came to have European languages-of-state. If they resembled the "American" model in this respect, they took from linguistic European nationalism its ardent populism, and from official nationalism its Russifying policy-orientation. They did so because Americans and Europeans had lived through complex historical experiences which were now everywhere modularly imagined, and because the European languages-of-state they employed were the legacy of imperialist official nationalism. This is why so often in the "nation-building" policies of the new states one sees both a genuine, popular nationalist enthusiasm and a systematic, even Machiavellian, instilling of nationalist ideology through the mass media, the educational system, administrative regulations, and so forth. In turn, this blend of popular and official nationalism has been the product of anomalies created by European imperialism: the well-known arbitrariness of frontiers, and bilingual intelligentsias poised precariously over diverse monoglot populations. One can thus think of many of these nations as projects the achievement of which is still in progress. . . .

It is generally recognized that the intelligentsias were central to the rise of nationalism in the colonial territories, not least because colonialism ensured that native agrarian magnates, big merchants, industrial entrepreneurs, and even a large professional class were relative rarities. Almost everywhere economic power was either monopolized by the colonialists themselves, or unevenly shared with a politically impotent class of pariah (non-native) businessmen — Lebanese, Indian and Arab in colonial Africa, Chinese, Indian, and Arab in colonial Asia. It is no less generally recognized that the intelligentsias' vanguard role derived from their bilingual literacy, or rather literacy and bilingualism. Print-literacy already made possible the imagined community floating in homogeneous, empty time. . . . Bilingualism meant access, through the European language-of-state, to modern Western culture in the broadest sense, and, in particular, to the models of nationalism, nation-ness, and nation-state produced elsewhere in the course of the nineteenth century.

In 1913, the Dutch colonial regime in Batavia, taking its lead from the Hague, sponsored massive colony-wide festivities to celebrate the centennial of the "national liberation" of the Netherlands from French imperialism. Orders went out to secure physical participation and financial contributions, not merely from the local Dutch and Eurasian communities, but also from the subject native population. In protest, the early Javanese-Indonesian nationalist Suwardi Surjaningrat (Ki Hadjar Dewantoro) wrote his famous Dutch-language newspaper article "Als ik eens Nederlander was" (If I were for once to be a Dutchman).

> *In my opinion, there is something out of place — something indecent — if we (I still being a Dutchman in my imagination) ask the natives to join the festivities which celebrate our independence. Firstly, we will hurt their sensitive feelings because we are here celebrating our own independence in their native country which we colonize. At the moment we are very happy because a hundred years ago we liberated ourselves from foreign domination; and all of this is occurring in front of the eyes of those who are still under our domination. Does it not occur to us that these poor slaves are also longing for such a moment as this, when they like us will be able to celebrate their independence? Or do we perhaps feel that because of our soul-destroying policy we regard all human souls as dead? If that is so, then we are deluding ourselves, because no matter how primitive a community is, it is against any type of oppression. If I were a Dutchman, I would not organize an independence cel-*

ebration in a country where the independence of the people has been stolen.

With these words Suwardi was able to turn Dutch history against the Dutch, by scraping boldly at the weld between Dutch nationalism and imperialism. Furthermore, by the imaginary transformation of himself into a temporary Dutchman (which invited a reciprocal transformation of his Dutch readers into temporary Indonesians), he undermined all the racist fatalities that underlay Dutch colonial ideology.

Suwardi's broadside—which delighted his Indonesian as much as it irritated his Dutch audience—is exemplary of a world-wide twentieth-century phenomenon. For the paradox of imperial official nationalism was that it inevitably brought what were increasingly thought of and written about as European "national histories" into the consciousnesses of the colonized—not merely via occasional obtuse festivities, but also through reading-rooms and classrooms. Vietnamese youngsters could not avoid learning about the *philosophes* and the Revolution, and what Debray calls "our secular antagonism to Germany." Magna Carta, the Mother of Parliaments, and the Glorious Revolution, glossed as English national history, entered schools all over the British Empire. Belgium's independence struggle against Holland was not erasable from schoolbooks Congolese children would one day read. So also the histories of the U.S.A. in the Philippines and, last of all, Portugal in Mozambique and Angola. . . .

. . . This in turn reminds us again of the unique role played by colonial school-systems in promoting colonial nationalisms.

The case of Indonesia affords a fascinatingly intricate illustration of this process, not least because of its enormous size, huge population (even in colonial times), geographical fragmentation (about 3,000 islands), religious variegation (Muslims, Buddhists, Catholics, assorted Protestants, Hindu-Balinese, and "animists"), and ethnolinguistic diversity (well over 100 distinct groups). Furthermore, as its hybrid pseudo-Hellenic name suggests, its stretch does not remotely correspond to any precolonial domain; on the contrary, at least until General Suharto's brutal invasion of ex-Portuguese East Timor in 1975, its boundaries have been those left behind by the last Dutch conquests (c. 1910).

Some of the peoples on the eastern coast of Sumatra are not only physically close, across the narrow Straits of Malacca, to the populations of the western littoral of the Malay Peninsula, but they are ethnically related, understand each other's speech, have a common religion, and so forth. These same Sumatrans share neither mother-tongue, ethnicity, nor religion with the Ambonese, located on islands thousands of miles away to the east. Yet during this century they have come to understand the Ambonese as fellow-Indonesians, the Malays as foreigners.

Nothing nurtured this bonding more than the schools that the regime in Batavia set up in increasing numbers after the turn of the century. To see why, one has to remember that in complete contrast to traditional, indigenous schools, which were always local and personal enterprises (even if, in good Muslim fashion, there was plenty of horizontal movement of students from one particularly well-reputed ulama-teacher to another), the government schools formed a colossal, highly rationalized, tightly centralized hierarchy, structurally analogous to the state bureaucracy itself. Uniform textbooks, standardized diplomas and teaching certificates, a strictly regulated gradation of age-groups, classes and instructional materials, in themselves created a self-contained, coherent universe of experience. But no less important was the hierarchy's geography. Standardized elementary schools came to be scattered about in villages and small townships of the colony; junior and senior middle-schools in larger towns and provincial centres; while tertiary education (the pyramid's apex) was confined to the colonial capital of Batavia and the Dutch-built city of Bandung, 100 miles southwest in the cool Priangan highlands.

Partha Chatterjee

The Nation and the Home

Nationalism has once more appeared on the agenda of world affairs. Almost every day, state leaders and political analysts in Western coun-

From *The Nation and Its Fragments: Colonial and Postcolonial Histories* by Partha Chatterjee. Copyright © 1993 by Princeton University Press. Excerpted by permission of Princeton University Press.

tries declare that with "the collapse of communism" (that is the term they use; what they mean is presumably the collapse of Soviet socialism), the principal danger to world peace is now posed by the resurgence of nationalism in different parts of the world. Since in this day and age a phenomenon has first to be recognized as a "problem" before it can claim the attention of people whose business it is to decide what should concern the public, nationalism seems to have regained sufficient notoriety for it to be liberated from the arcane practices of "area specialists" and been made once more a subject of general debate.

However, this very mode of its return to the agenda of world politics has, it seems to me, hopelessly prejudiced the discussion on the subject. In the 1950s and 1960s, nationalism was still regarded as a feature of the victorious anticolonial struggles in Asia and Africa. But simultaneously, as the new institutional practices of economy and polity in the postcolonial states were disciplined and normalized under the conceptual rubrics of "development" and "modernization," nationalism was already being relegated to the domain of the particular histories of this or that colonial empire. And in those specialized histories defined by the unprepossessing contents of colonial archives, the emancipatory aspects of nationalism were undermined by countless revelations of secret deals, manipulations, and the cynical pursuit of private interests. By the 1970s, nationalism had become a matter of ethnic politics, the reason why people in the Third World killed each other—sometimes in wars between regular armies, sometimes, more distressingly, in cruel and often protracted civil wars, and increasingly, it seemed, by technologically sophisticated and virtually unstoppable acts of terrorism. The leaders of the African struggles against colonialism and racism had spoiled their records by becoming heads of corrupt, fractious, and often brutal regimes; Gandhi had been appropriated by such marginal cults as pacifism and vegetarianism; and even Ho Chi Minh in his moment of glory was caught in the unyielding polarities of the Cold War. Nothing, it would seem, was left in the legacy of nationalism to make people in the Western world feel good about it.

This recent genealogy of the idea explains why nationalism is now viewed as a dark, elemental, unpredictable force of primordial nature threatening the orderly calm of civilized life. What had once been successfully relegated to the outer peripheries of the earth is now seen picking it way back toward Europe, through the long-forgotten provinces of the Habsburg, the czarist, and the Ottoman empires. Like drugs, terrorism, and illegal immigration, it is one more product of the Third World that the West dislikes but is powerless to prohibit.

In light of the current discussions on the subject in the media, it is surprising to recall that not many years ago nationalism was generally considered one of Europe's most magnificent gifts to the rest of the world. It is also not often remembered today that the two greatest wars of the twentieth century, engulfing as they did virtually every part of the globe, were brought about by Europe's failure to manage its own ethnic nationalisms. Whether of the "good" variety or the "bad," nationalism was entirely a product of the political history of Europe. Notwithstanding the celebration of the various unifying tendencies in Europe today and of the political consensus in the West as a whole, there may be in the recent amnesia on the origins of nationalism more than a hint of anxiety about whether it has quite been tamed in the land of its birth.

In all this time, the "area specialists," the historians of the colonial world, working their way cheerlessly through musty files of administrative reports and official correspondence in colonial archives in London or Paris or Amsterdam, had of course never forgotten how nationalism arrived in the colonies. Everyone agreed that it was a European import; the debates in the 1960s and 1970s in the historiographies of Africa or India or Indonesia were about what had become of the idea and who was responsible for it. These debates between a new generation of nationalist historians and those whom they dubbed "colonialists" were vigorous and often acrimonious, but they were largely confined to the specialized territories of "area studies"; no one else took much notice of them.

Ten years ago, it was one such area specialist who managed to raise once more the question of the origin and spread of nationalism in the framework of a universal history. Benedict Anderson demonstrated with much subtlety and originality that nations were not the determinate products of given sociological conditions such as language or race or religion; they had been, in Europe and everywhere else in the world, imagined into existence. He also described some of the major institutional forms through which this imagined community came to acquire concrete shape, especially the institutions of what he so ingeniously called "print-capitalism." He then argued that the historical experience of nationalism in Western Europe, in the Americas, and in Russia had supplied for all subsequent nationalisms a set of modular forms from which nationalist elites in Asia and Africa had chosen the ones they liked.

Anderson's book has been, I think, the most influential in the last few years in generating new theoretical ideas on nationalism, an influence that of course, it is needless to add, is confined almost exclusively to academic writings. Contrary to the largely uninformed exoticization of nationalism in the popular media in the West, the theoretical tendency represented by Anderson certainly attempts to treat the phenomenon as part of the universal history of the modern world.

I have one central objection to Anderson's argument. If nationalisms in the rest of the world have to choose their imagined community from certain "modular" forms already made available to them by Europe and the Americas, what do they have left to imagine? History, it would seem, has decreed that we in the postcolonial world shall only be perpetual consumers of modernity. Europe and the Americas, the only true subjects of history, have thought out on our behalf not only the script of colonial enlightenment and exploitation, but also that of our anticolonial resistance and postcolonial misery. Even our imaginations must remain forever colonized.

I object to this argument not for any sentimental reason. I object because I cannot reconcile it with the evidence on anticolonial nationalism. The most powerful as well as the most creative results of the nationalist imagination in Asia and Africa are posited not on an identity but rather on a *difference* with the "modular" forms of the national society propagated by the modern West. How can we ignore this without reducing the experience of anticolonial nationalism to a caricature of itself?

To be fair to Anderson, it must be said that he is not alone to blame. The difficulty, I am now convinced, arises because we have all taken the claims of nationalism to be a *political* movement much too literally and much too seriously.

In India, for instance, any standard nationalist history will tell us that nationalism proper began in 1885 with the formation of the Indian National Congress. It might also tell us that the decade preceding this was a period of preparation, when several provincial political associations were formed. Prior to that, from the 1820s to the 1870s, was the period of "social reform," when colonial enlightenment was beginning to "modernize" the customs and institutions of a traditional society and the political spirit was still very much that of collaboration with the colonial regime: nationalism had still not emerged.

This history, when submitted to a sophisticated sociological analysis, cannot but converge with Anderson's formulations. In fact, since it seeks to replicate in its own history the history of the modern state in Europe, nationalism's self-representation will inevitably corroborate Anderson's decoding of the nationalist myth. I think, however, that as history, nationalism's autobiography is fundamentally flawed.

By my reading, anticolonial nationalism creates its own domain of sovereignty within colonial society well before it begins its political battle with the imperial power. It does this by dividing the world of social institutions and practices into two domains—the material and the spiritual. The material is the domain of the "outside," of the economy and of statecraft, of science and technology, a domain where the West had proved its superiority and the East had succumbed. In this domain, then, Western superiority had to be acknowledged and its accomplishments carefully studied and replicated. The spiritual, on the other hand, is an "inner" domain bearing the "essential" marks of cultural identity. The greater one's success in imitating Western skills in the material domain, therefore, the greater the need to preserve the distinctness of one's spiritual culture. This formula is, I think, a fundamental feature of anticolonial nationalisms in Asia and Africa.

There are several implications. . . . [N]ationalism declares the domain of the spiritual its sovereign territory and refuses to allow the colonial power to intervene in that domain. . . .

. . . [B]ut it is not as though this so-called spiritual domain is left unchanged. In fact, here nationalism launches its most powerful, creative, and historically significant project: to fashion a "modern" national culture that is nevertheless not Western. If the nation is an imagined community, then this is where it is brought into being. In this, its true and essential domain, the nation is already sovereign, even when the state is in the hands of the colonial power. The dynamics of this historical project is completely missed in conventional histories in which the story of nationalism begins with the contest for political power.

. . . I wish to highlight here several areas within the so-called spiritual domain that nationalism transforms in the course of its journey. . . .

The first such area is that of language. . . . In Bengal, for instance, it is at the initiative of the East India Company and the European missionaries that the first printed books are produced in Bengali at the end of the eighteenth century and the first narrative prose compositions commissioned at the beginning of the nineteenth. At the same time, the first half of the nineteenth century is when English completely displaces Persian as the language of bureaucracy and emerges as the most powerful vehicle of intellectual influence on a new Bengali elite. The crucial moment in the development of the modern Bengali language comes, however, in midcentury, when this bilingual elite makes it a cultural project to provide its mother tongue with the necessary linguistic equipment to enable it to become an adequate language for "modern" culture. An entire institutional network of printing presses, publishing houses, newspapers, magazines, and literary societies is created around this time, *outside* the purview of the state and the European missionaries, through which the new language, modern and standardized, is given shape. The bilingual intelligentsia came to think of its own language as belonging to that inner domain of cultural identity, from which the colonial intruder had to be kept out; language therefore became a zone over which the nation first had to declare its sovereignty and then had to transform in order to make it adequate for the modern world. . . .

The desire to construct an aesthetic form that was modern and national, and yet recognizably different from the Western, was shown in perhaps its most exaggerated shape in the efforts in the early twentieth century of the so-called Bengal school of art. It was through these efforts that, on the one hand, an institutional space was created for the modern professional artist in India, as distinct from the traditional craftsman, for the dissemination through exhibition and print of the products of art and for the creation of a public schooled in the new aesthetic norms. Yet this agenda for the construction of a modernized artistic space was accompanied, on the other hand, by a fervent ideological program for an art that was distinctly "Indian," that is, different from the "Western." Although the specific style developed by the Bengal school for a new Indian art failed to hold its ground for very long, the fundamental agenda posed by its efforts continues to be pursued to this day, namely, to develop an art that would be modern and at the same time recognizably Indian.

Alongside the institutions of print-capitalism was created a new network of secondary schools. Once again, nationalism sought to bring this area under its jurisdiction long before the domain of the state had become a matter of contention. In Bengal, from the second half of the nineteenth century, it was the new elite that took the lead in mobilizing a "national" effort to start schools in every part of the province and then to produce a suitable educational literature. Coupled with print-capitalism, the institutions of secondary education provided the space where the new language and literature were both generalized and normalized—outside the domain of the state. It was only when this space was opened up, outside the influence of both the colonial state and the European missionaries, that it became legitimate for women, for instance, to be sent to school. It was also in this period, from around the turn of the century, that the University of Calcutta was turned from an institution of colonial education to a distinctly national institution, in its curriculum, its faculty, and its sources of funding.

Another area in that inner domain of national culture was the family. The assertion here of autonomy and difference was perhaps the most dramatic. The European criticism of Indian "tradition" as barbaric had focused to a large extent on religious beliefs and practices, especially those relating to the treatment of women. The early phase of "social reform" through the agency of the colonial power had also concentrated on the same issues. In that early phase, therefore, this area had been identified as essential to "Indian tradition." The nationalist move began by disputing the choice of agency. Unlike the early reformers, nationalists were not prepared to allow the colonial state to legislate the reform of "traditional" society. They asserted that only the nation itself could have the right to intervene in such an essential aspect of its cultural identity.

As it happened, the domain of the family and the position of women underwent considerable change in the world of the nationalist middle class. It was undoubtedly a new patriarchy that was brought into existence, different from the "traditional" order but also explicitly claiming to be different from the "Western" family. The "new woman" was to be modern, but she would also have to display the signs of national tradition and therefore would be essentially different from the "Western" woman.

The history of nationalism as a political movement tends to focus primarily on its contest with the colonial power in the domain of the outside, that is, the material domain of the state. This is a different history from the one I have outlined. It is also a history in which nationalism has no option but to choose its forms from the gallery of "models" offered by European and American nation-states: "difference" is not a viable criterion in the domain of the material.

In this outer domain, nationalism begins its journey (after, let us remember, it has already proclaimed its sovereignty in the inner domain) by inserting itself into a new public sphere constituted by the processes and forms of the modern (in this case, colonial) state. In the beginning, nationalism's task is to overcome the subordination of the colonized middle class, that is, to challenge the "rule of colonial difference" in the domain of the state. The colonial state, we must remember, was not just the agency that brought the modular forms of the modern state to the colonies; it was also an agency that was destined never to fulfill the normalizing mission of the modern state because the premise of its power was a rule of colonial difference, namely, the preservation of the alienness of the ruling group.

As the institutions of the modern state were elaborated in the colony, especially in the second half of the nineteenth century, the ruling European groups found it necessary to lay down—in lawmaking, in the bureaucracy, in the administration of justice, and in the recognition by the state of a legitimate domain of public opinion—the precise difference between the rulers and the ruled. If Indians had to be admitted into the judiciary, could they be allowed to try Europeans? Was it right that Indians should enter the civil service by taking the same examinations as British graduates? If European newspapers in India were given the right of free speech, could the same apply to native newspapers? Ironically, it became the historical task of nationalism, which insisted on its own marks of cultural difference with the West, to demand that there be no rule of difference in the domain of the state.

In time, with the growing strength of nationalist politics, this domain became more extensive and internally differentiated and finally took on the form of the national, that is, postcolonial, state. The dominant elements of its self-definition, at least in postcolonial India, were drawn from the ideology of the modern liberal-democratic state.

In accordance with liberal ideology, the public was now distinguished from the domain of the private. The state was required to protect the inviolability of the private self in relation to other private selves. The legitimacy of the state in carrying out this function was to be guaranteed by its indifference to concrete differences between private selves—differences, that is, of race, language, religion, class, caste, and so forth.

The trouble was that the moral-intellectual leadership of the nationalist elite operated in a field constituted by a very different set of distinctions—those between the spiritual and the material, the inner and the outer, the essential and the inessential. That contested field over which nationalism had proclaimed its sovereignty and where it had imagined its true community was neither coextensive with nor coincidental to the field constituted by the public/private distinction. In the former field, the hegemonic project of nationalism could hardly make the distinctions of language, religion, caste, or class a matter of indifference to itself. The project was that of cultural "normalization," like, as Anderson suggests, bourgeois hegemonic projects everywhere, but with the all-important difference that it had to choose its site of autonomy from a position of subordination to a colonial regime that had on its side the most universalist justificatory resources produced by post-Enlightenment social thought.

The result is that autonomous forms of imagination of the community were, and continue to be, overwhelmed and swamped by the history of the postcolonial state. Here lies the root of our postcolonial misery: not in our inability to think out new forms of the modern community but in our surrender to the old forms of the modern state. If the nation is an imagined community and if nations must also take the form of states, then our theoretical language must allow us to talk about community and state at the same time. I do not think our present theoretical language allows us to do this.

Suggestions for Further Reading

The bibliography of imperialism is vast, and therefore what follows is extremely selective.

For overviews of the background of modern imperialism consult:

C.A. Bayly, *Imperial Meridian: The British Empire and the World, 1780–1830* (London: Longman, 1989).

Robin Blackburn, *The Overthrow of Colonial Slavery, 1776–1848* (London: Verso, 1988).

Robin Blackburn, *The Making of New World Slavery: From the Baroque to the Modern, 1492–1800* (London: Verso, 1997).

D.K. Fieldhouse, *The Colonial Empires: A Comparative Study from the Eighteenth Century* (London: Weidenfeld and Nicolson, 1966).

Anthony Pagden, *Lords of All the World: Ideologies of Empire in Spain, Britain, and France, 1492–1830* (New Haven: Yale University Press, 1995).

J.H. Parry, *Trade and Dominion: The European Overseas Empires in the Eighteenth Century* (New York: Praeger, 1971).

Walter Rodney, *How Europe Underdeveloped Africa* (Washington, D.C.: Howard University Press, 1981 [1972]).

Eric Williams, *Capitalism and Slavery* (Chapel Hill: University of North Carolina Press, 1944).

Eric R. Wolf, *Europe and the People Without History*, 2d ed. (Berkeley: University of California Press, 1997 [1982]).

For European imperialisms of the nineteenth and early twentieth centuries consult:

Neil Ascherson, *The King Incorporated: Leopold II in the Age of Trusts* (Garden City: Doubleday, 1964).

Glen St. J. Barclay, *The Rise and Fall of the New Roman Empire: Italy's Bid for World Power, 1890–1943* (London: Sidgwick & Jackson, 1973).

Winfried Baumgart, *Imperialism: The Idea and Reality of British and French Colonial Expansion, 1880–1914* (Oxford: Oxford University Press, 1982).

Henri Brunschwig, *French Colonialism, 1871–1914: Myths and Realities* (New York: Praeger, 1966).

P.J. Cain and A.G. Hopkins, *British Imperialism: Innovation and Expansion, 1688–1914* (London: Longman, 1993).

Lance E. Davis and Robert A. Huttenback, *Mammon and the Pursuit of Empire: The Political Economy of British Imperialism, 1860–1912* (Cambridge: Cambridge University Press, 1986).

Michael W. Doyle, *Empires* (Ithaca: Cornell University Press, 1986).

D.K. Fieldhouse, *Economics and Empire, 1830–1914* (London: Weidenfeld and Nicolson, 1973).

E.J. Hobsbawm, *The Age of Empire, 1875–1914* (New York: Pantheon, 1987).

A.S. Kanya-Forstner, *The Conquest of the Western Sudan: A Study in French Military Imperialism* (Cambridge: Cambridge University Press, 1969).

Marten Kuitenbrouwer, *The Netherlands and the Rise of Modern Imperialism: Colonies and Foreign Policy* (New York: Berg, 1991).

Tekeste Negash, *Italian Colonialism in Eritrea, 1882–1941* (Uppsala: Acta Universitatis Upsaliensis, 1987).

David Northrup, *Indentured Labor in the Age of Imperialism, 1834–1922* (Cambridge: Cambridge University Press, 1995).

D.C.M. Platt, *Finance, Trade, and Politics in British Foreign Policy, 1815–1914* (Oxford: Oxford University Press, 1968).

Ronald Robinson, "Non-European Foundations of European Imperialism: Sketch for a Theory of Collaboration," in Roger Owen and Bob Sutcliffe (eds.), *Studies in the Theory of Imperialism* (London: Longman, 1972), pp. 117–142.

Ronald Robinson and John Gallagher, "The Imperialism of Free Trade," *Economic History Review* 6 (1953): 1–15.

Ronald Robinson and John Gallagher with Alice Denny, *Africa and the Victorians: The Official Mind of Imperialism* (London: Macmillan, 1961).

Bernard Semmel, *The Rise of Free Trade Imperialism: Classical Political Economy, the Empire of Free Trade and Imperialism, 1750–1850* (Cambridge: Cambridge University Press, 1970).

Woodruff D. Smith, *The German Colonial Empire* (Chapel Hill: University of North Carolina Press, 1978).

Hans-Ulrich Wehler, *The German Empire 1871–1918* (Leamington Spa: Berg, 1985 [1973]).

For American, Japanese, and Russian imperialisms in the nineteenth and early twentieth centuries consult:

W.G. Beasley, *Japanese Imperialism, 1894–1945* (Oxford: Clarendon Press, 1987).

Daniel R. Brower and Edward J. Lazzerini (eds.), *Russia's Orient: Imperial Borderlands and Peoples, 1700–1917* (Bloomington: Indiana University Press, 1997).

Peter Duus, *The Abacus and the Sword: The Japanese Penetration of Korea, 1895–1910* (Berkeley: University of California Press, 1995).

Dietrich Geyer, *Russian Imperialism: The Interaction of Domestic and Foreign Policy, 1860–1914* (New Haven: Yale University Press, 1987).

Barbara Jelavich, *A Century of Russian Foreign Policy, 1814–1914* (Philadelphia: Lippincott, 1964).

Amy Kaplan and Donald Pease (eds.), *Cultures of United States Imperialism* (Durham: Duke University Press, 1993).

John LeDonne, *Russian Empire and the World, 1700–1917* (Oxford: Oxford University Press, 1998).

Richard Pierce, *Russian Central Asia, 1867–1917: A Study in Colonial Rule* (Berkeley: University of California Press, 1960).

Peter W. Stanley (ed.), *Reappraising an Empire: New Perspectives on Philippine-American History* (Cambridge: Cambridge University Press, 1984).

William Appleman Williams, *The Roots of the Modern American Empire* (New York: Random House, 1969).

Louise Young, *Japan's Total Empire: Manchuria and the Culture of Wartime Imperialism* (Berkeley: University of California Press, 1998).

For the imperial mission and the discourses of Orientialism and racism consult:

William B. Cohen, *The French Encounter with Africans: White Response to Blacks, 1530–1880* (Bloomington: Indiana University Press, 1980).

Bernard S. Cohn, *Colonialism and Its Forms of Knowledge: The British in India* (Princeton: Princeton University Press, 1996).

Philip D. Curtin, *The Image of Africa: British Ideas and Action, 1780–1850* (Madison: University of Wisconsin Press, 1964).

Ronald Inden, *Imagining India* (Oxford: Blackwell, 1990).

V.G. Kiernan, *The Lords of Human Kind: Black Man, Yellow Man, and White Man in an Age of Empire* (Boston: Little, Brown, 1969).

Henrika Kuklick, *The Savage Within: The Social History of British Anthropology, 1885–1945* (Cambridge: Cambridge University Press, 1991).

Patricia Lorcin, *Imperial Identities: Stereotyping, Prejudice and Race in Colonial Algeria* (London: I.B. Tauris, 1995).

John M. MacKenzie, *Orientalism: History, Theory and the Arts* (Manchester: Manchester University Press, 1995).

Thomas R. Metcalfe, *Ideologies of the Raj* (Cambridge: Cambridge University Press, 1994).

Maxime Rodinson, *Europe and the Mystique of Islam* (Seattle: University of Washington Press, 1987 [1980]).

Edward W. Said, *Orientalism* (New York: Pantheon, 1978).

Bernard Semmel, *The Liberal Ideal and the Demons of Empire: Theories of Imperialism from Adam Smith to Lenin* (Baltimore: The Johns Hopkins University Press, 1993).

Eric Stokes, *The English Utilitarians and India* (Oxford: Clarendon Press, 1959).

Nicholas Thomas, *Colonialism's Culture: Anthropology, Travel and Government* (Princeton: Princeton University Press, 1994).

Tzvetan Todorov, *On Human Diversity: Nationalism, Racism, and Exoticism in French Thought* (Cambridge: Harvard University Press, 1993 [1989]).

For the colonial encounter, especially in terms of culture, gender, sexuality, and science consult:

Kenneth Ballhatchet, *Race, Sex, and Class under the Raj: Imperial Attitudes and Policies and Their Critics, 1793–1905* (New York: St. Martin's Press, 1980).

John G. Butcher, *The British in Malaya, 1880–1914: The Social History of a European Community in South-East Asia* (Kuala Lumpur: Oxford University Press, 1979).

Helen Callaway, *Gender, Culture and Empire: European Women in Colonial Nigeria* (Urbana: University of Illinois Press, 1987).

Nupur Chaudhuri and Margaret Strobel, *Western Women and Imperialism: Complicity and Resistance* (Bloomington: Indiana University Press, 1992).

Julia Clancy-Smith and Frances Gouda (eds.), *Domesticating the Empire: Race, Gender, and Family Life in French and Dutch Colonialism* (Charlottesville: University Press of Virginia, 1998).

John L. Comaroff and Jean Comaroff, *Of Revelation and Revolution* (Chicago: University of Chicago Press, 1991).

Philip D. Curtin, *Death by Migration: Europe's Encounter with the Tropical World in the Nineteenth Century* (New York: Cambridge University Press, 1989).

Daniel R. Headrick, *The Tools of Empire: Technology and European Imperialism in the Nineteenth Century* (Oxford: Oxford University Press, 1981).

Daniel R. Headrick, *The Tentacles of Progress: Technology Transfer in the Age of Imperialism, 1850–1940* (Oxford: Oxford University Press, 1988).

Ronald Hyam, *Empire and Sexuality: The British Experience* (Manchester: Manchester University Press, 1990).

Amirah Inglis, *The White Women's Protection Ordinance: Sexual Anxiety and Politics in Papua* (London: Sussex University Press, 1975).

Kumari Jayawardena, *The White Woman's Other Burden: Western Women and South Asia During British Rule* (London: Routledge, 1995).

Dane Kennedy, *Islands of White: Settler Society and Culture in Kenya and Southern Rhodesia, 1890–1939* (Durham: Duke University Press, 1987).

Dane Kennedy, *The Magic Mountains: Hill Stations and the British Raj* (Berkeley: University of California Press, 1996).

Claudia Knapman, *White Women in Fiji, 1835–1930: The Ruin of Empire?* (London: Allen and Unwin, 1986).

Billie Melman, *Women's Orients: English Women and the Middle East, 1718–1918* (Ann Arbor: University of Michigan Press, 1992).

Clare Midgley (ed.), *Gender and Imperialism* (Manchester: Manchester University Press, 1998).

David Prochaska, *Making Algeria French: Colonialism in Bône, 1870–1920* (Cambridge: Cambridge University Press, 1990).

Mrinalini Sinha, *Colonial Masculinity: The "Manly Englishman" and the "Effeminate Bengali" in the Late Nineteenth Century* (Manchester: Manchester University Press, 1995).

Gwendolyn Wright, *The Politics of Design in French Colonial Urbanism* (Chicago: University of Chicago Press, 1991).

For popular imperialism and colonial subjects in the metropole consult:

Antoinette Burton, *At the Heart of the Empire: Indians and the Colonial Encounter in Late-Victorian Britain* (Berkeley: University of California Press, 1998).

Annie E. Coombes, *Reinventing Africa: Museums, Material Culture and Popular Imagination in Late Victorian and Edwardian England* (New Haven: Yale University Press, 1994).

Peter Fryer, *Staying Power: The History of Black People in Britain* (London: Pluto Press, 1984).

Herman Lebovics, *True France: The Wars over Cultural Identity, 1900–1945* (Ithaca: Cornell University Press, 1992).

John M. MacKenzie, *Propaganda and Empire: The Manipulation of British Public Opinion, 1880–1960* (Manchester: Manchester University Press, 1984).

John M. MacKenzie (ed.), *Imperialism and Popular Culture* (Manchester: Manchester University Press, 1986).

Neil MacMaster, *Colonial Migrants and Racism: Algerians in France, 1900–1962* (New York: St. Martin's Press, 1997).

Susan Gilson Miller (ed.), *Disorienting Encounters: Travels of a Moroccan Scholar in France in 1845–46: The Voyage of Muhammad as-Saffar* (Berkeley: University of California Press, 1992).

Neil Parsons, *King Khama, Emperor Joe, and the Great White Queen: Victorian Britain through African Eyes* (Chicago: University of Chicago Press, 1998).

Jan Nederveen Pieterse, *White on Black: Images of Africa and Blacks in Western Popular Culture* (New Haven: Yale University Press, 1992).

Paul Rabinow, *French Modern: Norms and Forms of the Social Environment* (Cambridge: MIT Press, 1989).

Paul B. Rich, *Race and Empire in British Politics*, 2d ed. (Cambridge: Cambridge University Press, 1990).

Robert W. Rydell, *All the World's a Fair: Visions of Empire at American International Expositions, 1876–1916* (Chicago: University of Chicago Press, 1984).

William H. Schneider, *An Empire for the Masses: The French Popular Image of Africa, 1870–1900* (Westport: Greenwood Press, 1982).

Laura Tabili, *"We Ask for British Justice": Workers and Racial Difference in Late Imperial Britain* (Ithaca: Cornell University Press, 1994).

For anticolonial resistance and nationalism consult:

Michael Adas, *Prophets of Rebellion: Millenarian Protest Movements against the European Colonial Order* (Chapel Hill: University of North Carolina Press, 1979).

Margot Badran, *Feminists, Islam, and Nation: Gender and the Making of Modern Egypt* (Princeton: Princeton University Press, 1995).

A. Adu Boahen, *African Perspectives on Colonialism* (Baltimore: The Johns Hopkins University Press, 1987).

Partha Chatterjee, *Nationalist Thought and the Colonial World: A Derivative Discourse?* (London: Zed Press, 1986).

Michael Crowder (ed.), *West African Resistance* (London: Hutchinson, 1971).

Donald Crummey (ed.), *Banditry, Rebellion and Social Protest in Africa* (London: Heinemann, 1986).

Dagmar Engels and Shula Marks (eds.), *Contesting Colonial Hegemony: State and Society in Africa and India* (London: I.B. Tauris, 1994).

Ranajit Guha, *Elementary Aspects of Peasant Insurgency in Colonial India* (Delhi: Oxford University Press, 1983).

Ranajit Guha (ed.), *A Subaltern Studies Reader 1986–1995* (Minneapolis: University of Minnesota Press, 1997).

Thomas C. Holt, *The Problem of Freedom: Race, Labor, and Politics in Jamaica and Britain, 1832–1938* (Baltimore: The Johns Hopkins University Press, 1992).

Reynaldo C. Ileto, *Pasyon and Revolution: Popular Movements in the Philippines, 1840–1910* (Quezon City: Ateneo de Manila University Press, 1979).

Radha Kumar, *The History of Doing: An Illustrated Account of Movements for Women's Rights and Feminism in India, 1800–1990* (London: Verso, 1993).

J. Ayodele Langley, *Pan-Africanism and Nationalism in West Africa, 1900–1945: A Study in Ideology and Social Classes* (Oxford: Clarendon Press, 1973).

T.O. Ranger, "Connexions between 'Primary Resistance' Movements and Modern Mass Nationalism in East and Central Africa," *Journal of African History* 9, 3–4 (1968): 437–453, 631–641.

Robert Rotberg and Ali Mazrui (eds.), *Protest and Power in Black Africa* (New York: Oxford University Press, 1970).

Anil Seal, *The Emergence of Indian Nationalism: Competition and Collaboration in the Later Nineteenth Century* (Cambridge: Cambridge University Press, 1968).

For the interdisciplinary field of postcolonial cultural studies consult:

Bill Ashcroft, Gareth Griffiths, and Helen Tiffin (eds.), *The Post-Colonial Studies Reader* (London: Routledge, 1995).

Tani E. Barlow (ed.), *Formations of Colonial Modernity in East Asia* (Durham: Duke University Press, 1997).

Homi K. Bhabha, *The Location of Culture* (London: Routledge, 1994).

Frantz Fanon, *Black Skin, White Masks* (New York: Grove Press, 1967 [1952]).

Albert Memmi, *The Colonizer and the Colonized* (Boston: Beacon Press, 1991 [1957]).

Timothy Mitchell, *Colonising Egypt* (Cambridge: Cambridge University Press, 1988).

Ashis Nandy, *The Intimate Enemy: Loss and Recovery of Self Under Colonialism* (Delhi: Oxford University Press, 1983).

Gyan Prakash (ed.), *After Colonialism: Imperial Histories and Postcolonial Displacements* (Princeton: Princeton University Press, 1995).

Mary Louise Pratt, *Imperial Eyes: Travel Writing and Transculturation* (London: Routledge, 1992).

Edward W. Said, *Culture and Imperialism* (New York: Knopf, 1993).

Gayatri Chakravorty Spivak, "Can the Subaltern Speak?," in Cary Nelson and Larry Grossberg (eds.), *Marxism and the Interpretation of Culture* (Urbana: University of Illinois Press, 1988), pp. 271–313.

Gauri Viswanathan, *Masks of Conquest: Literary Study and British Rule in India* (New York: Columbia University Press, 1989).

Robert J.C. White, *Colonial Desire: Hybridity in Theory, Culture and Race* (London: Routledge, 1995).

Patrick Williams and Laura Chrisman (eds.), *Colonial Discourse and Post-Colonial Theory: A Reader* (New York: Columbia University Press, 1994).

Notes

Notes for Timothy Burke, *Colonialism, Cleanliness, and Civilization in Colonial Rhodesia* (p. 86).

1. Philip Molefe and Philip Van Niekerk, "Adventures of a Black Man in a White Town," *Weekly Mail*, 6:40, Oct. 19–Oct. 25, 1990, p. 1.

2. J. P. R. Wallis, ed., *The Matabele Journals of Robert Moffat*, 2 vols., Oppenheimer Series (London: Chatto & Windus, 1945), from "Moffat's Third Journey to Matabeleland," May–November 1854, vol. 1, p. 193.

3. Thomas Morgan Thomas, *Eleven Years in Central South Asia* (London: John Snow and Co., 1872), p. 171.

4. Crook Papers, Pitt Rivers Museum Archives, University of Oxford (1878).

5. Edward Tabler, ed., *To the Victoria Falls Via Matabeleland: The Diary of Major Henry Stabb*, 1875 (Cape Town: C. Struik Ltd., 1967).

6. Constance Fripp, ed., *Gold and the Gospel in Mashonaland* (London: Chatto & Windus, 1949), p. 54.

7. ZNA N 9/1/1–26, Native Department Annual Reports, Gutu District, 1909. (Native commissioners were asked by the chief native

commissioner to explicitly comment on African hygiene in 1909 and again periodically every few years.)

8. ZNA N 9/1/1–26, Native Department Annual Reports, Hartley District, 1909.

9. ZNA N 9/5/8, Native Department, Chief Native Commissioner's Office, Correspondence re: School Inspections, 1922–1923. See Carol Summers, *From Civilization to Segregation: Social Ideals and Social Control in Southern Rhodesia* (Athens: Ohio University Press, 1994) for some especially useful discussions of the term "civilization" in Rhodesian discourse.

10. See ZNA N 9/1/1–26 and S 2076, Native Department Annual Reports, esp. Ndanga District, 1899, for discussion of the infectious nature of hut taxes. Also see ZNA N 4/1/1, 23 July 1903, Chief Native Commissioner Circular, which was accompanied by packets of permanganate of potash "for the purpose of disinfecting all hut tax money collected." Also see Vaughan, *Curing Their Ills*, ch. 6.

11. Nathan M. Shamuyarira, *Crisis in Rhodesia* (London: Andre Deutsch Ltd., 1965), p. 119.

12. C. Frantz and Cyril Rogers, *Racial Themes in Southern Rhodesia: The Attitudes and Behavior of the White Population* (New Haven: Yale University Press, 1962), pp. 235 and 370.

13. "The Truth About the Colour Bar," *The Citizen* (Salisbury), February 24, 1956.

14. Dudley Kidd, *The Essential Kafir* (London: Adam and Charles Black, 1904), p. 34.

15. Jeannie M. Boggie, *First Steps in Civilising Rhodesia*, 4th ed. (Salisbury: Kingstons Ltd., 1966), p. 81.

16. Wilfred Robertson, *Rhodesian Rancher* (London: Blackie & Son Ltd., 1935), p. 36.

17. David Caute, *Under the Skin: The Death of White Rhodesia* (Evanston, Ill.: Northwestern University Press, 1983), p. 108.

18. Jacklyn Cock, *Maids and Madams: Domestic Workers under Apartheid* (London: Women's Press, 1989).

19. Boggie, *A Husband and a Farm in Rhodesia* (n.p.: Salisbury, 1939), p. 106.

20. Boggie, *First Steps*, p. 82.

21. Frantz and Rogers, *Racial Themes*, p. 370.

22. See John Pape, "Black and White: The 'Perils of Sex' in Colonial Zimbabwe," *Journal of Southern African Studies* 16:4 (December 1990); also see Jeater, *Marriage, Perversion, and Power.*

23. Margaret Wood, *Pastels under the Southern Cross* (London: Smith & Elder, 1911), p. 171.

24. Helen Caddick, *A White Woman in Central Africa* (London: T. Fisher Unwin, 1900), p. 83.

25. Felix Bryk, *Dark Rapture: The Sex Life of the African Negro* (New York: Walden Publications, 1939), pp. 50–51.

26. Wood, *Pastels*, pp. 125–126.

27. ZNA CA 1/1/1, diary of Algernon Capell, entry for April 1905.

28. Thomas Richards, *The Commodity Culture of Victorian England* (Stanford: Stanford University Press, 1990), pp. 2–3.

29. Grant McCracken, *Culture and Consumption: New Approaches to the Symbolic Character of Consumer Goods and Activities* (Bloomington: Indiana University Press, 1988), p. 28. Also see Appadurai, *The Social Life of Things*; William Reddy, *The Rise of Market Culture: The Textile Trade and French Society, 1750–1900* (Cambridge: Cambridge University Press, 1984); Neil McKendrick, *The Birth of a Consumer Society* (Bloomington: Indiana University Press, 1982); Chandra Mukerji, *From Graven Images* (New York: Columbia University Press, 1983); Rosalind H. Williams, *Dream Worlds: Mass Consumption in Late Nineteenth-Century France* (Los Angeles: University of California Press, 1982).

30. Ibid.

31. Hole, *Old Rhodesian Days*, p. 47.

32. "Raise Your Own Race," *Native Mirror* 2:3 (1934).

33. ZNA ZBJ 1/1/3, testimony of John Ralstein.

34. ZNA ZBJ 1/2/3, testimony of John Ralstein.

35. ZNA ZBJ 1/1/4, testimony of Jake Hanan.

36. ZNA ZBJ 1/2/1, testimony of the Mashonaland Kafir Truck Association.

37. ZNA ZBJ 1/2/1, testimony of the Salisbury Chamber of Commerce.

38. *Bantu Mirror*, August 24, 1946, p. 8.

39. *Bantu Mirror*, January 19, 1946, p. 7.

40. *Bantu Mirror*, October 2, 1948, p. 9.

41. *Bantu Mirror*, January 15, 1944, p. 5.

Notes for Ann Laura Stoler, *Gender, Race, and Class Boundaries in Southeast Asia* (p. 124).

1. At least one plausible accounting for this perspective is that it was extrapolated, as Victor Kiernan does, from "the run of officials" who populated the British civil service in India. Thus Kiernan writes:

   > [they] belong to the type of the gentleman who was evolving in Victorian England. An amalgam of the less flighty qualities of the nobility with the more stodgy of middle-class virtues, he had a special relevance to the empire, and indeed was partly called into existence by its requirements, made to measure for it by England's extraordinary public school education." The Lords of Human Kind *(London: Wiedenfeld and Nicolson, 1969) 37.*

   But even in India, this knighted bourgeoisie was not in the majority. David Arnold calculated that "nearly half the European population [living in India by the end of the nineteenth century] could be called "poor whites" (104). "European Orphans and Vagrants in India in the Nineteenth-Century," *The Journal of Imperial and Commonwealth History* 7.2 (January 1979): 104–127. Also see Hugh Ridley's detailed and subtle analysis of the myth of an "aristocratic democracy" of whites in German, French, and British colonies in *Images of Imperial Rule* (London: St. Martin's Press, 1983) esp. 124–145.

2. Homi Bhabha's provocative analysis of a difference that is "almost the same but not quite" ("Of Mimicry and Man: The Ambivalence of Colonial Discourse," *The Location of Culture* [London: Routledge, 1994]) has spawned a profusion of studies that examine the inherent ambivalence of specific colonial institutions that at once incorporated and distinguished colonized populations without collapsing the critical difference between ruler and ruled. My point is that this sort of colonial ambivalence was also a national one, directed at a much broader population whose class differences literally colored their perceived and proper racial membership as designated by colonial authorities.

3. Eric Hobsbawm, *The Age of Capital: 1845–1878* (New York: Scribner, 1975) 244.

4. See Michael Taussig's "Culture of Terror—Space of Death," *Comparative Studies in Society and History* 26 (1984): 467–97

and my "In Cold Blood: Hierarchies of Credibility and the Politics of Colonial Narratives," *Representations* 37 (Winter 1992): 151–89 that both broach the "epistemic murk," the incomplete sorts of knowledge, and the terror of rumor through which many colonial officials operated.

5. Divers quoted in Hugh Ridley, *Images of Imperial Rule* (London: St. Martin's Press, 1983) 129.

6. George Woodcock, *The British in the Far East* (New York: Atheneum, 1969) 163; Robert Hughes, *The Fatal Shore* (New York: Knopf, 1987) 323.

7. Benedict Anderson, *Imagined Communities* (London: Verso, 1983).

8. W. L. Ritter, *De Europeanen in Nederlandsche Indie* (Leyden: Sythoff, 1856) 6.

9. These categories were further complicated by the fact that the Indies was never wholly a Dutch-populated colony and certainly not from its beginning when many of its European inhabitants spoke no Dutch, were unfamiliar with Dutch cultural conventions, and were not Dutch by birth. In the seventeenth century, Portuguese served as the lingua franca "on the streets, in the markets, in church and in the households where European men kept Asian mistresses." Jean Taylor, *The Social World of Batavia* (Madison: U of Wisconsin P, 1983) 18–19. In the nineteenth and twentieth centuries, the colonial enclave was an international community made up of temporary and permanent expatriates who used Malay more easily than Dutch and many of whom had never been to Holland.

10. J. Kohlbrugge, "Het Indische kind en zijne karaktervorming," *Blikken in het zielenleven van den Javaan en zijner overheerschers* (Leiden: Brill, 1907).

11. W. L. Ritter, *Be Europeanen in Nederlandsche Indie* (Leyden: Sythoff, 1856) 30.

12. See Charles van Onselen, "Race and Class in the South African Countryside: Cultural Osmosis and Social Relations in the Sharecropping Economy of the South-Western Transvaal, 1900–1950," *American Historical Review* 95 (1990): 99–123 who argues for a more complex view of South African racial history that challenges prevailing assumptions about the homogeneity of race relations

by attending to the divergent alliances and interests of a broader class spectrum of subaltern whites.

13. A. Van Marle, "De group der Europeanen in Nederlands-Indie," *Indonesia* 5.2 (1952): 77–121; 5.3 (1952): 314–341; 5.5 (1952): 481–507.

14. Algemeen Rijksarchief, Verbaal 9 July 1860. Governor-General's summary report to the Minister of Colonies concerning the establishment of a technical/craft school in Surabaya: J. H. F. van de Wall, "Het Indoisme," *De Reflector* 39 (1916): 953.

15. This point is detailed in Chapter 5 of *Carnal Knowledge and Imperial Power* (Berkeley: U of California P, forthcoming).

16. On the fact that a "European upbringing" was considered "necessary to cultivate love for the fatherland and to strengthen the ties binding the colony to the motherland" see Algemeen Rijksarchief, Kol. 1848 geheim, no. 493, and the additional reports cited therein where this discourse on subversion, national security and upbringing is explicitly expressed.

17. See Fasseur who, while not taking note of this paradox, does provide evidence of the rationales for barring "inlandse kinderen" and the simultaneous emphasis placed on native language acquisition in the Indies colonial civil service (*De Indologen* 112–129).

18. Hans Rigart, "Moraliseringoffensief in Nederland in de periode 1850–1880," *Vijf Eeuwen van Gezinsleven* ed. H. Peeters, et al. (Nijmegen: SUN, 1986) 194–208.

19. Stuurman, 1993 360.

20. Ali de Regt, *Arbeidersgezinnen en beschavingsarbeid* [Working-class families and the civilizing mission] (Boom: Amsterdam, 1984) 151.

21. On the living conditions of village-based Europeans as compared to the housing of the poor in Amsterdam see H. C. H. Gunning, "Het Woningvraagstuk," *Koloniale Studien* 2 (1918): 109–126.

PROBLEMS IN EUROPEAN CIVILIZATION

New editions now available, in chronological order:

Other Wadsworth, Cengage Learning Series of Interest

PROBLEMS IN WORLD HISTORY

Latin America and the World Economy, Richard Salvucci (1996, 35174-1)
The Atlantic Slave Trade, David A. Northrup (1994, 33145-7)

MAJOR PROBLEMS IN EUROPEAN HISTORY

Major Problems in the History of the Italian Renaissance, Benjamin Kohl and Alison Smith (1995, 28002-X)
Major Problems in the History of Imperial Russia, James Cracraft (1994, 21497-3)

SOURCES IN MODERN HISTORY

From the South African Past: Narratives, Documents, and Debates, John A. Williams (1997, 28789-X)
Revealing America: Image and Imagination in the Exploration of North America, James P. Ronda (1996, 35175-X)
World War I and European Society, Marilyn Shevin-Coetzee and Frans Coetzee (1995, 33470-7)
The Civilization of the Italian Renaissance, Kenneth R. Bartlett (1992, 20900-7)
Eastern Europe: Transformation and Revolution, 1945–1991, Lyman H. Legters (1992, 24994-7)
Inside Hitler's Germany: A Documentary History of Life in the Third Reich, Benjamin Sax and Dieter Kuntz (1992, 25000-7)
Movements, Currents, Trends: Aspects of European Thought in the Nineteenth and Twentieth Centuries, Eugen Weber (1992, 27881-5)
Antisemitism in the Modern World, Richard Levy (1991, 24340-X)
1492: Discovery, Invasion, Encounter, Martin Lunenfeld (1991, 21115-X)